A Century of Global Economic Crises

Lúcio Vinhas de Souza

A Century of Global Economic Crises

Monetary Policy in Search of An Anchor

Lúcio Vinhas de Souza
61 Kirkland St.
Havard University
Cambridge, MA 02138, MA, USA

ISBN 978-3-031-53459-1   ISBN 978-3-031-53460-7   (eBook)
https://doi.org/10.1007/978-3-031-53460-7

© The Editor(s) (if applicable) and The Author(s), under exclusive license to Springer Nature Switzerland AG 2024
This work is subject to copyright. All rights are solely and exclusively licensed by the Publisher, whether the whole or part of the material is concerned, specifically the rights of translation, reprinting, reuse of illustrations, recitation, broadcasting, reproduction on microfilms or in any other physical way, and transmission or information storage and retrieval, electronic adaptation, computer software, or by similar or dissimilar methodology now known or hereafter developed.
The use of general descriptive names, registered names, trademarks, service marks, etc. in this publication does not imply, even in the absence of a specific statement, that such names are exempt from the relevant protective laws and regulations and therefore free for general use.
The publisher, the authors and the editors are safe to assume that the advice and information in this book are believed to be true and accurate at the date of publication. Neither the publisher nor the authors or the editors give a warranty, expressed or implied, with respect to the material contained herein or for any errors or omissions that may have been made. The publisher remains neutral with regard to jurisdictional claims in published maps and institutional affiliations.

This Palgrave Macmillan imprint is published by the registered company Springer Nature Switzerland AG.
The registered company address is: Gewerbestrasse 11, 6330 Cham, Switzerland

Paper in this product is recyclable.

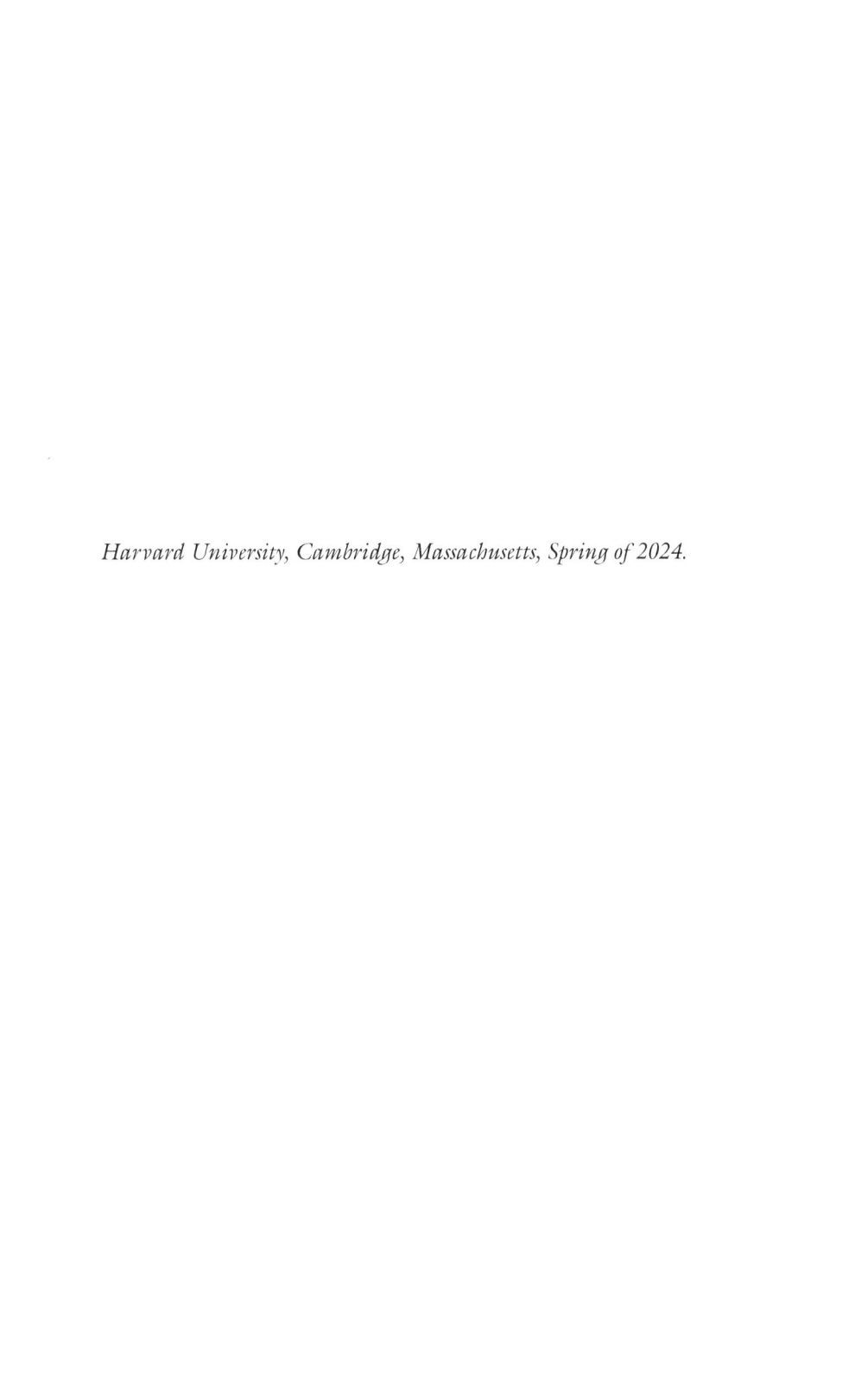

Harvard University, Cambridge, Massachusetts, Spring of 2024.

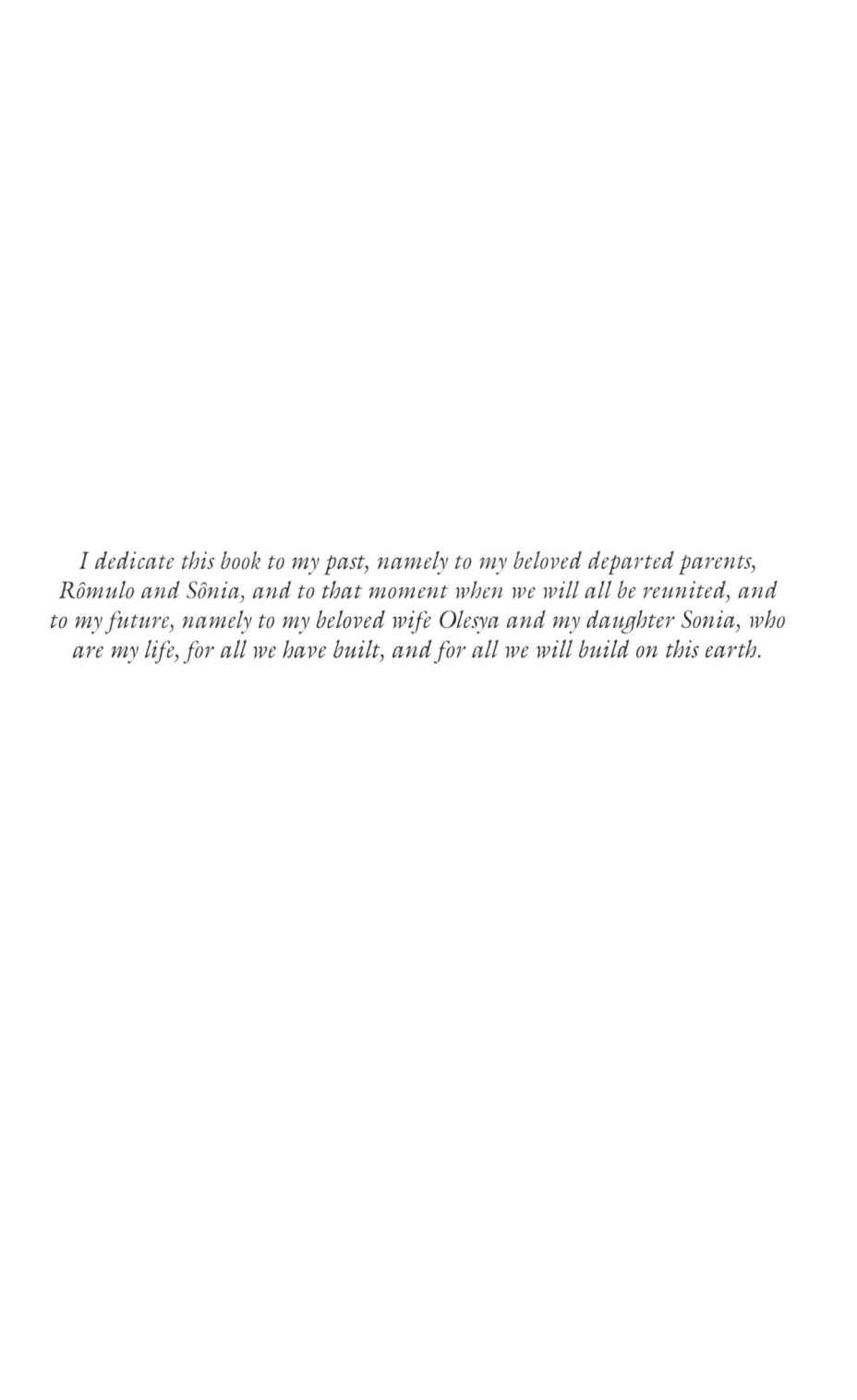

I dedicate this book to my past, namely to my beloved departed parents, Rômulo and Sônia, and to that moment when we will all be reunited, and to my future, namely to my beloved wife Olesya and my daughter Sonia, who are my life, for all we have built, and for all we will build on this earth.

Acknowledgements

This author would like to thank the valuable comments and discussions by/with, among others, Richard Clarida, Karen Dynan, Karolina Ekholm, Marcelo Kfoury Muinhos, Reiner Martin, Eric Parrado, Ted Truman, (Sir) Paul Tucker, and Peter Praet, and by the students of my "Financial Crises" course at Brandeis University (who "road tested" the chapters of this book) and the participants of seminars held at Harvard. My profound gratitude also to particular persons that have been important in different stages of my professional and academic life in both sides of the Atlantic (and sometimes literally on both sides, albeit in different moments), António Borges,[1] Jorge Braga de Macedo, Linda Bui, Otaviano Canuto, Cristina Corado, Sonia Dahab, Karen Donfried, José Manuel Durão Barroso, Joseph Francois, Vitor Gaspar, Indermit Gill, Erin Goodman, Sergei Guriev, Ricardo Hausmann, Ivailo Izvorski, Jean-Claude Juncker, Rolf Langhammer, Catherine Mann, Antonio de Lecea, Ann Mettler, António Nogueira Leite, Lucjan Orlowski, Adam Posen, Klaus Regling, Paul Wachtel, and many, many others. The comments of anonymous reviewers that measurably improved this book are also gratefully appreciated, as is the great work by the Palgrave Macmillan editorial team throughout this process. All and any remaining omissions and mistakes are my sole responsibility.

The institutional support of the Weatherhead Center for International Affairs at Harvard University and of Brandeis University is equally gratefully recognized.

[1] António sadly passed away after fighting a cruel disease in 2013.

Disclaimer

Harvard University and Brandeis University. The opinions expressed in this work do not necessarily reflect the views of any institution with which the author is or was associated with. All usual disclaimers apply.

Contents

1. Introduction and definitions: thirty years in the ramparts   1
   References   9

2. The long goodbye of the gold standard and the "Great Depression"   11
   2.1 *The Classic Gold Standard*   11
   2.2 *The Great Depression and the End of the "Gold Exchange Standard"*   15
   2.3 *Beyond the "Great Depression": Bretton Woods and that "Barbarous Relic"*   22
   2.4 *The US "Great Inflation" and the End of the "Bretton Woods" System*   25
   Annex 2.A: Formalizing Price Level Determination under the Gold Standard   28
   Annex 2.B: Global Participation in the "Classical Gold Standard"   31
   References   33

3. The "Great Inflation" Arrives   35
   3.1 *The "Great Inflation" and Domestic US Policies*   35
   3.2 *External Price Shocks*   39
   3.3 *Domestic US Monetary Policy Responses*   41
   Annex 3.A Was the "Great Inflation" Global?   42

4 From Volcker to China: The "Great Moderation" Begins — 45
4.1 Big Shoes that Needed to Be Filled — 45
4.2 But What Was the "Great Moderation"? — 47
4.3 What Caused the Great Moderation? — 48
    4.3.1 Monetary Policy and the Great Moderation — 50
4.4 The Great Moderation That Wasn't: Developing Countries — 52
4.5 That Other American Giant: The Federal Republic of Brazil — 53
4.6 Latin America Beyond Brazil: The Case of Chile — 60
Annex 4.A: Economic Models Incorporating Expectations — 62
References — 64

5 Houses Built on Sand: The "Global Financial Crisis" — 67
5.1 From Humble Beginnings: How It All Started — 67
5.2 How It Spread — 73
5.3 What the Fed (and Others) Did: The Policy Response — 77
    5.3.1 Federal Reserve — 81
    5.3.2 BoE — 81
    5.3.3 BoJ — 82
    5.3.4 ECB — 82
5.4 More Granularity on the Regulatory Response — 84
5.5 Effects in and Policy Actions of Developing Countries — 87
Annex 5.A: Spotting a Bubble — 88
Annex 5.B: Creating Future Vulnerabilities While Dealing with a Crisis — 90
References — 94

6 Trojan Horses: The Long Shadow of the Euro Area Sovereign Crisis — 95
6.1 The Very Progressive Take-Off of the European Bumblebee — 95
6.2 Why Did It Happen? — 96
6.3 What the ECB (and Others) Did: The Policy Response — 104
6.4 The Incompleteness of EMU — 108
Annex 6.A: Let's Talk a Little More about Sovereign Ratings — 114
    6.A.1. First Things First: A Brief History of Sovereign Ratings — 114
    6.A.2. Euro Area Periphery Ratings — 117
Annex 6.B: Modeling the Euro Area Crisis Using Expectations — 118
References — 120

7 COVID-19: The Fiscal and Monetary Responses to a Global Pandemic 121
7.1 *Faster Than a Speeding Train: The "Light Switch" Recession* 121
7.2 *The Policy Reaction: There We Go Again (But Now with Even More Fiscal Support)* 124
    7.2.1 *The US Policy Response* 125
    7.2.2 *The Policy Response of a (Less Fragmented) Euro Area* 127
7.3 *The (Short-Term) Effectiveness of Policy Measures* 129
7.4 *The Pandemic Policy Response in Developing Economies* 131
    7.4.1 *India* 131
    7.4.2 *Brazil* 132
Annex 7.A: What Is Inflation Targeting after All? 135
Annex 7.B: China's Limited Role in Global Financial Crises 139

8 Shadows from the Past: Inflation and War 143
8.1 *No Good Deed Ever Goes Unpunished* 143
8.2 *Fiscal Side Effects* 143
8.3 *Price Side Effects* 145
8.4 *The (Initial) Monetary Policy (Non) Reaction* 147

9 Looking Back, Looking Forward: Monetary, Fiscal and Structural Policies for an Older, Indebted and More Fragmented World 151
9.1 *So, What Worked (and Must be Preserved)?* 152
9.2 *What Did Not Work?* 153
9.3 *What Can (Credibly) Change?* 155
    9.3.1 *An Older, More Indebted, More Fragmented, Slower Growing and More Digital Economy* 155
9.4 *Conclusion: Frugal Suggestions for a Possible Path Forward* 164

References 169

Index 183

About the Author

Lúcio Vinhas de Souza a Brazilian/Portuguese (and almost American…) national, is currently a Fellow at the Weatherhead Center for International Affairs at Harvard University, a Visiting Professor at Brandeis University in Boston and a Board Member of the National Economic Club in Washington, DC. Before that, he was an Advisor to the leadership of the European External Action Service (the EU's joint Ministry of Foreign Affairs and Defense) in Brussels, Belgium, and he led the Economics Department of the European Political Strategy Centre (EPSC), an internal advisory body to the European Commission President Jean-Claude Juncker, a position he joined from Moody's Investors Service headquarters in New York City, where he was Managing Director and Global Chief Economist.

Before Moody's, Dr. Vinhas de Souza was at the World Bank in Washington, DC, and prior to that he was Coordinator for economic relations between the EU and the countries of the Western Commonwealth of Independent States (the loose successor of the Soviet Union) at the European Commission in Brussels. He joined the European Commission from the Kiel Institute for the World Economy in Germany, but started his career at the United Nations. He holds a PhD in Economics from the Erasmus University in Rotterdam, the Netherlands and a Master in Economics from the NOVA University in Lisbon, Portugal (of which he was also a proud donor for its new economics faculty campus). He has over a 100 different publications in several languages.

List of Figures

Fig. 1.1	Share of countries in debt crises (external default or restructuring)	4
Fig. 2.1	Long-term GDP growth rates for a sample of developed economies	13
Fig. 2.2	US GDP and GDP per capita, real, 1929–1945	17
Fig. 2.3	US unemployment, percentage of civilian labor force	18
Fig. 2.4	Global GDP during the Great Depression (real $ thousands)	21
Fig. 2.5	The US external balance under Bretton Woods (% of GDP)	24
Fig. 2.6	US gold reserves/money in circulation, end-of-the-year (eoy), %	26
Fig. 3.1	US CPI inflation, eoy	36
Fig. 3.2	Total US Government expenditures and receipts (% of GDP)	38
Fig. 3.3	Total US Government military and social expenditures ($ billions)	39
Fig. 3.4	Crude oil, average ($/barrel)	40
Fig. 3.5	CPI in different regions of the world	43
Fig. 4.1	Re-anchoring expectations with non-accommodative monetary policy	46
Fig. 4.2	Share of manufacturing and services in US gross value added (% of GDP)	49
Fig. 4.3	CPI in different groups of countries (eoy)	52
Fig. 4.4	A century of inflation in the US and in Brazil (log scale)	55
Fig. 4.5	Overall fiscal balance as a GDP percentage, 1900–2022	56
Fig. 4.6	Brazil and Latin America and the Caribbean external balance (percentage of GDP)	58
Fig. 4.7	Brazil (left) & Chile (right) compared: II	62
Fig. 5.1	Purchase-only house price index, US, yearly change	68
Fig. 5.2	Federal funds rate (in %) and "subprime" mortgages (in $ trillion)	71
Fig. 5.3	Real GDP growth, yoy	74

Fig. 5.4	Selected central banks' policy rates	78
Fig. 5.5	Selected central banks' balance sheets, % of GDP	78
Fig. 5.6	Selected interbank rates (3-month or 90-day rates and yields)	80
Fig. 5.7	The pillars of Basel II and III	86
Fig. 5.8	Using monetary policy to reduce accumulated fiscal imbalances in the US	92
Fig. 6.1	Sovereigns 10-year benchmark government bond yield (% p.a., daily data)	98
Fig. 6.2	Banks 5-years CDS spreads (daily data)	99
Fig. 6.3	Euro area, Core and Periphery current account dynamics. ("Core" includes Austria, Belgium, Germany, Finland and Luxembourg—largely, the euro area capital-exporting countries, while "periphery" includes Cyprus, Greece, Ireland, Italy, Portugal and Spain. The series are simple averages of the countries' current account balances)	100
Fig. 6.4	Fiscal balances in the euro area, Greece and Portugal, percentage of GDP	101
Fig. 6.5	Net public and private savings, euro area as a whole and core and periphery, % of GDP	102
Fig. 6.6	Decomposition of the euro area Periphery Current Account Balance, percentage of GDP	103
Fig. 6.7	Sovereign debt held by domestic banks, end 2013 (% of all government debt)	104
Fig. 6.8	ECB main policy rate (pp) and balance sheet to GDP (%), and effects in market stresses	105
Fig. 6.9	Public debt stock, euro area, core and periphery, percentage of GDP	113
Fig. 6.10	Total number of Sovereigns, developed and developing, rated, 1949–2013	116
Fig. 6.11	Moody's rating of selected euro area Sovereigns	118
Fig. 7.1	Google mobility data (index)	122
Fig. 7.2	"Weekly Tracker", GDP growth proxy. (See source and the explanation of how this series is constructed at OECD, Tracking GDP growth in real time, Paris)	123
Fig. 7.3	Quarterly GDP in selected economies (percentage change, previous period)	124
Fig. 7.4	Scale of fiscal measures in response to the Pandemic (% of GDP). (The IMF has a very comprehensive policy tracker of the economic measures applied by each individual country during the Pandemic: see, IMF, Policy Responses to COVID-19, Washington, DC)	125
Fig. 7.5	Fed and ECB systemic stress indicators (January 2009 set to 1)	130

Fig. 7.6	Fed and ECB balance sheets ($ and € trillion)	130
Fig. 7.7	Balance sheet, RBI and CBB (₹ & R$)	134
Fig. 7.8	Policy rates, RBI and CBB	134
Fig. 7.9	Growth in the number of inflation targeting monetary authorities	138
Fig. 7.10	Expansion of inflation targeting in developing regions	138
Fig. 7.11	Shares of main currencies in payments (September 2023) and reserves (Q2 2023)	140
Fig. 8.1	Disposable income and savings ($ billions)	144
Fig. 8.2	Global Supply Chain Pressure Index	145
Fig. 8.3	Monthly CPI series	146
Fig. 8.4	Individual CPI items, whole OECD	146
Fig. 8.5	Average policy rates, selected developed and developing countries	149
Fig. 8.6	CPI inflation and policy rates, selected countries	149
Fig. 9.1	Different estimates of r_t^*	155
Fig. 9.2	Global GDP shares, developed & developing countries (current $)	156
Fig. 9.3	Global population shares, developed and developing and emerging countries	157
Fig. 9.4	Trade as a share of global GDP (%)	158
Fig. 9.5	Less (eventually) and older: life expectancy and fertility	159
Fig. 9.6	Percentage of public and private debt in global GDP	162

List of Tables

Table 1.1	Definitions of economic crisis types	3
Table 2.1	Global participation in the "Classical Gold Standard"	31
Table 4.1	US inflation (1914–2007)	47
Table 4.2	US Real GDP growth (1914–2007)	48
Table 4.3	Brazil's (many and mostly failed) stabilization plans, 1986–1994	58
Table 4.4	Brazil and Chile compared	60
Table 5.1	Shares of global financial markets, 2006 (in $ billion)	75
Table 5.2	GFC-related policies in selected developing countries	87
Table 5.3	Decomposition of post–WWII large debt reductions in advanced economies (1945–1975)	93
Table 6.1	An overview of the unconventional monetary policies of the ECB and the FED	106
Table 6.2	Early Sovereign ratings	115
Table 7.1	Pandemic-related fiscal support in the US	127
Table 8.1	Estimating the price effects of fiscal support	147

CHAPTER 1

Introduction and definitions: thirty years in the ramparts

While writing this book, between the Fall of 2022 and the Winter of 2023/2024, I was struck by the sheer number (and scale) of crises that the global economy and the global monetary system had experienced just during my lifetime, which led me to wonder what was common (and connected) among those, and what was different (if anything). Hence the title I chose.

First things first: What is a crisis? Well, a crisis can be thought of as an extreme version of the downward part of the **normal economic cycle**. Of course, this in its turn begs the definition of what is an economic cycle, so here we go: all economies experience significant periodic changes in economic activity, from periods of expanding production, employment and consumption (a.k.a. the expansion part of the cycle) to other periods where the economy operates below capacity and unemployment is higher (the contraction or at least deceleration part of the cycle). This combination of expansions and contractions is called **the economic (or business) cycle**.

Business cycles occur because shocks, rigidities or disturbances—endogenous or exogenous, real or nominal, policy or technologically induced—to the economy push it off a stable and sustainable equilibrium path (e.g., making it grow above or below the "full employment" of its

© The Author(s), under exclusive license to Springer Nature Switzerland AG 2024
L. Vinhas de Souza, *A Century of Global Economic Crises*, https://doi.org/10.1007/978-3-031-53460-7_1

available endowment of resources). Their first formal analysis is to be found in the Burns and Mitchell seminal 1946 book, "Measuring Business Cycles".[1] This work was written while both authors were at the US National Bureau of Economic Research (NBER), and this private independent economic research body was later mandated to formally "date" US business cycles, a function it still performs today.

While "an unstable or crucial time or state of affairs in which a decisive change is impending" is the Merriam-Webster dictionary definition of a **crisis**, there is no real agreed or standard definition of what an **economic crisis** is. The used classifications of crises usually rely on a combination of quantitative and qualitative criteria, and normally differentiate between inflation, currency, debt and banking crises (see Table 1.1). However, economic crises are overwhelmingly multidimensional (e.g., one crisis type is related to, happens parallel or leads to another type—or types—of crises) and additionally, noneconomic crises (geopolitical, military) can lead to economic/financial crises (or, alternatively, economic/financial crises can lead to geopolitical/military crises: e.g., the "Great Depression" and its relationship with World War II).

We do, however, know crises are exceedingly common (as pointed out in the very first paragraph of this book, and also on its title). Using Reinhart and Rogoff (2009) data, 17% of their country sample was classified as in external **debt crisis** each year between 1970 and 2012 (or 11 countries per year experienced an external default or restructuring just during that period, see Fig. 1.1: on the other hand, this same figure shows us that this share during the "Classic Gold Standard"—see Chap. 2—was a mere 5%), while Laeven and Valencia (2018) estimates 151 **banking crises** between 1970 and 2017 (or over three banking crises per year).[2] However—and fortunately for all of us, of these many, many crises, just a few can be considered as **truly globally systemic** (so, affecting the majority of the global economy, in number of countries or GDP share).

---

[1] Burns, A. and Mitchell, W. (1946), "Measuring Business Cycles," National Bureau of Economic Research (NBER). (Arthur) Burns was then at Columbia University in New York City and the NBER in Cambridge, Massachusetts, but will later reappear in this book as the Chairman of the Federal Reserve from 1970 to 1978, during the so-called Great Inflation period.

[2] The numerically more precise Laeven and Valencia (2018) framework aims to reduce the use of subjective criteria in dating these events, compared with, for example, Reinhart and Rogoff (2009).

Table 1.1 Definitions of economic crisis types

Crisis Type	Threshold
Inflation	An annual inflation rate of 20% or higher.
Currency (Crash)	An annual depreciation versus the US dollar (or relevant anchor currency—historically the UK pound, the French franc, the German mark or the euro) of 15% or more.
Currency (Debasement)	
Type I	A reduction in the metallic content of coins in circulation of 5% or more.
Type II	A currency reform whereby a new currency replaces a depreciated earlier currency.
Debt Crisis	
External	A sovereign default is defined as the failure of a government to meet a principal or interest payment on the due date (or within the specified grace period). These episodes include instances in which rescheduled debt is ultimately extinguished in terms less favorable than the original obligation.
Domestic	The definition given above for an external debt crisis also applies. In addition, domestic debt crises have involved the freezing of bank deposits and/or forcible conversions of such deposits from dollars to local currency.
Banking Crises	
Type I—systemic (severe)	Banking crises are marked by two types of events (1) bank runs that lead to the closure, merging, or takeover of one or more financial institutions and (2) if there are no runs, the closure, merging, takeover, or large-scale government assistance of an important financial institution/group that marks the start of similar outcomes for other financial institutions.
Type II—financial distress (milder)	
Banking Crises (Laeven and Valencia, 2018)	(A) Significant signs of financial distress in the banking system (as indicated by significant bank runs, losses in the banking system, and/or bank liquidations). B) Significant banking policy intervention measures in response to significant losses in the banking system. Quantitatively, (A) happens if (1) a country's banking system exhibits significant losses resulting in a share of nonperforming loans above 20% of total loans or bank closures of at least 20% of banking system assets or (2) fiscal restructuring costs of the banking sector are sufficiently high, exceeding 5% of GDP, while for (B) at least three out of the following six measures are used: (1) deposit freezes and/or bank holidays; (2) significant bank nationalizations; (3) bank restructuring fiscal costs (at least 3% of GDP); (4) extensive liquidity support (at least 5% of deposits and liabilities to nonresidents); (5) significant guarantees put in place; and (6) significant asset purchases (at least 5% of GDP).

Sources: Reinhart and Rogoff (2009) and Laeven and Valencia (2018)

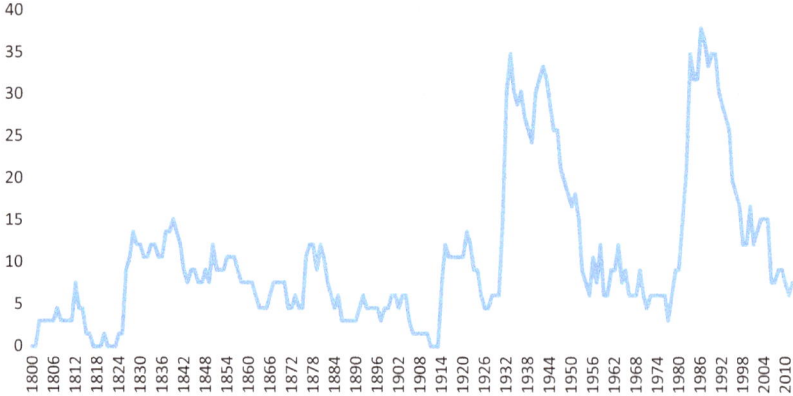

Fig. 1.1 Share of countries in debt crises (external default or restructuring). (Source: Author, based on Reinhart and Rogoff (2009) data for a sample of 66 developed and developing economies. (The countries are: Algeria, Angola, Argentina, Australia, Austria, Belgium, Bolivia, BrazilBrazil, Canada, Central African Republic, ChileChile, ChinaChina, Colombia, Costa Rica, Cote d'Ivoire, Denmark, Dominican Republic, Ecuador, Egypt, El Salvador, Finland, France, GermanyGermany, GreeceGreece, Guatemala, Honduras, Hungary, IndiaIndia, Indonesia, ItalyItaly, JapanJapan, Kenya, Korea, Malaysia, Mauritius, Mexico, Morocco, Myanmar, Netherlands, New ZealandNew Zealand, Nicaragua, Nigeria, Norway, Panama, Paraguay, Peru, Philippines, Poland, PortugalPortugal, Romania, RussiaRussia, Singapore, South Africa, SpainSpain, Sri Lanka, Sweden, Taiwan, Thailand, Tunisia, Turkey/Ottoman Empire, United KingdomUnited Kingdom (UK), United States, Uruguay, Venezuela, Zambia and Zimbabwe)

Inflation crises are also included on Table 1.1 (albeit the definition should also include *deflationary episodes*), which allows me to follow up by replying to another very basic question: **Why is price stability important?** Well, for several important reasons (and here I speak based on personal and family experience). First, price stability reduces distortions in economic decisions concerning savings and investment. Second, there are the so-called shoe-leather costs of holding money (e.g., when inflation is high, currency and non-interest-bearing checking accounts are constantly declining in value, so people will use scarce economic resources—time and "shoe leather"—to optimize the use of their monetary balances, misallocating those scarce resources and reducing productivity and growth). Third, price stability improves the transparency of the price mechanism and make economic agents (e.g., governments, firms, households, individuals) in general less uncertain about the future. There are, therefore, many good reasons why one should be concerned about price stability, and therefore to eventually decide to allocate the responsibility over this important matter to a dedicated institution (in this case, a "central bank", which are bodies originally designed with other functions in mind, as the name suggests).

I was both a witness to and an actor in some of the decisions that led to a number of the conundrums now facing monetary (and fiscal) authorities globally and, above and beyond these years as an international policy maker and practitioner, I spent my formative years in a hyperinflationary environment in a Developing country, which gives me a concrete experience of the costs that unstable prices have for real individuals, households, firms and governments.

From the Great Depression, which started in 1929 (and which is described in Chap. 2) until now, we had almost a hundred years of instability and global systemic crises, punctuated by the collapse of several global monetary frameworks and occasional inflationary and deflationary waves and largely limited stable periods. This overall turbulent period replaced the remarkable monetary (and real) stability that characterized the earlier era of the **"Classic Gold Standard"** (see also in Chap. 2).

However, for a whole generation it seemed monetary stability had been achieved around the world: this golden age of monetary policy under *fiat* regimes was dubbed the "Great Moderation" (see Chap. 4), in reference to a long period of low and stable price increases (and low GDP variability). This outcome was seen as largely the result of actions by newly empowered monetary authorities—*assumed* as bodies capable of affecting inflation dynamics, made independent from "fiscal dominance" (the tendency of Governments to make fiscal commitments that constrain the room for maneuver of their monetary authorities) and endowed with clear and legally protected mandates by their governments, and was a rection to the instability of the "Great Inflation" (see Chap. 3). Even several major global shocks that will be described here did not fundamentally change that perception of "well-anchored" prices during this period. However, a series of developments in 2021–2023 brought inflation back as a worldwide phenomenon, and this book aims to use this as an opportunity to tell the story of how that golden age came about, and what may lie ahead.

The explicit notion behind the "Great Moderation" was the belief in an **effective technical understanding of the business cycle and price formation dynamics**, embodied in frameworks like the Taylor rule, inflation targeting and growingly sophisticated macro models (with micro fundaments and rational expectations that in-built stylized versions of the behavior of different economic agents) and entrusted those to increasingly **formally and effectively independent monetary authorities**, free from the bane of "fiscal dominance", which was also made possible by a world of overall more limited fiscal pressures (certainly compared to the realities during both world wars).[3] As we will see in this book, this was not the first time economic practices would fall prey to hubris of this kind.

While this greater institutional quality (and complexity) was certainly part of the explanation for the "Great Moderation", it is likely that underlying long-term trends underpinned it: those go from **demographic trends** (an older global population with—initially, at least—a large pool of savings available for investment) to the positive and long-standing deflationary effects of the **reentry of China into the global economy** (and to a smaller degree, of Eastern Europe and the resulting nations of the breakup of the Soviet Union), a **greater digitalization** of aspects of economic and financial life—leading to developments like faster price discovery and digital currencies, and the related **changing micro and macro behavior of economic agents.**

While the actual comprehension of the underlying business cycle and price-formation dynamics was always incomplete, it now also seems that some of those long-term trends are ebbing away (see Chap. 9): for example, China's deflationary impact into global markets appears to be ending, or be made to end (and it is not apparent that a growing India can be a "second China" in terms of global prices), while the global economy seems to be partially re-fragmenting into blocks. Additionally, new pressures are appearing and some unresolved ones are finally showing their costs.

Namely, the mispricing of risk behind the "Global Financial Crisis" (or GFC, which was eventually followed by significant increases in the regulatory burden on the financial sector, as financial stability increasingly became part of an expanded formal mandate for many monetary authorities: see Chap. 5) and its regional successor and variant, the euro area sovereign crisis (see Chap. 6), was associated with **large increases in the indebtedness of economic agents around the world, both public and private**, to levels not seen since the last world war. Those much larger

---

[3] One can already anticipate here how much more "governance heavy" the current system is compared with the "Classic Gold Standard".

stocks of debt were accommodated by much bigger balance sheets of monetary authorities following a so-called **"quantitative easing"** (QE) approach—buying a large share of the newly issued Government debt, and made bearable by policy interest rates that were, in some cases, nominally negative, and as a rule **negative in real terms** (given inflation levels above the nominal interest rate). The presumed "exit strategy" from this situation was a progressive "normalization" of both interest rates and of the size of the balance sheets of monetary authorities: this "normalization" has proved to be very progressive indeed, and had hardly started (if at all, for instance, in the euro area) when the next shock, COVID-19, hit in early 2020 (see Chap. 7).

The policy response to a global pandemic was a series of "lockdowns" of whole economies and populations around the world, paralyzing economic and human interactions around the planet, and creating long-lived price shocks due to the disruption of global supply chains. To cushion the deep effects of those worldwide "lockdowns"—a real economy shock, which caused again another global recession of a dimension last seen during a world war—**a replay of the GFC "policy script" for a financial crisis was effectively chosen**: even more massive and on occasion untargeted fiscal spending, supported by balance sheet (re)expansion and negative real interest rates by monetary authorities. This delayed further an already protracted "normalization" path and would further create inflationary pressures that would interact with those created by the lockdown-driven supply chains disruptions.

Finally, in early 2022, Russian troops invaded a neighboring country, Ukraine (see Chap. 8). This fragrantly illegal act against the international rule of law led to *additional* price shocks—as price increases had started already *a year before the conflict began*—on traded energy and agricultural commodities that reverberated globally, interacting with the previous sources of inflationary dynamics. Importantly, from a sectoral point of view, the exit from the lockdown-induced global recession **inherently implies a "transitional" price shock that can be very long-lived** (the reordering of the global energy matrix away from fossil fuels pursued by major economic areas around the world is an additional and prolonged "transitional" shock).

Only when faced with this last shock, and a possible unmooring of price expectations, monetary authorities implemented a policy of steady interest rate increases: given the level of accumulated price pressures by then, repeated worldwide rounds of those became necessary until late 2023.

After this historic "tour d'horizon", the final chapter of the book (Chap. 9) looks at **what lies ahead for monetary policy**. This is a global matter, as monetary (and fiscal) authorities around the world grapple with how to fulfill their price stability mandates, while uncertain about the magnitude and duration of the ongoing shocks (e.g., demographics, the potential re-fragmentation of the global economy in competing blocks, technological developments), the related fiscal behavior of their governments, with historically high debt loads and facing possibly large and long-duration conflict-related expenses, suggesting a structurally larger role for Governments going forward, and finally more indebted and financially fragile public and private sectors facing policy reversals, entailing additional pressures on the financial stability mandate of monetary authorities.

This implies at least a review of the theoretical and analytical underpinnings used by central banks since the "Great Moderation" era, to assess what is and what may not be "fit for purpose" in this new environment: this is already ongoing, and also happened after other major crises. This does not imply "throwing the baby out with the bathwater", but instead to recognize the shortcomings of any monetary policy framework—especially ones that lack stable endogenous anchors, as is the case with *fiat* money, and that therefore have to rely on sophisticated and non-transparent models to set where to lay the anchor. This is even more problematic given the limitations and uncertainty those models face when presented with "structural breaks"—including those of a geopolitical nature—that ultimately affect the behavior of economic agents, and the consequent need to see monetary policy and its implementers, central banks, as part of a policy mix that is underpinned by a dynamic political, economic, technological and societal compact.

The main conclusion of this book is that crises usually do not come out of nowhere (albeit occasionally exogenous shocks from a noneconomic nature do occur, as if "God is testing humanity"). Rather, **crises, on most occasions, reflect real people taking imperfect policy decisions in real time, and doing so guided by frameworks that progressively reveal themselves to be incorrect** (from the "real bills doctrine" in 1929 to the stable "Phillips curve" during the 1970s to "forward guidance" in 2020).

There is no analysis that looks comprehensively at how we got here, and what may lie ahead. This synthetic book, mixing history, economic theory and personal memory, and deliberately covering the "missing link" of Developing countries throughout its narrative arch, while building on works produced through different stages of my over 20-year-long professional career, aims to help fill this gap. At the same time, I pepper the book with examples of explicit model frameworks that relate to the different periods in questions, with the objective of making this work even more useful for both practitioners, academic users and economics and finance students (the latter demonstrated by my own students at Brandeis). So, enjoy reading the rest of this book!

References

Laeven, L., and F. Valencia. 2018. *Systemic Banking Crises Revisited*. IMF Working Paper No. 18/206.

Reinhart, C., and K. Rogoff. 2009. *This Time Is Different: Eight Centuries of Financial Folly*. Princeton University Press.

CHAPTER 2

The long goodbye of the gold standard and the "Great Depression"

2.1 The Classic Gold Standard

In an open economy, monetary policy cannot be understood separately from the exchange rate regime, or from the fiscal stance of a government. In this chapter, these statements will be illustrated in historical terms.

The world economies and monetary system are in a status of perpetual change, which implies that the same is true for monetary policy. However, all stories—and histories—must have a starting point for the narratives they aim to tell, if for no other reason than to make the process of storytelling manageable. So, our history here starts with the so-called gold standard, arguably the first (quasi) global monetary system.

The gold standard was a global system through which participating countries (and, in some cases, their associated empires, as it came about during an age of mostly European-led global empires) agreed to fix the prices of their domestic currencies in terms of a given amount of particular commodity, namely, gold—a durable, divisible, transportable and relatively rare element, and those national currencies were then (largely) freely convertible into gold at that fixed amount: these features would give this system—at least in principle—a binding quasi-automatic mechanism to correct balance-of-payments imbalances between all participating monetary areas, via inflows and outflows of gold reserves that transmitted the price and competitiveness shocks behind those imbalances, while

© The Author(s), under exclusive license to Springer Nature Switzerland AG 2024
L. Vinhas de Souza, *A Century of Global Economic Crises*, https://doi.org/10.1007/978-3-031-53460-7_2

compensating for those shocks via real exchange rate adjustments (see Annex 2.A for an elegant formalized model of the gold standard operation as concerning the price level). This process was enabled by the existing respective national monetary authorities pursuing passive, accommodative policies.[1]

This system's main advantages were its **automatic and system-wide provision of long-term price stability**, which underpinned the convertibility needs of a global economy that was then both growing and integrating. Of course, economies under the gold standard were vulnerable to real and monetary shocks—*as all economies are, under any monetary or exchange rate regime*—and prices could still be unstable in the short run. However, because the gold standard deliberately constrained monetary authorities' (if such existed) discretion to use policy tools, economies in a gold standard were consequently less able to cushion monetary or real shocks, and therefore real output *could* in principle, if not in practice, be more unstable under it than under other frameworks.[2] This said, the state apparatus in those times was far less developed than currently[3] and had therefore a much smaller set of tools to stabilize an economy: more than that, the very notion that the state has a *responsibility* to cushion the business cycle is actually a fairly recent development.

While historical analysis do confirm the price stabilizing properties of the gold standard (see Bordo 1981), **it is simply not apparent that data series actually bears out a higher volatility of real GDP then under other regimes**: data with GDP growth for a sample of 16 developed

---

[1] Bloomfield, A. (1959), "Monetary Policy Under the Gold Standard, 1880 to 1914", Federal Reserve Bank of New York, and Dutton J., 1984, "The Bank of England and the Rules of the Game under the International Gold Standard: New Evidence", in Bordo M. and Schwartz A. (eds.), *A Retrospective on the Classical Gold Standard*, NBER.

[2] Bordo, M. (1981), "The Classical Gold Standard—Some Lessons for Today", Federal Reserve Bank of St. Louis Review, 5: 2–17.

[3] For instance, "central banks" as what one thinks of them now just did not exist, as they were not needed under the gold standard. Additionally, institutions that later evolve to become central banks, for instance, the appropriately named "Bank of England" (originally a privately owned body), had as their main original function to *bankroll their national governments*. Their later first and main institutional mandate (as the name suggests) *was not related to price stability, but to financial stability, namely, the provision of liquidity to the broader financial system*, that is, acting as a bank for banks, or as a "central bank". And do not start me on the fiscal fine-tuning of the economic cycles…

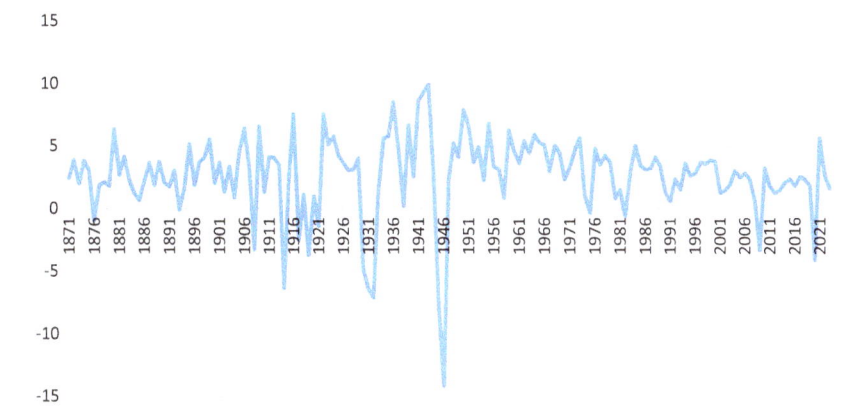

Fig. 2.1 Long-term GDP growth rates for a sample of developed economies. (Sources: Author, based in Maddison (2001) and IMF)

economies[4] from 1870 onward essentially shows the same GDP variability for the periods of the "Classic Gold Standard" and the post 1973 period[5] (using a post-Gold Standard sample starting *after* any of the two world wars results in a standard deviation that is measurably higher: just "eyeballing" the data in Fig. 2.1 already suggests that conclusion).

This system, as it were, developed gradually. The core of it, the United Kingdom (UK)—then the largest economy and the largest empire in the world, and also the country that spearheaded the industrial revolution, first adopted a *de facto* gold standard in 1717, and a formal one shortly after the end of the Napoleonic Wars in 1819, together with some of its colonies.[6] Other countries joined progressively: for instance, Portugal joined already in 1854,[7] almost 20 years before larger European

---

[4] These 16 economies are Australia, Austria, Belgium, Canada, Denmark, Finland, France, Germany, Italy, Netherlands, New Zealand, Norway, Sweden, Switzerland, the UK and the US.

[5] Using Bank of England GDP data for Britain since **1210** shows that GDP variability during the "Classic God Standard" is not only actually lower than that in the later periods, **but it is also lower than in all the preceding periods**.

[6] Bordo, M. (1981), ibid.

[7] Duarte, A. and Andrade, J., (2012), "How the Gold Standard Functioned in Portugal: An Analysis of Some Macroeconomic Aspects", Applied Economics, 44(5): 617–629.

economies—led by Germany in 1872, the year after its unification made it the second largest economy in the continent—did so. By the end of the nineteenth century, the Kingdom of Spain was the only European country that kept a nonconvertible paper money (or *fiat* money, from the Latin for "let it be done"). Outside of Europe, the United States (US) had a *de facto* gold standard since 1834, which became formal in 1900, and countries as diverse and far apart as Brazil and Japan adopted versions of the standard (Box 2.1 and Annex 2.B).

Box 2.1 The (Quasi) Universality of the Classical Gold Standard
The gold standard history is typically told from the point of view of the largest Developed economies of North America and Europe. However, even if its apogee coincided with the age of Empires (outside of Europe, only the American continent was then made-up of mostly independent polities), it was a truly global system, albeit with particular national and regional dynamics (see Annex 2.B). To illustrate that, below are two examples from independent nations in Latin America and Asia:

Brazil: From the currency reform of 1846 onward, Brazil informally followed the gold standard with the then Brazilian currency, the "milreis", kept around a parity of 27d (or 27 pence, which implied a fixed parity to the gold-backed British pound), temporally moving below this parity during major crisis like the Paraguayan War.[8] However, only in 1906 Brazil formally joined the gold standard, at a revalued 15d parity (adjusted to 16d a few years later) and remained on the gold standard until World War I (briefly returning to it from 1926 to 1930).[9]

(*continued*)

---

[8] The Paraguayan War, also known as the War of the "Triple Alliance", is the deadliest war in Latin American history, lasting from 1864 to 1870. It was fought between Paraguay and the so-called Triple Alliance" of the Republic of Argentina, the Empire of Brazil, and the Oriental Republic of Uruguay.

[9] Schulz, J. (2017), "Around the British Gold Standard: Portugal and Brazil. Two satellites?", História e Economia, Vol. 19 and Fritsch, W and Franco, G. (1992), "Aspects of the Brazilian Experience with the Gold Standard".

Box 2.1 (continued)
Japan: After the (re) opening of Japan to international trade in 1853, the new Meiji government enacted a "New Currency Law" in 1871 that created the yen as a currency and made it equal to 1.5 grams of gold. Albeit the yen was actually placed on a silver-standard from 1885 until 1897, Japan finally formally adopted the gold standard that year, in a parity that would be maintained, with a few interruptions, until December 1931.[10]

The period lasting from 1870 (or 1880, depending on the author) to 1914 is known as the "classical gold standard", and it was also a period of largely global free trade in goods, labor, and capital, the "First Globalization" period in human history, which was underpinned by this largely stable and convertible global monetary system. However, it broke down during the major systemic upheavals brought about by World War I, due to the monetary financing of the large conflict-related expenses (the *de facto* gold standard had also been suspended during earlier conflicts, for instance, during the Napoleonic Wars, and some countries left the formal system before World War I, for example, Portugal, which exited the system in 1891 in response to a domestic economic and political crisis) and the changes in the global economic order that underpinned the system.

2.2 THE GREAT DEPRESSION AND THE END OF THE "GOLD EXCHANGE STANDARD"

A *quasi*-gold standard system was partially and briefly reinstated after the end of World War I as the so-called Gold Exchange Standard, which lasted between 1925 and 1931. Under it, participating countries could hold gold, US dollars or British pounds as reserves backing convertible currencies: on the other hand, the US and the UK—the "anchors" of this new system—could hold reserves only in gold: given that core monetary authorities, and notably the Federal Reserve (or "Fed", the US monetary

---

[10] Metzler, M. (2006), "Japan and the British Gold Standard, ca. 1715–1885", in *Lever of Empire*, 14–28, University of California Press.

authority, which had been created only in 1913, originally as a system of regional "bank of banks" to provide market liquidity after the US banking crisis of 1907) **engaged in frequent sterilizing operations of gold flows that fundamentally negated the automatic adjustment properties of the gold system**, this period is probably better described as a "managed monetary period".[11] Importantly, this was also **a structural break concerning agents expectations about inflation**: *with the demise of the "Classic Gold Standard" came the end of its nominal and real stabilization properties described above, and economic agents eventually internalized that on their behavior, even if not immediately.*

This limited (and internally contradictory) attempt to reassert the gold standard was also simply inconsistent with the realities of the post-World War I global economy, and some authors link its' eventual demise to—with hindsight, misguided—not only Fed but also US legislative and policy actions that facilitated the onset of global deflationary pressures, that, on their turn, helped create the profoundest and most prolonged economic downturn of the twentieth century, the appropriately called **Great Depression**.[12]

The Great Depression began almost a century ago, in August 1929, when an 8-year-long economic expansion known as "Roaring Twenties"—unleashed by the end of World War I dislocations and the ebbing away of the 1918–1920 "Spanish Flu" Pandemic—came to an end. A series of financial crises punctuated this contraction, including the famous stock market crash in 1929 that signals its beginning, which followed by a series of US regional banking panics in 1930 and 1931 and US and international financial crises from 1931 through 1933.

The downturn hit bottom in March 1933, when deep stresses in the US commercial banking system led to then President Franking Delano

---

[11] Bordo, M. (1981), ibidem.

[12] Mundell, R. (2000), "A Reconsideration of the Twentieth Century", American Economic Review (AER), 90 (3): 327–340. This AER piece is a reprint of Mundell's Nobel Prize lecture of 1999, where he singles out not only Fed actions—following Friedman and Schwartz, 1963—but trade protectionism, including the US' Smoot-Hawley Tariff Act of 1930, as culprits of what came later (one could think of this piece as an international economy extension of the Friedman and Schwartz critique of Fed policies during the "Great Depression"). As a personal recollection, this author wrote his PhD dissertation as an application of the Mundell-Fleming optimal currency area theory to the creation of the European common currency, the euro, and had the honor of having Robert Mundell signing a copy of it. He passed away in 2021.

Roosevelt to declare, just 36 hours into his presidency a national banking holiday that would last for four days. Systemic reforms of the US financial system accompanied the economic recovery, which was interrupted by another GDP contraction in 1937, with sustained growth only finally returning during World War II.

The Great Depression is, quite simply, the deepest cumulative economic contraction in US history. Between 1929 and 1933, GDP fell by a shocking over 20% and GDP per capita fell by almost 30%, while unemployment surpassed 25% of the total civilian labor force (and reached an astounding **almost 38%** of the non-farm civilian employment in 1933): see Figs. 2.2 and 2.3.

The Great Depression also dramatically expanded the role of the US government: before it, the US federal government spending accounted for less than 5% of GDP, already by 1939 this figure had more than doubled. It also significantly increased its regulatory footprint, from expanded powers to the Federal Reserve to the creation of the Federal Deposit Insurance Corporation (FDIC)—the organism that provides bank deposit insurance in the US, of state-owned corporations like the Tennessee Valley Authority, of the US Social Security System and the first national US minimum wage.

How did the "Great Depression" come about? There are many explanations, but a short, snappy, theoretically rigorous (and honest) one is given by none other than Ben Bernanke in 2002 (he was then a member

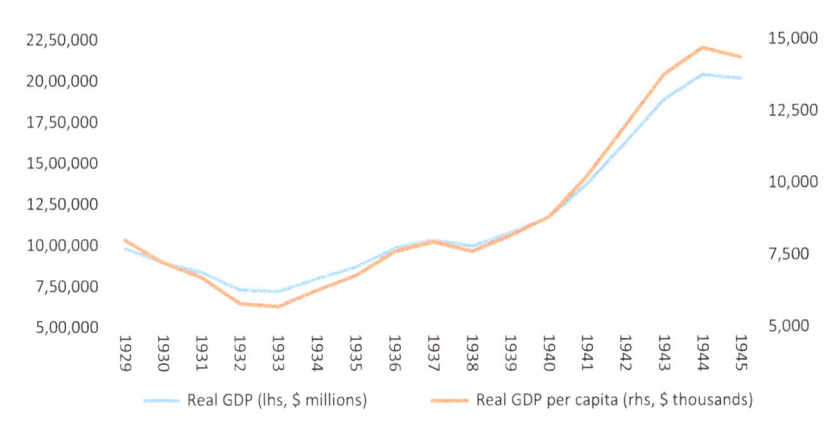

Fig. 2.2 US GDP and GDP per capita, real, 1929–1945. (Source: US Bureau of Economic Analysis [BEA])

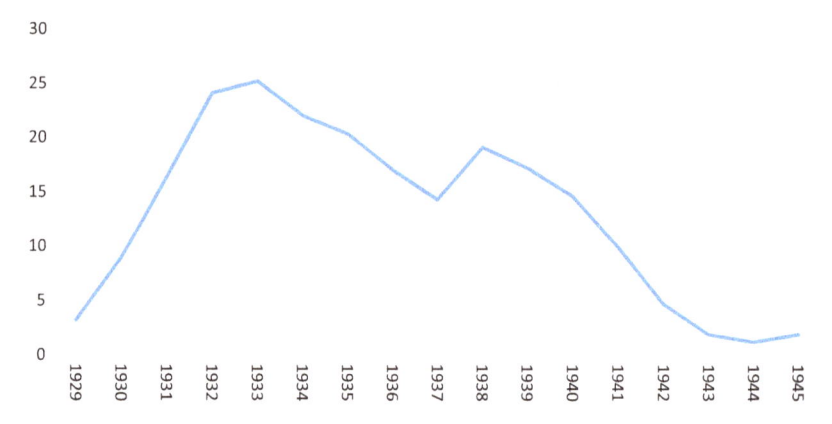

Fig. 2.3 US unemployment, percentage of civilian labor force. (Source: US Bureau of Labor Statistics)

of the Federal Reserve Board of Governors, only becoming Chairman of the Board in 2006): "…we did it. We're very sorry. … We won't do it again".[13] In this piece, he—channeling the monumental and seminal work by Friedman and Schwartz, 1963[14]—acknowledged that **repeated** Federal Reserve's mistakes fundamentally contributed to the "worst economic disaster in American history", while also claiming that the Fed had "learned its lessons" (Bernanke 2002). As it turns out, this book will later add some nuance to his last point on the Fed "learning lessons" from crises.

The list of Fed policy mistakes during the "Great Depression" is indeed quite extensive, in number and in persistency.[15] At the start of the Depression, the Federal Reserve's decision-making structure was rather decentralized and arguably of limited effectiveness. Each of the 12 regional "districts" (clusters of US Federal states) had a governor who set policies for his district, although some decisions required approval of the Fed Board. However, the Board lacked the authority, personalities and tools to

---

[13] Bernanke, B., speech given at "A Conference to Honor Milton Friedman on the Occasion of His 90th Birthday", November 8, 2002.

[14] Friedman, M. and Schwartz, A., 1963, "A Monetary History of the United States, 1867–1960", Princeton University Press.

[15] The corresponding section in Friedman and Schwartz, 1963, ibid., is telling, actually entitled "Why Was Monetary Policy so Inept?" (pp. 407).

fully formulate policy or to coordinate policies across districts, effectively acting more as a secretariat, and with the New York Fed frequently acting as the *actual* policy setter for the system.

The New York Fed was the most important among the Fed districts, due to the size of New York's bank system and related institutional responsibilities but also due to the strong personality of Benjamin Strong (sic), the head of the New York Federal Reserve since its creation in 1914 until his death in 1928, just before the onset of the "Great Depression". To this day, the New York Fed as a body has the monopoly on implementing of Fed monetary policy (via its "Open Market Trading Desk"), is the sole fiscal agent of the US Treasury Department, the custodian of the US gold reserves and holder of the primary responsibility for international monetary relations in the Fed system. The NY Fed was so dominant during Strong's tenure (and for a short time afterward) that it would even act unilaterally without the other Fed districts.

Beyond the absence of a common diagnostic of the situation among Board members and the lack of Board leadership capable of and willing to provide effective policy guidance (and that under two successive Chairmen, Roy Young, from October 1927 to August 1930 and Eugene Meyer, September 1930 to May 1933), sheer policy mistakes were committed in the lead up and during the Great Depression—even if unintentionally, as is usually the case with mistakes. An example is the Fed's decision **to raise interest rates in 1928 and 1929**, as an attempt to limit speculation in the US securities markets and to stem the outflow of gold reserves: the Fed repeated this error when responding to the international financial stresses caused by the UK's exit from the "Gold Exchange Standard" in 1931. Another example is the Fed's **failure to act as a lender of last resort during the several domestic banking runs that lasted from 1930 until the banking holiday of 1933**: this was a direct result of the Federal Reserve's internal policy disagreements on *if* to provide liquidity to the financial system and *to whom* this liquidity should be provided, and of the continued ineffectiveness of the Fed Board in enforcing coordination.[16]

---

[16] Friedman and Schwartz, 1963, ibid., provide a detailed description of the repeated attempts by the NY Fed between 1929 and 1933 in providing additional liquidity to the economy and bank system being stimmed by the opposition from particular Presidents of Fed districts, in parallel to persistent Fed Board institutional limitations. One of the effects of this was that between 1929 and 1933, 10,763 of the 24,970 commercial banks in the US closed (or over 43% of all existing U.S. banks at the time).

If these were not enough, the likely most egregious policy mistake of the Fed was its **failure to stem the decline in money supply: from 1929 to 1933, M1** (a measure of money that includes physical currency, demand deposits, travelers' checks and other checkable deposits) **shockingly fell by almost a third.** Prices fell by a similar amount, all the way into disinflationary territory, increasing debt burdens and distorting economic decisions, pushing all types of economic agents into bankruptcy and brutally increasing unemployment.

The Fed could have prevented deflation by expanding the monetary base and/or by providing liquidity to the banking system: it did neither of those things. Its policy makers misinterpreted signals about the state of the economy, either because of the adherence of some Board members to a "real bills doctrine"[17] or due to a perceived need to uphold the "Gold Exchange Standard" by raising interest rates.

These costly and repeated policy flaws and the design shortcomings in the Federal Reserve's governance ultimately led to several regulatory reforms: the Reconstruction Finance Corporation Act and the Banking Act of 1932 (so, passed already under the Hoover administration), and the Emergency Banking Act of 1933, the Glass-Steagall act of 1933, the Gold Reserve Act of 1934 and the Banking Act of 1935 (those under the Roosevelt administration).

These policy deficiencies made the US very much the epicenter of the "Great Depression": while undoubtedly a global, systemic crisis, most other economies contracted by considerably less than the US. For instance, the US cumulative 1929–1933 GDP contraction was five **times larger than that of Western Europe, and three and a half times that of Latin America**. Only in countries like Australia, Canada, Germany, Mexico and New Zealand the average contraction was somewhat closer to the US one, at between 15% and 20% of GDP. Also, ex-US, global GDP fell by around 8%, and the through was already in 1932, not 1933, and there was no "double-dip recession" as in the US (see Fig. 2.4).

---

[17] The founders of the Fed understood it as a decentralized system of reserve banks that would allow the expansion and contraction of money supply and therefore of credit, based on discounting paper issued by its member banks (so-called bills) for financing real, productive activities (therefore, "real bills"). By discounting these real bills that would finance loans for "productive" trade and goods related activities, the Fed would have fulfilled its institutional responsibilities (as understood by those Board members), namely, provide the reserves required to finance only legitimate, nonspeculative, demands for credit.

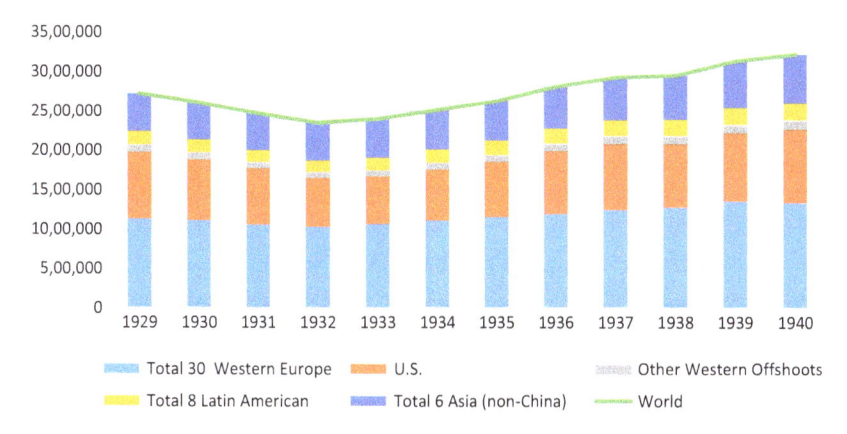

Fig. 2.4 Global GDP during the Great Depression (real $ thousands). (Source: Author, based on Maddison 2001)

But what made the "Great Depression" in the US **both deeper and longer than in most parts of the world?** The policy mistakes—emanating largely from the US monetary authority—described earlier are a large part of the explanation, but mostly for the extent and depth of the *contraction phase* of this particularly extreme business cycle: for the length and relative mildness of the *recovery phase*, additional elements are likely needed. Cole and Ohanian (2007)[18] estimate that by 1933 the negative effects of the monetary shock had effectively ended in the US, and that the length of the weak recovery was largely due **to the labor and industrial policies of the Roosevelt administration**: namely, the National Industrial Recovery Act of 1933 allowed much of the US economy to **cartelize** via different types of regulations affecting over 500 economic sectors, including manufacturing, and that these policies increased relative prices and real wages by 25% or more in the cartelized sectors. Using their model, they conclude that these policies, by preventing markets from clearing at full employment levels **accounted for about 60% of the weakness of the US recovery from the "Great Depression"**.

---

[18] Cole, H. and Ohanian, L. (2007), "A Second Look at the U.S. Great Depression from a Neoclassical Perspective", in *Great Depressions of the Twentieth Century*, Kehoe, T. and Prescott, E. (eds) (2007), Federal Reserve Bank of Minneapolis, pp. 21–57.

As the effects of the 1929 Great Depression spread globally, the "Gold Exchange Standard", that short-lived, partial and internally inconsistent replacement to the gold standard eventually broke down after the 1931 British exit of the system (itself a consequence of the failure of the Vienna Kreditanstalt, Austria's largest bank, that year and the subsequent German banking crisis). Finally, in 1933, the US also suspended its own participation in the system, leading to its final end.[19] The collapse of the gold standard also meant the end of the "first globalization" era, as international capital and trade flows collapsed. This slump in global integration will persist throughout the many stresses caused by the overlapping global shocks of the "Great Depression" and World War II, and was replaced by a patchwork of national, largely nonconvertible *fiat* currencies subject to national monetary policies and operating under restricted capital and goods international flows.[20]

2.3 Beyond the "Great Depression": Bretton Woods and that "Barbarous Relic"

With the "Great Depression" firmly behind and the end of the World War II approaching, a conference was organized by the US (and the UK, as a very much "minority partner") in July 1944 in Bretton Woods, New Hampshire, US, to effectively (re)shape the global postwar economic order.[21] The core question at the conference was what would be the new global economic, monetary and financial order and how it would be governed. Although 730 delegates from 44 allied countries met, the US and

---

[19] By Executive Order 6102 of April 5, 1933 (an amendment of the Emergency Banking Act of March 1933), US President Franklin Delano Roosevelt required US citizens to *turn their gold coins and bullion over to the Federal Reserve and prohibited exports of gold*. The US Congress then followed with a law overriding gold payment requirements in public and private contracts (Graetz, M., and Briffault, O. [2016], "A 'Barbarous Relic': The French, Gold, and the Demise of Bretton Woods", Columbia University Law School). The prohibition of US citizens holding gold would be removed **only in 1974**, by President Gerald Ford.

[20] For the US case, see Wheelock, D. (1977), "Monetary Policy in the Great Depression and Beyond: The Sources of the Fed's Inflation Bias", Federal Reserve Bank of St. Louis Working Paper 1997-011.

[21] For an entrancing history of this episode and the lead up to it, see Steil, B. (2013), "The Battle of Bretton Woods: John Maynard Keynes, Harry Dexter White, and the Making of a New World Order", Princeton University Press.

UK fully dominated the proceedings, led by respectively, Harry Dexter White (a senior US Treasury Department official) and John Maynard (Baron) Keynes, one of the most famous and influential economists of the twentieth century.[22]

The "White Plan" advocated a central status for the dollar as a surrogate for gold, while Keyne's eschewed the "barbarous relic",[23] proposing what effectively was an international *fiat* money, the "bancor" (one of the aims of Keynes' proposal was actually to avoid a US-centric global monetary system). The two plans agreed, however, on the need for an international institutional framework for the coordination of monetary and exchange rate policies (which was to become the International Monetary Fund, or IMF). In the end, the countries represented at Bretton Woods largely supported (or were "incentivized" to support) the US plan—as that country was now the undisputed core of the global economy, being spared the widespread devastation unleashed by World War II. The IMF "Articles of Agreement"—its founding treaty—were signed in December 1945 and the IMF became operational in March 1947.[24]

Even though this so-called Bretton Woods System (after the city where the conference was held) was tested as soon as 1949 by a progressive crisis of the British pound,[25] its participating countries (which were the large majority of the market economies in the world) mostly operated under it

---

[22] His classic work is Keynes, J. (1936), "The General Theory of Employment, Interest, and Money", First Harvest Hacourt Brace, UK, and it provided the dominant analytical framework for the macroeconomic policies used in market economies to counteract the "Great Depression". The British Sovereign, King George VI, awarded him in 1942 the title "Baron Keynes, of Tilton, in the County of Sussex".

[23] The full quote is "In truth, the gold standard is already a barbarous relic", see Keynes, J. (1923), "A Tract on Monetary Reform", Macmillan and Co. (the predecessor of the publisher of this book), UK, p. 172.

[24] The US centrality in the new system was demonstrated even geographically, as the two new "Bretton Woods" institutions, the IMF and the World Bank, were **both** to be headquartered in Washington, DC. As aside, this author, a former World Bank staffer, –the other "Bretton Woods" institution, is fond of the old quip that the Bretton Woods institutions are misnamed, as the IMF is actually a *bank* (as it lends money to its members, who make its' lendable capital via deposits, a.k.a., as "quotas", and receives principal and interest repayment on those loans), while the World Bank is at least partially a *fund* (as it makes nonreimbursable grants from its pooled funds to its poorer members, albeit admittedly it makes loans, too).

[25] The Pound was ultimately forced to devalue by 30% in September 1949, a move that was followed within days by 30 other countries also devaluing their currencies (see Steil 2013, ibid.).

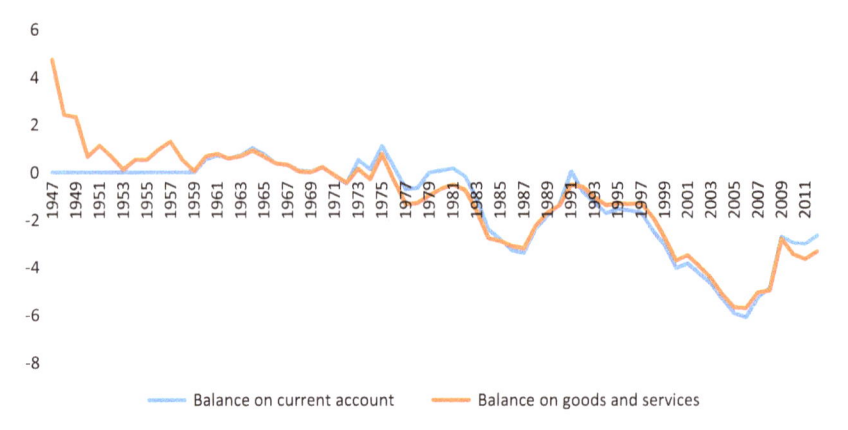

Fig. 2.5 The US external balance under Bretton Woods (% of GDP). (Sources: BEA, U.S. Census Bureau, calculations by the Author)

until 1971, settling their international balances in US dollars,[26] as the US government committed to redeem other central banks' holdings of dollars for gold at a fixed rate of $35 per ounce.[27] However, a progressively worsening US balance-of-payments' position[28] after the end of World War II (Fig. 2.5) steadily reduced US gold reserves and, on August 15, 1971, the US announced that it would no longer redeem its currency for gold. The "gold standard" and its derivates was soon to be no more, and the age of floating exchange rates managed by monetary authorities ("central banks", the new "anchors" of this decentralized set of monetary systems) issuing *fiat* money and pursuing national monetary policies was up on us.[29]

---

[26] The IMF Articles of Agreement actually define international currencies parities **with reference to gold**, with members committing to maintain those within a 1% variation margin, by either buying or selling dollars at their gold-pegged value to maintain the value of their currencies within that margin.

[27] In 1934, US President Roosevelt set the price of gold at $35 an ounce (effectively devaluing the US dollar in gold term by nearly 60%, as the previous dollar gold price was $20.67 an ounce).

[28] Reinbold, B. and Wen, Y. (2019), "Historical U.S. Trade Deficits", Federal Reserve.

[29] Or, again, not (quite) yet: actual (truly) free floating *fiat* currencies will be mostly restricted to some developed economies for many years to come. Most other economies (including some smaller developed ones) will largely opt for several reasons for variations of pegged currency regimes (so, even after 1973, pegged systems lived to fight another day). For the seminal paper in this literature, see Calvo, G. and Reinhart, C, (2000), "Fear of Floating", NBER Working Paper 7993, and for an application to very open small economies, see Vinhas de Souza, L. (2002), "Integrated Monetary and Exchange Rate Frameworks: Are There Empirical Differences?", Working Paper Series, n° 2/2002, Bank of Estonia.

2.4 The US "Great Inflation" and the End of the "Bretton Woods" System

It was not an easy birth: the end of the gold-backed Bretton Woods system can be aptly described by the famous quote from Ernest Hemingway's 1926 novel "The Sun Also Rises", in which a character asks another how he went bankrupt, the reply being "gradually, then suddenly". Gradually, imbalances were building up under this US-led afterlife of the "gold standard" (Fig. 2.5). Henry Dexter White was wrong when he said that "dollar and gold are … .synonymous",[30] as what would come to be known as the "Triffin dilemma" eventually asserted itself (in 1959, Belgian economist Robert Triffin told the US Congress that the use of "national currencies in international reserves" was a destabilizer to "world monetary arrangements").

That was because foreign governments that accumulated US dollars eventually either lent any excess dollars (i.e., over and above their imports' needs) back to the US or held them as reserves, implying that there was no effective way for the US to provide sufficient dollars to satisfy the world's liquidity needs for trade and capital flows, while simultaneously limiting the number of dollars that could be redeemed for gold at a fixed price (hence the "dilemma").[31]

Accordingly, from a post–World War II high of almost 81% of US dollars in circulation covered by US gold reserves, this had dwindled to around 16% in 1971 (Fig. 2.6). The same fundamental weakness of the system was also detected by French economist Jacques Rueff,[32] who would later become an adviser to French President Charles de Gaulle on monetary and financial matters. Rueff's analysis that an alternative system would

---

[30] Henry Dexter White to the House Committee on Banking and Currency, during the Bretton Woods ratification debate in March 1945 "[T]o us, and to the world, the United States dollar and gold are synonymous. … It is a mere matter of convenience of expression rather than significance other than reiteration of the fact that dollars and gold are virtually synonymous" (as quoted by Steil, B., 2013, ibid., p. 256). In another misreading of economic theory *and* history, White was later unmasked as a Soviet collaborator (see Steil, B., ibid.).

[31] Graetz and Briffault, ibid. That abstracts from domestic US currency needs.

[32] Rueff, J. and Hirsh, F. (1965), "The Role and the Rule of Gold: An Argument", Princeton Essays on International Finances, 47: 2–3 and Rueff, J. (1972), "The Monetary Sin of the West", New York, Macmillan.

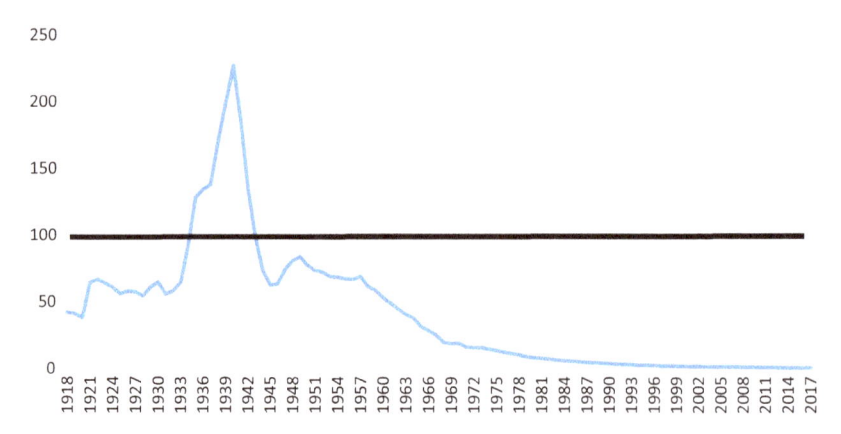

Fig. 2.6 US gold reserves/money in circulation, end-of-the-year (eoy), %. (Source: FRED (Federal Reserve Economic Data), calculations by the Author. The line at 100 shows when money in circulation is fully covered by gold reserves)

be needed would be one of the building blocks that would eventually lead to the creation of the common European Union currency, the euro (see Chap. 6: the euro was a project in which this author—humbly—also worked on).

As said above, the final demise of "Bretton Woods"—like the gold standard before it—was a (*dixit*) very gradual process, even as its internal contradictions were becoming increasingly apparent (the popular expression "slow motion train wreck" may come to mind). For instance, given the growing imbalances, already in 1961 nine central banks—the US plus eight European countries—created the so-called London Gold Pool[33] in

---

[33] Upholding the gold-pegged Bretton Woods system may have helped the US Federal Reserve deliver on low and stable inflation (domestically and abroad) from the early 1950s to the mid-1960s. The transfer of main responsibility for the US external balance from the Fed to the US Treasury with the creation of the "gold pool", especially after 1965, possibly weakened this constraint—and therefore the Fed's commitment to low and stable inflation in the US—even before Bretton Woods formal end (see Bordo, M. and Eichengreen, B. (2008) "Bretton Woods and the Great Inflation", NBER Working Paper Series n. 14532).

an attempt to maintain fixed convertible values for their currencies at the $35 price for an ounce of gold (half the required supply of gold for the pool came from the US).[34]

However, already by 1965 the "pool" could no longer stem the outflow of gold, accelerated by the growing external and internal US imbalances, so the "pool" ultimately collapsed in May 1968, being replaced by a two-tiered system with separate private and public (in the sense of trading between public bodies like central banks) gold markets: governments traded gold in the public market at a fixed price, while in the private market the price of gold was a market one (this transformed market stresses from speculative attacks on a gold-backed standard to more traditional speculative attacks against a fixed exchange rate regime, this one centered on a fiat currency, the US dollar: see Garber 1991).[35] Bretton Woods and the "gold"-linked era will finally end a little more than three years after that, in August 1971.[36]

---

[34] Another (half-hearted) attempt to preserve some features of the Bretton Woods *quasi*-gold standard was the creation of the IMF's "Special Drawing Rights", or SDRs, an international reserve asset based on an evolving basket of IMF members' currencies, somewhat similar to Keynes' "bancor" proposal of a generation earlier (the political agreement on the SDRs was reached in the summer of 1967, but they only became operational in 1969).

[35] Garber, P. (1991), "The Collapse of the Bretton Woods Fixed Exchange Rate System" in *A Retrospective on the Bretton Woods System: Lessons for International Monetary Reform*, Bordo, M. and Eichengreen, B. (eds), University of Chicago Press: 461–494.

[36] Well, again, not quite yet: even then the global (quasi) gold standard was not finished, as in December 1971 monetary authorities from the world's leading developed countries met at the Smithsonian Institution in Washington, DC, to try *one more time* to preserve the system. With the so-called Smithsonian Agreement, the US agreed to devalue the dollar to $38 per ounce of gold, and participants agreed to future talks on reforms of the international monetary system. This did not stabilize the system and renewed pressures on European currencies ultimately led to capital controls being imposed by the affected countries. In February 1973, the US devalued the dollar in relation to gold one more time, but this again failed to reduce market pressures, and within a month currencies were finally (mostly…) freely floating against the US dollar: that event—the "sudden" part of Hemingway's quote—is what marks the real end of the "Bretton Woods" gold-linked monetary system.

Annex 2.A: Formalizing Price Level Determination under the Gold Standard

A simple and elegant model of how the gold standard actually endogenously anchors the price level is given by Barro (1979).[37] In it, the stock of money, denoted by M, represents a liability of the central bank, which is assumed to be ready to buy or sell any amount of gold at a fixed price, P_g. If G_m represents the stock of gold held by the central bank, then the supply of money would equal $P_g G_m$ under a strict gold standard (it would differ under a partial gold standard). Total money supply is

$$M^s = (1/\lambda) P_g G_m, \qquad (2.1)$$

where the parameter λ, which as $0 \leqslant \lambda \leqslant 1$, measures the gold "backing" of the monetary issuance (there have been periods of a backing above 1, as seen in Fig. 2.6).

The demand for money in circulation M^d is assumed to depend on P, on real income y and on the opportunity cost of holding money. The opportunity cost for holding money is measured by the expected rate of inflation, $\pi \equiv E(\dot{P}/P)$, where a dot denotes a time derivative. Formally, money demand is represented by

$$M^d = k\underset{(-)}{(\pi)} P y, \qquad (2.2)$$

where the minus sign denotes a negative derivative, as expected inflation and desired money holding are inversely related, while k is money velocity. Money supply and demand from (Eq. 2.1) and (Eq. 2.2) imply the price level condition

$$P = \frac{P_g G_m}{\lambda k(\cdot \pi) y} \qquad (2.3)$$

---

[37] Barro, R. (1979), "Money and the Price Level under the Classical Gold Standard", Economic Journal, 89: 13–33. Bob Barro is currently a colleague of this author at Harvard: he is an economist with a truly insightful analytical mind, as Barro regularly demonstrates in our internal seminars.

Since Eq. (2.3) holds at all times, variations of P around P_g reflect movements in the right-hand-side variables, as represented in $G_m/(\lambda k y)$. The two key determinants of monetary gold stock are gold production and the extent to which gold is held for nonmonetary purposes. With g being the rate at which new gold is extracted (and an estimated 75% of all gold on earth has already been extracted), the production function for the gold industry can be expressed by the (real) cost function $c(g)$, which describes the cost of producing gold at rate g. Production is assumed to involve positive and increasing marginal costs—that is, c', $c'' > 0$. The nominal cost for producing gold at rate g is $Pc(g)$, while the nominal revenue is $P_g g$ (with a common price for gold in monetary and nonmonetary uses). Revenue-maximizing behavior by gold producers with P_g and P exogenous implies

$$c'(g) = P_g / P \tag{2.4}$$

generating the supply function for new gold in (Eq. 2.5) below

$$g^s = g^s \underset{(-)}{\left(P / P_g \right)} \tag{2.5}$$

Let G_n denote the stock of gold that is held for non-monetary (e.g., industrial) uses, which depreciate at the constant rate δ (gold held by the central bank is assumed not to depreciate): δG_n measures the steady-state demand for gold. Total demand would also include the growth in G_m and G_n linked to growth in y. Non-monetary uses of gold would fall given a higher current relative price, P_g/P, but would increase due to expectations of higher future values of P_g/P. With P_g constant, expected future values of P_g/P vary inversely with π. Net changes in G_n at any point in time are given by

$$\dot{G}_n = g_n^d - \delta G_n = (\alpha + \delta) \left[\underset{(+)(-)}{\left(\underset{(-)}{PP_g}, \pi \right)} y - G_n \right] \tag{2.6}$$

With the monetary authority standing ready to buy or sell any amount of gold at price P_g, the steady state of the system described by the equations above corresponds to

$$\dot{P} = \dot{G}_m = \dot{G}_n = 0 \tag{2.7}$$

It can also be supposed that π, the expected value of $\dot{P}/P$, is equal to zero in the steady state. To simplify the analysis, it is assumed that π is fixed at zero even when P is changing over time. The steady-state values of P, G_m and G_n, which will be denoted by asterisks, determined from the equations above and by $\dot{G}_m = \dot{G}_n = 0$, imply

$$g^s\left(P^*_{(-)}P_g\right) = \delta f\left(P^*_{(+)}P_g, \pi^*_{(-)}\right)y \tag{2.8}$$

This condition (together with π* = 0 determines the steady-state value, P^*/P_g—and, hence, P^*—from the equality between gold production and the replacement demand for nonmonetary gold.

Additionally, as said above, in a model where y is continually increasing, the steady-state demand for gold would have other components, as given by

$$G^*_n = f\left(P^*_{(-)}/P_g, \pi^*\right)y \atop {\scriptstyle (+)} \tag{2.9}$$

This, with Eq. (2.3), implies

$$G^*_m = \lambda k\left(\pi^*\right)yP^*/P_g \tag{2.10}$$

which determines the steady-state value G^*_m and the money stock $M^* = (1/\lambda)P_g G^*_m$.[38]

---

[38] More complex model formulations are of course possible: Chappell and Dowd, 1997, developed a model of the gold standard in which technology and preferences are modeled more explicitly and which takes into account gold's durability and exhaustibility, while Fernández-Villaverde and Sanches (2022) add microfoundations (so, incorporating the behavior of different types of economic agents) and the transmission of financial crises, which makes the gold standard nonsustainable for peripheral countries (see, respectively, Chappell, D. and Dowd, K. (1997), "A Simple Model of the Gold Standard", Journal of Money, Credit and Banking, 29(1): 94–105 and Fernández-Villaverde, J. and Sanches D. (2022) "A Model of the Gold Standard," WP 22–33, Federal Reserve Bank of Philadelphia).

In other terms, **the gold standard delivers an endogenous, stable and determined (price) equilibrium**: one should compare this result with those of models for other monetary frameworks described later in this book.

ANNEX 2.B: GLOBAL PARTICIPATION IN THE "CLASSICAL GOLD STANDARD"

Table 2.1 Global participation in the "Classical Gold Standard"

Country	Type of Gold Standard	Period
Center Country		
Britain[a]	Coin	1717–1797[b], 1819–1914
Other Core Countries		
United States[c]	Coin	1834–1917[d]
France[e]	Coin	1878–1914
Germany	Coin	1872–1914
British Colonies and Dominions		
Australia	Coin	1852–1915
Canada[f]	Coin	1854–1914
Ceylon	Coin	1901–1914
India[g]	Exchange (British pound)	1898–1914
Western Europe		
Austria-Hungary[h]	Coin	1892–1914
Belgium[i]	Coin	1878–1914
Italy	Coin	1884–1894
Liechtenstein	Coin	1898–1914
Netherlands[j]	Coin	1875–1914
Portugal[k]	Coin	1854–1891
Switzerland	Coin	1878–1914
Scandinavia		
Denmark[l]	Coin	1872–1914
Finland	Coin	1877–1914
Norway	Coin	1875–1914
Sweden	Coin	1873–1914
Eastern Europe		
Bulgaria	Coin	1906–1914
Greece	Coin	1885, 1910–1914
Montenegro	Coin	1911–1914
Romania	Coin	1890–1914
Russia	Coin	1897–1914
Middle East		
Egypt	Coin	1885–1914

(*continued*)

Table 2.1 (continued)

Country	Type of Gold Standard	Period
Turkey (Ottoman Empire)	Coin	1881^m–1914
Asia		
Japan^n	Coin	1897–1931
Philippines	Exchange (US dollar)	1903–1914
Siam	Exchange (British pound)	1908–1914
Straits Settlements^o	Exchange (British pound)	1906–1914
Mexico and Central America		
Costa Rica	Coin	1896–1914
Mexico	Coin	1905–1913
South America		
Argentina	Coin	1867–1876, 1883–1885, 1900–1914
Bolivia	Coin	1908–1914
Brazil	Coin	1906–1914, 1926–1930
Chile	Coin	1895–1898
Ecuador	Coin	1898–1914
Peru	Coin	1901–1914
Uruguay	Coin	1876–1914
Africa		
Eritrea	Exchange (Italian lira)	1890–1914
German East Africa	Exchange (German mark)	1885^p–1914
Italian Somaliland	Exchange (Italian lira)	1889^p–1914

Source: Officer, L. (2008), "Countries and Dates on the Gold Standard", adapted by the author. (a) Including colonies (except British Honduras) and possessions without a national currency: New Zealand and certain other Oceanic colonies, South Africa, Guernsey, Jersey, Malta, Gibraltar, Cyprus, Bermuda, British West Indies, British Guiana, British Somaliland, Falkland Islands, other South and West African colonies. (b) Or perhaps 1798. (c) Including countries and territories with US dollar as exclusive or predominant currency: British Honduras (from 1894), Cuba (from 1898), Dominican Republic (from 1901), Panama (from 1904), Puerto Rico (from 1900), Alaska, Aleutian Islands, Hawaii, Midway Islands (from 1898), Wake Island, Guam, and American Samoa. (d) Except August—October 1914. (e) Including Tunisia (from 1891) and all other colonies except Indochina. (f) Including Newfoundland (from 1895). (g) Including British East Africa, Uganda, Zanzibar, Mauritius, and Ceylon (to 1901). (h) Including Montenegro (to 1911). (i) Including Belgian Congo. (j) Including Netherlands East Indies. (k) Including colonies, except Portuguese India. (l) Including Greenland and Iceland. (m) Or perhaps 1883. (n) Including Korea and Taiwan. (o) Including Borneo. (p) Approximate date

References

Barro, R. 1979. Money and the Price Level under the Classical Gold Standard. *Economic Journal* 89: 13–33.

Bernanke, B. 2002. Speech given at "A Conference to Honor Milton Friedman on the Occasion of His 90th Birthday", November 8.

Bordo, M. 1981. The Classical Gold Standard—Some Lessons for Today. *Federal Reserve Bank of St. Louis Review* 5: 2–17.

Chappell, D., and K. Dowd. 1997. A Simple Model of the Gold Standard. *Journal of Money, Credit and Banking* 29 (1): 94–105.

Cole, H., and L. Ohanian. 2007. A Second Look at the U.S. Great Depression from a Neoclassical Perspective. In *Great Depressions of the Twentieth Century*, ed. T. Kehoe and E. Prescott, 21–57. Federal Reserve Bank of Minneapolis.

Fernández-Villaverde, J., and D. Sanches. 2022. *A Model of the Gold Standard*. WP 22–33, Federal Reserve Bank of Philadelphia.

Friedman, M., and A. Schwartz. 1963. *A Monetary History of the United States, 1867–1960*. Princeton University Press.

Garber, P. 1991. The Collapse of the Bretton Woods Fixed Exchange Rate System. In *A Retrospective on the Bretton Woods System: Lessons for International Monetary Reform*, ed. M. Bordo and B. Eichengreen, 461–494. Press: University of Chicago.

Maddison, A. 2001. *The World Economy: A Millennial Perspective*. OECD.

Steil, B. 2013. *The Battle of Bretton Woods: John Maynard Keynes, Harry Dexter White, and the Making of a New World Order*. Princeton University Press.

Wheelock, D. (1977), "Monetary Policy in the Great Depression and Beyond: The Sources of the Fed's Inflation Bias", Federal Reserve Bank of St. Louis Working Paper 1997-011.

CHAPTER 3

The "Great Inflation" Arrives

3.1 The "Great Inflation" and Domestic US Policies

Overlapping with the latter part of the very gradual demise of gold-backed or gold-pegged monetary systems, the so-called Great Inflation was one of the defining macroeconomic period of the second half of the twentieth century in the US (and, by extension, of the rest of the world). Usually dated as having lasted from 1965 to 1982—albeit initial signs of an inflationary acceleration were already observable as of the early 1960s, it ultimately led to (another) revision of global monetary policy frameworks. Given the centrality of the US dollar to the global monetary system, and the large share of US GDP in global terms, this chapter will initially describe this process with a US focus, later covering other economies.

While Chap. 2 described the policy mistakes and external framework and constraints for monetary policy due to the usage of gold-derivate monetary systems, inflationary pressures in the US were also linked to purely **domestic economic policy choices and their direct and indirect effects on price dynamics and monetary policy**: those would lead US inflation to go from below 1% *pa* (per annum) in 1959 to almost 14% in 1984 (Fig. 3.1).

But let's start with a little more on the history of the US institutional framework for monetary policy. As said previously, the Federal Reserve, a US federal body, was only created in 1913, after a series of bank panics in

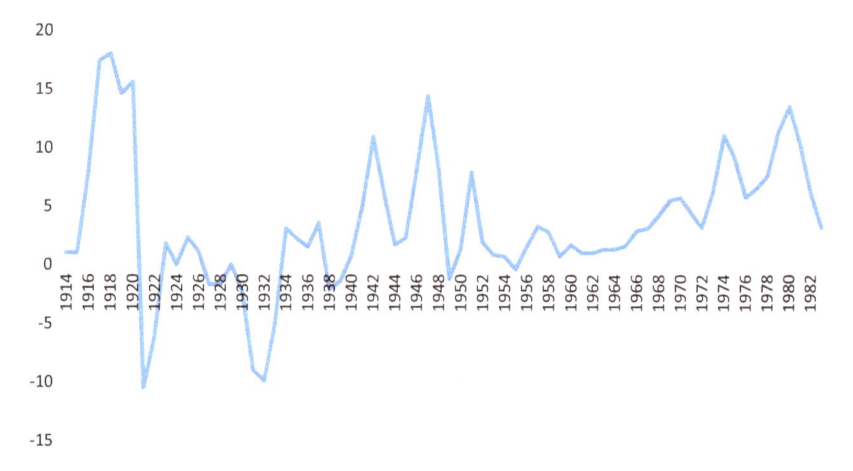

Fig. 3.1 US CPI inflation, eoy. (Source: US Bureau of Economic Analysis [BEA])

1873, 1884, 1890, 1893 and finally 1907 (when a single private citizen, namely, J. P. Morgan, used its personal resources to stabilize the whole US financial system)[1] made apparent the need of a "central bank", for example, a body to assure *financial and banking stability* (as the US was then still under the gold standard, the automatic mechanism of that system determined price dynamics, see Annex 2.A), which happened with the "Federal Reserve Act" of 1913[2]: this parallels the large expansion of Government powers in many different areas throughout the 20th Century. Importantly, the Fed was created as a "system" of largely autonomous regional "reserve banks" that would be coordinated by a secretariat-like body, based in Washington, DC.

After the initial bouts of large Great Depression–related institutional changes mentioned earlier, the Fed would experience further major changes with the "Employment Act" of 1946, which still largely defines its current institutional features: namely, this act declared it a responsibility of the US federal government "to promote maximum employment" (beyond price and financial stability), which is the basis for the Fed somewhat unusual "dual mandate" (only in 1977 the US Congress actually amended the original Fed 1913 Act with the so-called Humphrey-Hawkins Act

---

[1] Bruner, R. and Carr, S. (2009) "The Panic of 1907", Darden Case No. UVA-G-0619, University of Virginia, Darden School of Business.

[2] It is noteworthy to reflect that the US experienced most of its history as country *without a formal monetary authority* (the same is true for other nations in the Americas, for instance, Brazil, as we will see later in this book).

specifying explicit unemployment and inflation goals: this is the *formal* basis for the Fed dual mandate).

Now, the dominant economic policy framework used in most market economies—including the US, since the Great Depression was the active management of the business cycle by fiscal policies (usually referred to as Keynesian policies, in a reference to John Maynard—Baron—Keynes and his "*opus magnum*", and which provide one of the key analytical justifications for the expansion of Government powers in the economic arena mentioned above).[3] One of the *erroneous* assumption of those policies was that there exists a stable "Phillips curve"[4] that could be exploited to deliver the dual mandate of maximum unemployment and price stability. However, the empirical observation of increasing inflation mentioned above led to two separate but almost simultaneous analytical breakthroughs by US economists Edmund Phelps and Milton Friedman, who explained this dynamics via the **embedding of expectations into the behavior of economic agents**.[5] Therefore, mistakenly attempting to exploit an incorrectly assumed lack of trade-off between unemployment ("managed" largely via fiscal-side Keynesian policies) and prices would ultimately lead to inflationary spirals. Crucially, for this to happen, **one would need accommodative policies by a monetary authority.**

How did it actually happen? First, US government expenditures increased constantly, from around a quarter to a third of US GDP,[6] between the early 1960s and the early 1980s (while receipts remained largely constant: Fig. 3.2).

---

[3] This strand of the profession is best represented in the US by the group of economists linked to the Kennedy and Lyndon Johnson administrations, collectively referred to under the "New Economics" tag: using Keynesian models, they were characterized by a trust in the level of development of economic science that would enable the active technocratic management of aggregate demand, by counteracting shortfalls or excesses relative to the potential of an economy (alas, this type of hubris will also reappear later…). For (an arguably sometimes rose-tinted) view of this period, see Tobin, J. (1972), "New Economics One Decade Older", Princeton University Press: Tobin, who was a member of this group, even uses the word "Camelot" to describe the period in the Kenedy Administration.

[4] The Phillips curve supposes a negative statistical relationship between nominal wage growth (as a proxy for inflation) and the rate of unemployment. It is named after New Zealander economist Alban Phillips (see Phillips, A., (1958), "The Relationship between Unemployment and the Rate of Change of Money Wages in the United Kingdom 1861–1957", Economica, 25(100): 283–99).

[5] Phelps, E. (1967), "Phillips Curves, Expectations of Inflation and Optimal Unemployment Over Time", Economica, 34(135): 254–81 and Friedman, M. (1968), "The Role of Monetary Policy", American Economic Review, 58(1): 1–17.

[6] Compare that with the about 5% of GDP when the Fed was created.

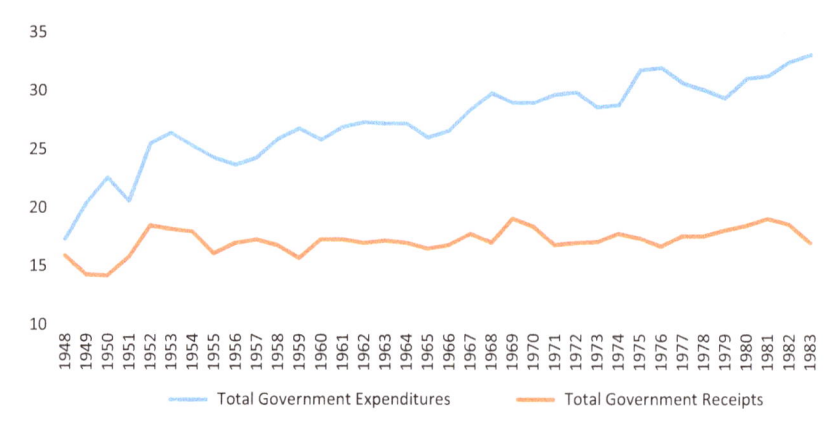

Fig. 3.2 Total US Government expenditures and receipts (% of GDP). (Source: US Office of Management and Budget [OMB])

It is worthwhile to point out that these developments were largely driven by a very significant expansion of social policies (and not by military expenditures, even as the US was involved in major military operations in Northeast and Southeast Asia from the 1950s till mid-1970s): **from 1960 to 1980, expenditures with social policies in the US increase by a factor of 12 in nominal US dollars, roughly doubling as a share of government expenditures and reaching over 53% of the total** (Fig. 3.3).[7]

As Phelps and Friedman could have said, it takes two to tango: faced with these fiscal developments, the US monetary authority openly pursued a deliberately accommodative behavior, formalized in the so-called even-keel policy, which effectively meant not rising rates as not to disrupt the (now larger and more frequent) issuance of US federal debt necessary to finance those bigger fiscal expenditures.[8]

---

[7] One feels tempted to assess the effectiveness of this very large and continued increases in social expenditures, but that is not the objective of this book.

[8] The "even keel" policy evolved progressively since the 1951 Fred-Treasury accord that marks the end of the post–World War II "financial repression" policies in the US (see Annex 5.B), replacing it with a policy in which the Fed would "support" Treasury actions around the period in which debt auctions would take place, via, for example, avoiding interest rate moves. For more on the "even keel", see Meltzer, A. (2002), "Origins of the Great Inflation", Federal Reserve Bank of St. Louis *Review*, 87(2): 145–75. Other works have a somewhat kinder take on the "even keel" policy: see Consolvo, V., Humpage, O. and Mukherjee, S. (2020), "Even Keel and the Great Inflation", Federal Reserve Bank of Cleveland, Working Paper n. 20–33.

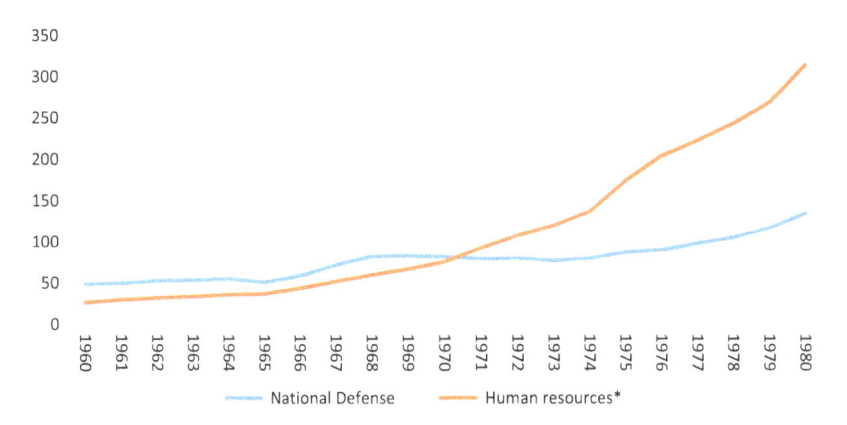

Fig. 3.3 Total US Government military and social expenditures ($ billions). Source: OMB *This aggregate budget item includes education, training, employment, social services, health, Medicare, income and social security programs.

3.2 EXTERNAL PRICE SHOCKS

Added to this domestic policy developments (and choices) were the effects of two external energy price shocks caused by actions of major oil-producing countries in the Middle East.[9] The first one started from an oil export embargo that began in October 1973 by the members of the Organization of Arab Petroleum Exporting Countries (OAPEC, the forebear of OPEC), initially targeted at the nations that had supported Israel during the Yom Kippur War (which was fought that year between Israel and a coalition of Arab states)—for example, Canada, Japan, the Netherlands, the UK and the US: **the upshot was that between 1972 and 1974 average global oil prices increased by a factor of 6**. This was followed by a second oil price shock in 1979, this one brought about by the so-called Iranian revolution, where the Imperial State of Iran was replaced by the theocratic Islamic Republic of Iran, which further increased oil prices **by a factor of 3. As a result, between 1972 and 1980 nominal oil prices grew over 20 times** (Fig. 3.4). These were truly global shocks, with inflationary implications throughout the world (Annex 3.A).

---

[9] Interestingly, Barsky and Kilian (2004) argue to the possibly (partial) **endogeneity of the 1970s price shocks**, linking those to excess demand create by the expansionary fiscal actions that were sanctioned by monetary policies (including those in the US): see Barsky, R. and Kilian, L. (2004), "Oil and the Macroeconomy Since the 1970s", Journal of Economic Perspectives, 18(4): 115–134.

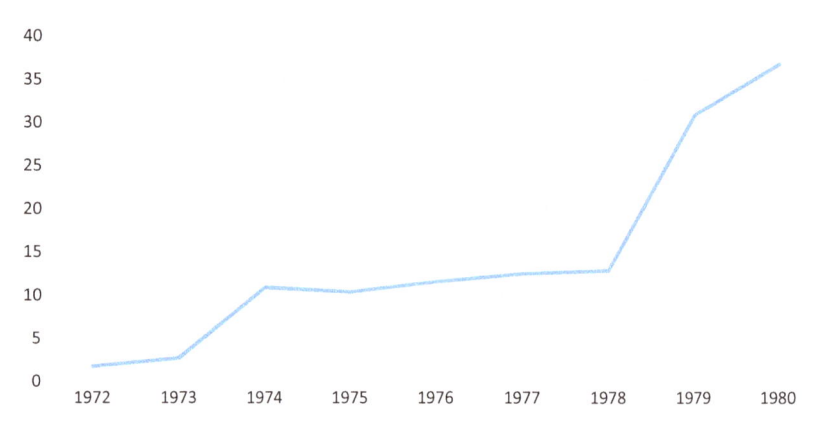

Fig. 3.4 Crude oil, average ($/barrel). (Source: World Bank)

The fiscal policy actions of the US government described in Sect. 3.1 were what economists would now call a "demand side" shock, which resulted from policies that created a level of demand in excess of what the economy could supply—an apparent case for a straightforward non-accommodative monetary policy stance. However, if oil price shocks were interpreted as global exogenous "supply shocks", those could present a more complex analytical case, especially in the case of a monetary authority with a dual mandate[10]: namely, as global supply shocks, they reflected one-off changes in relative prices outside of the control of monetary authority, so a case could potentially be made for policy inaction (or "looking through"), while, on the other hand, potential long-lasting increases in unemployment resulting from these relative price changes could call for a more accommodative response, but, however, second-round effects in terms of wages and price increases could suggest a non-accommodative policy (so, to the further distress of former US President Harry Truman, who once famously clamored for a one-handed economist, this central banking advisor unfortunately had three).

---

[10] Gordon, R. (1975), "Alternative Responses of Policy to External Supply Shocks", Brookings Papers on Economic Activity, 1:183–204, and Phelps, E. (1978), "Commodity-Supply Shock and Full-Employment Monetary Policy", Journal of Money, Credit and Banking, 10: 206–221.

3.3 Domestic US Monetary Policy Responses

Leaving aside those admittedly complex analytical considerations, the US Federal Reserve policy choice was to **expand money supply, ultimately leading to an inflationary spiral (while, incidentally—*dixit* Phelps and Friedman—failing to reduce unemployment).** This happened notably during the Chairmanships of William McChesney Martin Jr., who remained as Chairman of the Federal Reserve for almost 20 years, from 1951 to 1970, and of Arthur Burns (of business cycle fame, as described earlier), Chairman of the Federal Reserve from 1970 to 1978.

Martin[11] (who famously would frequently make a point of saying "I am not an economist"), while a fiscal conservative who understood the needs of stable money and external balance, did not follow formal models to guide policy actions: the same is true in general for the Fed Board secretariat and its Members, the district Governors.[12] A tendency to short-term "data dependency" on potentially random movements and a lack of reflection on how their short-term decisions related to the Fed long-term aims compounded the earlier largely atheoretical approach.[13] Finally, governance frameworks, namely, Martin's belief in the importance of coordinating Fed actions with the US Government—mainly the Treasury and the President's office, leading to a progressively overriding importance of the "maximum employment" component of the Fed's 1946 Employment Act dual mandate (Martin's prized policy coordination became "one sided", that is, the US President and its Treasury expected the Fed to coordinate its actions with theirs, but not necessarily the other way around…).[14] Ultimately, the combination of those three elements, especially notable during the final five years of Martin's mandate (e.g., 1965–1970) led to the *start* of the Great Inflation (*and* the run on the US dollar that led to the ultimate collapse of the Bretton Woods system).[15]

---

[11] Martin served under US Presidents Truman, Eisenhower, Kennedy, Johnson and Nixon. Not only the "Great Inflation" actually started under his Chairmanship of the Fed, but the pressures of the US external position in the Bretton Woods framework were also already clear. In his earlier as a US Treasury official, Martin was also involved in the development of the "even keel" policy (from the Treasury side).

[12] Of course, the same cannot be said of the group of economists belonging to the "New Economics" group: they did have a model in their minds.

[13] Which, remarkably, even conveyed a lack of perceived difference between nominal and real rates in FOMC decisions. Beyond that, Martin had established what he called a "Riefler rule", stating that the Fed Board **"didn't make or discuss forecasts"** (Meltzer, 2002, ibid.: the name refers to Winfield Riefler, assistant to Martin and Secretary of the FOMC).

[14] Meltzer, A. (2002), ibidem.

[15] Meltzer, A. (2002), ibidem.

How the "Great Inflation" continued (and grew…) after starting is a different but related story. Burns became Chairman of the Fed in February 1970, and he was the first economist to hold that position (and a distinguished one at that). However, as a policy maker in this function, he was notable for his effective **adherence to "maximum employment" as the main mandate of the US monetary authority** and for a seemingly limited concern with the independence of the central bank.[16] Contrary to Martin's atheoretical approach, Burns, like the "New Economics" group, also did have a model for assessing monetary policy actions, albeit one that also reflected his personal and political beliefs and that unfortunately was incorrect: the same Keynesian model based on a stable "Phillips curve". This, among other things, led him to interpret the energy price shocks (endogenous or exogenous) not as one-off relative price adjustments but as causing long-lasting unemployment increases that "needed" to be counteracted.

The eventual (in the US English usage of the word, therefore as a process "ultimately resulting" in an outcome, and not as a probabilistic, possible result) consequence was that economic agents of all types now expected prices to continue to increase and adjusted their behavior accordingly (in central bank lingo, their inflation expectations had become "unanchored"). So, a prolonged and significant domestic fiscal expansion and large and persistent external price shocks were *both* consistently accommodated by US monetary policy decisions, resulting in changes in agents' expectations: with this, the "Great Inflation" was now in full swing.

Annex 3.A Was the "Great Inflation" Global?

Yes, to a degree, at least when it comes to the (global…) oil price shocks, be those endogenous or exogenous: to show that, the graph below compares the CPI dynamics in the US with the other developed economies of the OECD and developing regions for the period 1970–1983 (Fig. 3.5).

As one can see, the price increases linked to the *two global oil price shocks* are indeed largely common among the depicted countries/regions, both Developed and Developing ones. However, there are important differences on the persistence of the shock: for instance, in Germany—where

---

[16] On this, you can read Burns in his own words: Burns, A. (1979), "The Anguish of Central Banking", Per Jacobsson Lecture, reprinted at Federal Reserve Bulletin, September 1987, 73(9):689–98.

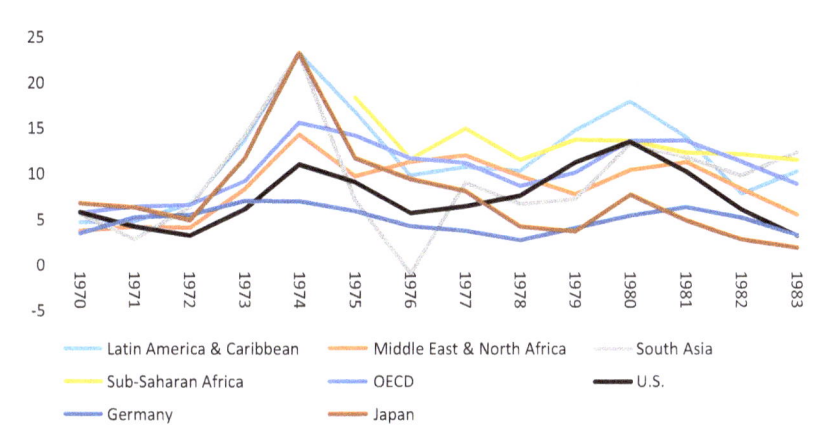

Fig. 3.5 CPI in different regions of the world. (Sources: OECD and World Bank)

the (then west) German monetary authority, the Deutsche Bundesbank, run a more non-accommodative policy, with the result that the effects of the price shocks were considerably more muted[17]—and in Japan,[18] where, after a punctual jump during the first oil shock, inflation was speedily brought under control (additionally, one must remember that both these countries are much more dependent on energy imports than the US was or is).

---

[17] Lehment, H. (1982), "Economic policy response to the oil price shocks of 1974 and 1979: The German Experience", European Economic Review, 18 (2): 235–242 and Beyer, A., Gaspar, V., Gerberding, C. and Issing, O. (2009), "Opting Out of the Great Inflation: German Monetary Policy after the Breakdown of Bretton Woods", Discussion Paper Series 1: Economic Studies, Deutsche Bundesbank (the latter paper also makes the point that Switzerland also followed the German example and equally eschewed the "Great Inflation"): The Bundesbank (an institution that this author twice visited as a Fellow) was a price stability single-mandate monetary authority consistently following a targeting of monetary aggregates (which the Beyer *et al.* paper models as a Taylor-like rule).

Of course, several other factors beyond just monetary policy–from the pricing of oil imports in US dollars to the usage of energy per unit of GDP, the energy mix of a given country and its reliance on import hydrocarbons—potentially also explain the different price sensitives to external oil price shocks (see Summers, P., (2005), "What Caused The Great Moderation? Some Cross-Country Evidence", Federal Reserve Bank of Kansas City, Economic Review).

[18] Ito, T. (2013), "Great Inflation and Central Bank Independence in Japan", in Bordo, M. and Orphanides, A. (eds), *The Great Inflation: The Rebirth of Modern Central Banking*, University of Chicago Press, pp. 357–387.

Also noteworthy is the continued increase of inflation in some Developing regions, and notably in Latin America and the Caribbean **after the oil price shocks**. This is another significant observation that points to the importance of specific regional/national dynamics, and will be elaborated on in Chap. 4, which discusses the so-called Great Moderation.

CHAPTER 4

From Volcker to China: The "Great Moderation" Begins

4.1 BIG SHOES THAT NEEDED TO BE FILLED

As described in Chap. 3, the effects of another "policy mistake", this one persistently overly accommodative US monetary policy (the opposite of what was done during the "Great Depression") to both external price shocks and domestic fiscal expansion soon became apparent. Administrative attempts to control price increases, from the Nixon administration wage and price controls[1] to the Ford administration 1974 "Whip Inflation Now" program failed (as they would later in Latin America, see Sects. 4.4 and 4.5). As said in Chap. 3, by the late 1970s inflation expectations had become "unanchored" (see Fig. 4.1), and therefore economic agents expected further price increases.

Then, in August 1979, Paul Volcker, formerly the president of the Federal Reserve Bank of New York, became Chairman of the Federal Reserve Board. Volcker adroitly framed the need to fight inflation as necessary for the Federal Reserve to *deliver on its dual mandate*.[2] While some

---

[1] Those policies were urged by none other than Arthur Burns in his 1970 so-called "incomes policy speech", shortly after his appointment as Fed Chaiman: see Burns, A., (1970) "The Basis for Lasting Prosperity" address at Pepperdine College in the US.

[2] "Over time we have no choice but to deal with the inflationary situation because over time inflation and the unemployment rate go together. ... Isn't that the lesson of the 1970s?": Paul Volcker, as quoted in Meltzer, A. (2010), "A History of the Federal Reserve. Volume 2, Book 2, 1970–1986", University of Chicago Press. Mr. Volcker sadly passed away in 2019.

© The Author(s), under exclusive license to Springer Nature Switzerland AG 2024
L. Vinhas de Souza, *A Century of Global Economic Crises*,
https://doi.org/10.1007/978-3-031-53460-7_4

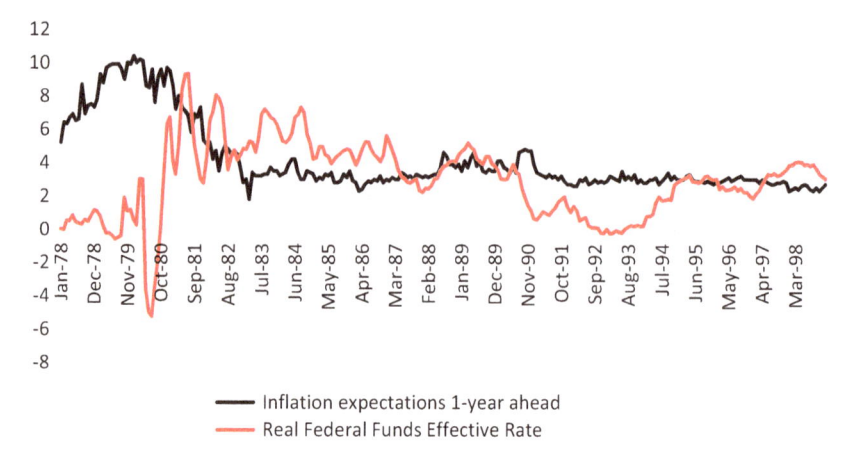

Fig. 4.1 Re-anchoring expectations with non-accommodative monetary policy. (Source: FRED)

new tools were added to the Federal Reserve tool kit, **it essentially went about this by pursuing a rather orthodox policy of higher interest rates**[3] **and slower reserve growth, reversing the previous accommodative policies: between August 1979 and April 1980, the Federal Funds Effective Rate (the Fed policy rate) increased from below 11% to almost 18%.** The US duly experience a brief economic slowdown that lasted until mid-1980, with the Fed policy rate adjust downward to 9%, but by January 1981 it had been raised again, and this time to 19.1%, its highest level ever. This re-anchored expectations of future inflation (see Fig. 4.1).[4] While inflation was brought down speedily already from 1979 onward, **the Fed policy rate had to stay above the 10% mark for several years, until late 1982, for expectation to be truly re-anchored at low and stable levels**: by that time price increases had fallen to around 3% *pa*. The "Great Inflation" had ended, and the "Great Moderation" had begun.[5]

---

[3] But not only "higher", but *higher than expected inflation*, so real *ex post* positive rates.

[4] The inflation expectations used on Fig. 4.1 are the 1-year ahead formal market expectations data series produced by the University of Michigan, which are only available from 1978 onwards, while the real Federal Funds Effective Rate series is a "naïve" measure estimated using contemporaneous CPI. Inflation expectations data series for earlier periods can be *proxied* using, for example, yields series.

[5] Hakkio, C., 2013, "The Great Moderation", Federal Reserve Bank of Kansas City.

Having the right people in the right place at the right moment is clearly very important, but advances in economic theory and monetary policy practice underpinned these policy efforts of the Fed, and of other monetary authorities around the world too.[6] For instance, the Phelps and Friedman insights referred to in Chap. 3 concerning expectations and the behavior of economic agents were progressively refined and incorporated into economic models (see Annex 4.A), and policy implementation was later complemented by the usage of numerical objectives for inflation (so-called inflation targeting) to anchor monetary policy and enhance communication with economic agents.

4.2 But What Was the "Great Moderation"?

The Great Moderation (GM) from the mid-1980s to 2007 was a period when average inflation was lower and more stable than during the "Great Inflation", or GI (even if not really lower when compared to the period *preceding* the GI), while GDP growth was higher and equally showed a lower standard deviation than before (Tables 4.1 and 4.2). This very significant decline in macroeconomic volatility has been documented by many studies.[7]

Table 4.1 US inflation (1914–2007)

	Average	Median	Standard deviation
Full sample	3.3	2.7	4.7
Pre–WWII	1.6	1.0	7.6
Post–WWII	4.7	3.3	4.0
WWII-GI	2.9	1.4	3.8
GI	6.7	6.0	3.2
GM	3.1	3.0	1.0

Source: BEA

---

[6] The "right" practices Include the fundamental primacy of independency for the monetary authority: if central banks know what to do to assert monetary stability, and are willing to do so, but cannot because of the institutional dominance of their fiscal principals, they will be unable to deliver on their mandate. Concerning this, the US Presidential administration during the Reagan years had a more balanced approach to "policy coordination" with the Fed than that was followed during the period from the mid-1960s to the late 1970s.

[7] The best-known reference in this literature is Stock, J. and Watson, M. (2003), "Has the Business Cycle Changed? Evidence and Explanations", Federal Reserve Bank of Kansas City.

Table 4.2 US Real GDP growth (1914–2007)

	Average	Median	Standard deviation
Full sample	3.3	3.1	4.9
Pre–WWII	2.7	2.7	7.0
Post–WWII	3.1	3.7	3.7
WWII-GI	3.1	4.1	4.6
GI	3.0	3.3	2.5
GM	3.4	3.5	1.4

Sources: BEA and Johnston and Williamson

However, while this moderation was not just a US experience, it was far from a global phenomenon: it occurred around the same time in several other high and in *some* middle-income economies, **but it was largely not experienced by lower-income economies** (which admittedly do face other types of structural and institutional constraints when dealing with inflation, see Sect. 4.4).

4.3 What Caused the Great Moderation?

Monetary authorities doing their jobs by pursuing non-accommodative policies to reduce inflation and reestablishing price stability are part of the explanation for the Great Moderation. However, when looking for a more comprehensive set of possible explanations, economists generally proposed three possible ones: **changes in the structure of the economy, good luck, and third, better policies** (as mentioned above).

Changes in the structure of the economy can indeed *potentially* reduce volatility, and likely played a role in the very significant decline in volatility documented in Tables 4.1 and 4.2. Since manufacturing tends to be more volatile than other economic sectors, a global shift away from manufacturing toward services would in principle reduce volatility (manufacturing more than halved as a share of value added to US GDP since the late 1940s (Fig. 4.2), while globally it fell from about a third to around 28% between 1991 and 2022). Optimizing "just in time" inventory practices supported by advances in information and financial technology may also have helped reduce volatility in production and in GDP, while more international trade and capital flows (including China's integration in the world economy after its 2001 WTO accession) may also have helped make the

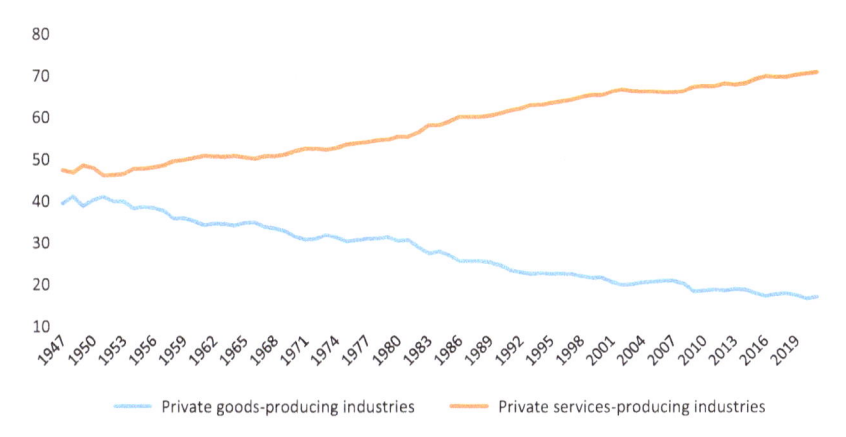

Fig. 4.2 Share of manufacturing and services in US gross value added (% of GDP). (Source: BEA)

economy more stable. However, as we will see later in this book, the Global Financial Crisis (GFC) and the Russian invasion of Ukraine illustrate the potentially large downsides of greater interconnectedness, while the value chains stresses during the Pandemic "lockdowns" periods equally show the problems associated with "just in time" manufacturing and stocks.

On the "good luck" explanation, the shocks hitting the global economy during the Great Moderation era may have been on average smaller and more region-/country-specific than the large, adverse global shocks of the 1960s and 1970s—of which the oil price shocks are the most obvious example (Stock and Watson, ibid., are proponents of this view, as they estimate that over half of the fall in volatility during the GM comes from smaller shocks). However, also here, just a limited list of both US-specific and global shocks with economic and financial implications during this period—for example, the series of Latin American debt crisis of the 1980s, the US stock market crashes of 1987 and 2000, the German reunification in 1990, the collapse of the Soviet Union in the early 1990s, Iraq's invasion of Kuwait in 1990 and posterior US military operations in those two countries, the US savings and loans crisis through the 1990s, the EU's "Exchange Rate Mechanism" crisis of 1992–1993, the Asian financial crisis in 1997, the Russian financial crisis of 1998, the 9/11 terrorist strikes on US territory and the US-led coalition invasions of Afghanistan in 2001 and of Iraq in 2003—suggest that the global economy was hit by many and at least "largish" shocks during the time of the "Great Moderation". This said, the lack of a major global shock also likely played a role in the volatility fall.

Now let us go us back to "good policy" (or at least "less bad policies"), and especially monetary policy, as a one of the main explanation for the Great Moderation.

4.3.1 Monetary Policy and the Great Moderation

A by now traditional (albeit admittedly pre-GFC) view tends to place a (reasonably) large role for improvements in monetary policy for the GM.[8] The narrative—correctly—states that during the Great Moderation, the Federal Reserve simply responded more systematically than it had before to deviations of inflation and output from their desired levels, in a way broadly consistent with what is now known as a Taylor-type rule.[9] Under this kind of rule, a monetary authority tightens monetary policy **over proportionately** (so, more than 1:1) when output is above potential or inflation is not at its desired target, and eases policy when the circumstances are reversed. Such Taylor-type rules are reasonably simple to implement, and they are also transparent, understandable and easy to communicate to the public at large.

Additionally, changes in the Fed's approach to communicating its monetary policy are also seen as having contributed to the GM, by helping to better anchor inflation expectations by explaining more clearly the Fed's aims and strategies to the general population. Surprisingly, before February 1994 the Federal Reserve's rate-setting body, the Federal Open Market Committee (FOMC) **did not announce its policy decisions**: decisions had to be *inferred* by market participants from the actions taken by the Open Market Desk of the New York Fed (as indicated before, the Fed

---

[8] For a representative example of this literature, see Clarida, R., Gali, J. and Gertler, M. (2000), "Monetary Policy Rules and Macroeconomic Stability: Evidence and Some Theory", Quarterly Journal of Economics, 115(1): 147–80.

[9] The so-called Taylor rule is basically a numerical formula that relates the US FOMC's target for the federal funds rate to the current state of the economy (which is captured by measures of GDP and inflation deviations from desired/sustainable levels): Taylor, J. (1993), "Discretion versus Policy Rules in Practice", Carnegie Rochester Conference Series on Public Policy, no 39: 195–214.

"district" among its 12 ones in charge of open market operations).[10] To complement the transparent announcement of policy actions as they were made, from 2000 onward the FOMC progressively increased a so-called forward guidance component of its communications with market participants, aiming to convey the *expected* path of future actions (this said, the last crisis may have shown some limitations on the practical usefulness of this communication practice; see Chap. 8).

However, as shown by Stock and Watson (2003), one can make counterarguments to the importance of monetary policy in the GM. Namely, for a change in monetary policy regime to both reduce GDP and inflation volatility effects requires not just more consistent anti-inflationary policies, but a policy that reduces the output volatility costs of disinflation.[11] Also, low and stable inflation is far from being a post-Volcker phenomenon[12]: leaving aside the classic gold standard period described in Chap. 2, inflation for the period 1946–1965 is actually lower, even if more unstable (Table 4.1). Romer and Romer (2002), for instance, also argue that policy in the 1950s was similar to the post-1983 policy (**implying that the policy from the late 1960s through the 1970s was actually an outlier**).[13]

This suggests a somewhat more complicated tale, beyond central bankers just fulfilling their mandate as expected. Monetary policy can be subject to "regime changes", and as an example of that, since the 1980s many central banks around the world adopted so-called inflation targeting regimes that arguably involve a structural break from earlier policies. However, while Clarida et al. (2000; ibid.) do provide evidence that the US monetary regimes pre-1979 and post-1983 were different, the former resulting in both inflation and output instability, Sims and Zha (2006)[14] argue that changes in US monetary policy were somewhat limited and happened at the same time as the changes in inflation and volatility (there-

---

[10] Albeit the decisions (or, more precisely, the directives to the "Manager of the System Open Market Account" at the New York Fed) would be eventually formally published at the Fed Board's Annual Report, but sometimes as much as **15 months after being taken**.

[11] Davis, S and Kahn, J. (2008), "Interpreting the Great Moderation: Changes in the Volatility of Economic Activity at the Macro and Micro Levels", Journal of Economic Perspectives, 22(4): 155–180.

[12] Friedman and Schwartz (1963), ibid.

[13] Romer, C. and Romer, D. (2002) "The Evolution of Economic Understanding and Postwar Stabilization Policy", NBER Working Paper 9274.

[14] Sims, C. and Zha, T. (2009), "Were There Regime Switches in U.S. Monetary Policy?", American Economic Review, 2006, 96(1): 54–81.

fore, without necessarily implying causality, and suggesting a larger role for structural changes and "luck"). International evidence (more on that in the next section) also supports (some) skepticism on an *exclusive* role of monetary policy during the "Great Moderation", as since the early 1980s, most developed economies experienced reduced GDP and inflation volatility, but not necessarily connected to meaningful—or at least within a time frame that could credibly imply causality—changes in monetary policy.

Consequently, evidence does suggest that *policy mistakes* during the 1960s and 1970s raised volatility for a period, and that returning to policies similar to those pursued earlier allowed volatility to recover an underlying postwar trend toward lower price and output volatility, with important roles for structural changes and (on average) smaller global shocks. Importantly, **this conclusion does not diminish the relative importance of appropriate monetary policies, but rather highlights more the costs of pursuing inconsistent ones.**

4.4　The Great Moderation That Wasn't: Developing Countries

Additionally, one must qualify all the statements above, as the very notion of a "Great Moderation" simply does not apply to many Developing countries (or at least arrives much later for those; see Fig. 4.3).

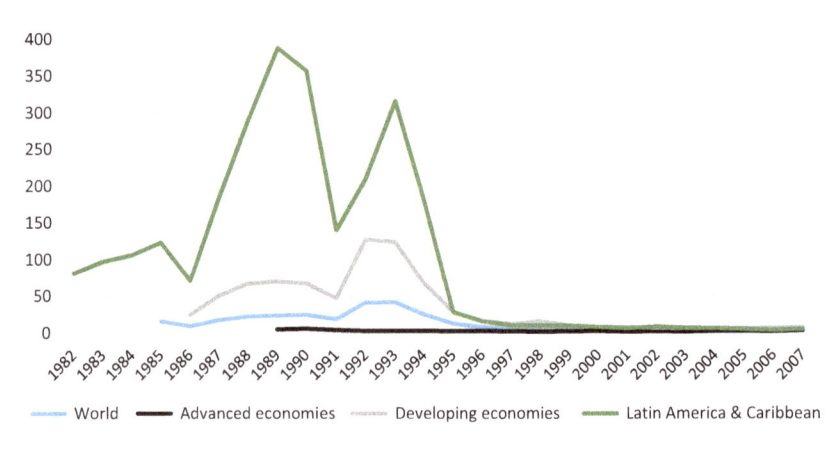

Fig. 4.3 CPI in different groups of countries (eoy). (Source: IMF)

Figure 4.2 shows that Developing countries' average CPI is *orders of magnitude higher* than that in Developing economies: **this is essentially because of a particular group of Developing countries, namely Latin American and Caribbean economies**, who suffered several bouts of hyperinflation (in some particular cases, with prices increases of over a **1000% in a multi-year period**) during the "Great Moderation". As a matter of fact, while inflation rates in other Developing regions are "mere" multiples of that in Developed nations, those in Latin America and the Caribbean can be **between two and three orders of magnitude higher**. Inflation as also much more unstable, with its standard deviation in this region during the period above a **whopping 72 *times* that in Developed economies** (compared to 23 times for the whole Developing economies sample, a figure that falls to less than six when the Developing economies sample excludes Latin American and Caribbean countries). What may lie behind those disparities will be described in Sect. 4.5, by looking at the experiences of two very different Latin American countries, Brazil and Chile.[15]

4.5 That Other American Giant: The Federal Republic of Brazil

Brazil is the tenth-largest economy in the world, with the third biggest GDP among developing nations, after China and India. The GDP of this country in current $ dollars equals a whole third of the one of the whole Latin America and Caribbean region. This large country, where this author was born, has a complex story, also on the monetary sphere.

Central banks—that is, institutions that have a state monopoly in the supply of currency, credit and monetary policy in a given country (or in a monetary union of several countries)—as we now understand, are largely a twentieth-century development. The same is true for Brazil: while the Brazilian Mint ("Casa da Moeda do Brasil", in Portuguese), was created in 1694, still during colonial times, commercial banks had to wait until 1808 to appear, when the Portuguese Royal family and a large part of the Portuguese Royal Court escaped from Portugal to Brazil, high on the heels of the invading French Napoleonic troops. The city of Rio de Janeiro,

---

[15] Most of the literature of the Latin American hyperinflation links it to a "fiscal dominance" narrative, but more general analysis mixing different analytical schools can be found in Cardoso, E. (1989), "Hyperinflation in Latin America", Challenge, 32(1): 11–19.

where the Royal family eventually settled, was elevated to capital of the Kingdom of Portugal and of the Portuguese Empire that same year (Brazil and Portugal would be formally declared a "United Kingdom" in 1815).

The same year of 1808 saw a flurry of policy actions by the just-arrived Portuguese "Prince Regent" (who would become King only in 1816, with the death of his mother, the Queen), including the creation of the "Banco do Brasil", a mixed institution that was not only the first commercial bank of the (no longer) colony, but also responsible for the issuance of currency, credit and the selling of government bonds. Unfortunately, when the (now) Portuguese King was eventually forced to return to Portugal 1821 by the threat of the overthrow of the monarchy, the King took with him much of the assets of the original Banco do Brasil, which eventually went bankrupt in 1829.[16] However, he did leave behind his son and heir, who would proceed to declare Brazilian independence from Portugal the following year, but as a monarchy with him as Emperor.

The "Banco do Brasil" was re-founded in 1851 as a private bank with a currency issuance monopoly (different private banks jointly performed currency issuance functions between 1829 and 1851), and, while experiencing occasional financial crisis and mergers with other institutions along the way, largely kept traditional monetary authority functions until 1945. That year, the Superintendence of Currency and Credit (SUMOC, from its acronym in Portuguese) was created, a forerunner to a full-fledged monetary authority, taking over some central banking functions related to monetary policy and supervision (the Banco do Brasil—to this day the largest Brazilian commercial bank, remained as a "government bank", while a department of the Brazilian Ministry of Finance became responsible for currency issuance). Only in 1964 was the Central Bank of Brazil (CBB) actually created (and only became legally autonomous in 2021).

Their similarly complex institutional histories apart (two previous forerunners of the Fed went under during the first half of the nineteenth century), a long-term examination of the price dynamics in the two largest economies (in PPP terms) of the Americas, Brazil and the US, shows that inflation was roughly similar for the two, both in terms of trend, scale and variability, between the beginnings of the twentieth century and the end of World War II: this was not only because the external shocks faced by those economies were mostly similar, but because the monetary

---

[16] Cardoso, J., (2010), "Novos Elementos para a História do Banco do Brasil (1808-1829): Crónica de um Fracasso Anunciado", Revista Brasileira de História, 30(59):167–192.

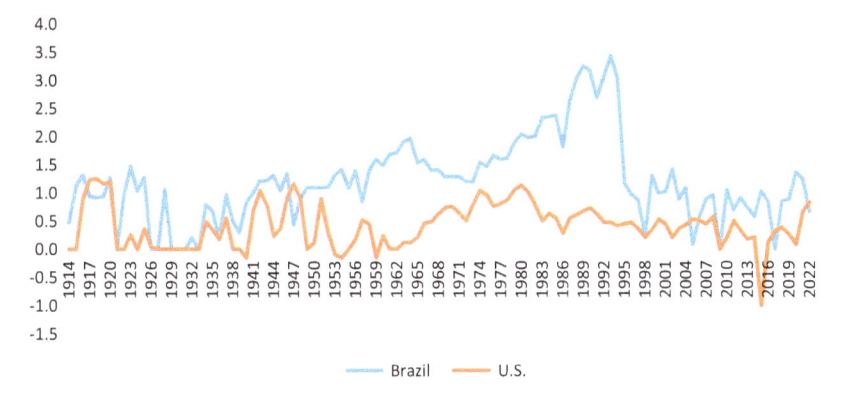

4 FROM VOLCKER TO CHINA: THE "GREAT MODERATION" BEGINS   55

Fig. 4.4 A century of inflation in the US and in Brazil (log scale). (Source: Author, based on IBGE and FGV (IBGE Instituto Brasileiro de Geografia e Estatística, Brazilian Institute of Geography and Statists, the official Federal Brazilian Statistical Office and Fundação Getúlio Vargas, Getúlio Vargas Foundation, a body akin to the U.S. BEA), BEA and Johnston and Williamson (2023), "What Was the U.S. GDP Then?", in *MeasuringWorth*) data. Data for Brazil between 1914 and 1944 is the GDP deflator, used as a proxy for CPI and logs are used to enable an easier visualization, given the Brazilian hyperinflation)

framework was also similar, as both were during most of the time following variations of a "gold standard". However, there is a clearer divergence of paths from 1948 onward, and especially with a protracted hyperinflationary period in Brazil starting around the time of the 1973 oil price shock (Fig. 4.4), with stabilization only coming after the mid-1990s.[17]

The most common explanation of the Latin America "exceptionalism" concerning inflation is largely based on the inability, or unwillingness, of governments in the region to limit their fiscal spending, with macroeconomic stability from the 1990s onward conversely associated with more fiscal restraint, and, as will be seen, even largely weathering later crises (at least on the monetary side), from the GFC to the Pandemic–Russian invasion of Ukraine inflationary spike: this is told, therefore, largely as a **"fiscal dominance"** story (see Kehoe and Nicolini 2021).[18] Some cross-country

---

[17] Garcia Munhoz, D., (1997), "Inflação Brasileira: Os Ensinamentos desde a Crise dos Anos 30", Revista de Economia Contemporânea, 1(1), UFRJ, Brazil.

[18] Kehoe, T. and Nicolini, J. (eds.), (2021), "A Monetary and Fiscal History of Latin America, 1960-2017", University of Minnesota Press.

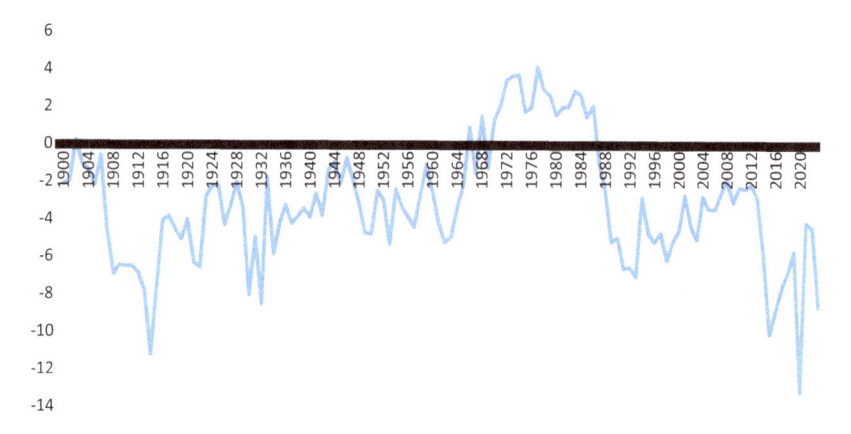

Fig. 4.5 Overall fiscal balance as a GDP percentage, 1900–2022. (Source: IBGE, Séries históricas e estatísticas, modified by the author)

analyses do conclude that those countries in Latin America with large and sustained fiscal deficits have more monetary instability, while other works highlight the institutional development of monetary policy frameworks in the region to counteract those vulnerabilities (see Langhammer and Vinhas de Souza 2005).[19] Other works, like Cardoso, 1989, mentioned earlier, address the continued structural and policy shortcomings that have prevented macro stabilization to be achieved to this day in some countries, of which Argentina is a perennial example.[20]

This said, Brazil's story has many nuances, first due to relatively limited budget deficits–for the standards of the region and at until around 1986 (Fig. 4.5)[21]—and second due to its comprehensive domestic nominal indexation framework. The Brazilian experience came about as the two cumulative oil shocks of 1973 and 1979 and the external imbalances they

---

[19] Langhammer, R. and Vinhas Souza, L. (eds), (2005), "Monetary Policy and Macroeconomic Stabilization in Latin America", Springer.

[20] See McCandless, G. (2005), "Argentina: Monetary Policy by Default", pp. 87–112, in Langhammer, R. and Vinhas Souza, L. (eds), (2005), "Monetary Policy and Macroeconomic Stabilization in Latin America", Springer and Pesce, M. and Feldman, G. (2023), "Monetary Policy Challenges over Two Decades: a View from Argentina", pp. 21–39, in "Central Banking in the Americas: Lessons from Two Decades", BIS, Basel.

[21] Secretaria do Tesouro Nacional, Brazil (2009), "Dívida Pública: A Experiência Brasileira".

engendered ended a long period of robust economic growth and unleashed years of very high inflation rates and successive failed stabilization plans (dubbed the "lost decade") that lasted until the mid-1990s (Table 4.1).[22]

The origins of this complex price indexation framework harken back to the mid-twentieth century: as inflation in Brazil had been elevated since the 1950s, to shelter different social groups and industries a formal indexation system was progressively developed from 1964 onward—the same year in which Brazil became a military dictatorship, with the so-called PAEG (Portuguese acronym for "Plano de Ação Econômica do Governo", or Government Plan for Economic Action) and the introduction of official price indexations structures.[23] While the oil shocks of the 1970s further accelerated the indexation process, they also implied that initially the main policy concern of Brazilian policy makers (including those at the central bank, who housed the Brazilian hard currency reserves) was the need to assure external funding flows to support not only economic activity in general but also economic development[24] (external funding constraints are another traditional Brazilian—and Latin American—economic problem: see Fig. 4.6).[25]

As a result, inflation continued to increase, until it reached truly hyperinflationary levels of almost 1400% on average yearly during the period 1988–1994. Only then policy actions were taken: unfortunately, the sequence of so-called heterodox stabilization plans that began in 1986 (the year after the end of the military dictatorship) to address this matter shared the flawed underlying notion that "inertial inflation"—in the economic parlance used in Brazil in those days—due to indexation was the core of the inflationary process, and breaking that inertia should be the

---

[22] For a revealing–and rather personal–behind the curtains description of those adjustment plans from the point of view of both Brazilian policy makers and common citizens, see Leitão, M. (2011), "Saga Brasileira: A Longa Luta de um Povo por Sua Moeda", Editora Record, Brazil. The family of this author—among millions of other ones—was one of those that had its financial assets frozen in one of those failed stabilization plans.

[23] Bastian, E., (2013),"O PAEG e o Plano Trienal: Uma Análise Comparativa de suas Políticas de Estabilização de Curto Prazo", Estudos Econômicos, 43,(1):139–166.

[24] Monetary authorities in the region frequently pursued (hard and soft) pegged regimes to a "hard currency", effectively using the exchange rate as an intermediate target for price stability.

[25] Some authors question the relative importance of the external funding constraint in the Latin American 1980s debt crisis: see Truman, E., (2021), "The Road to the 1980s Write-Downs of Sovereign Debt", Financial History Review, Cambridge University Press, 28(3): 281–299.

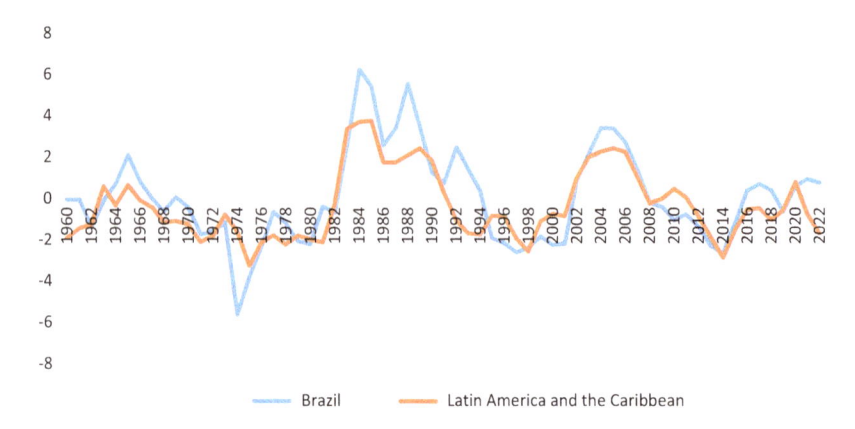

Fig. 4.6 Brazil and Latin America and the Caribbean external balance (percentage of GDP). (Source: World Bank)

Table 4.3 Brazil's (many and mostly failed) stabilization plans, 1986–1994

1986	Cruzado Plan	1990	Collor Plan I
1987	Bresser Plan	1991	Collor Plan II
1989	"Verão" Plan	**1994**	**Real Plan**

Source: Author

focus of the stabilization plans (with ideally neutral distributional effects for different economic agents) (Table 4.3).

However, the staggering of wages and other prices' increases meant that when price freezes were introduced, agents with similar nominal prices would have *different real prices*, depending on when the last adjustment had happened, and ultimately each successive stabilization plan floundered shortly after being introduced amidst the extra sectoral distortions it had caused. Additionally, and much more fundamentally, the "heterodox" moniker in those plans implied they commonly lacked a commitment to the "orthodox", old-fashioned macroeconomic adjustment needs of monetary and fiscal variables.[26] For example, **different economic agents had mechanisms to effectively act as *quasi* monetary authorities** (e.g., as legacy of its role as the monetary authority, the Banco do Brasil, and later also newly created federal states' development banks all **had accounts at the CBB, which were used as parallel channels for money creation**), ultimately effectively forcing the central bank to monetize those quasi-fiscal actions.[27]

Only when those elements—indexation, fiscal dominance and the monopoly in issuance of money by a reformed and reinforced CBB—were comprehensively and simultaneously addressed (by the rather more "orthodox" Plano Real in 1994–1995),[28] and helped by an eventually more supportive external environment (e.g., the cushion provided by successive IMF programs in 1992–1993 and then during 1998–2005, renewed commodity exports to a booming China, which speedily became the largest single external trade partner of Brazil) did stabilization finally take hold.[29] The "Great Moderation" had finally arrived at the largest Latin American economy, even if 12 years later than in the US.

---

[26] It is human nature to dream about costless ways to address problems: Gustavo Franco, a former Governor of the CBB, in one of his books tells the story of a Brazilian President responsible for one of those unsuccessful "heterodox" plans inviting two famous Brazilian economists to the Presidential palace, the "Alvorada" (Sun dawn), for an informal talk. They explained to him that he needed fiscal and monetary adjustment, or disinflation would not work. The President replied: "But I know that! For this sort of solution, I do not need brilliant economists!": see Franco, G. (2017), "A Moeda e a Lei: Uma História Monetária Brasileira, 1933-2013", Editora Zahar, Brazil, pp. 414.

[27] Ayres, J, Garcia, M., Guillén, D. and Kehoe, P. (2019), "The Monetary and Fiscal History of Brazil, 1960-2016", NBER Working Paper 25,421. These authors produce an adjusted budget balance series that, when taking into account some of those factors, is substantially worse than the official IBGE figures presented in Fig. 4.4.

[28] Portugal, M. (2017), "Política Fiscal na Primeira Fase do Plano Real, 1993–1997", in *A Crise Fiscal e Monetária Brasileira*, Bacha, E., Rio de Janeiro, Civilizacão Brasileira, Brazil.

[29] Bacha, E. (2003), "Brazil's Plano Real: A view from the Inside", in *Development Economics and Structuralist Macroeconomics: Essays in Honor of Lance Taylor*, Edward Elgar, UK.

4.6 Latin America Beyond Brazil: The Case of Chile

Of course, Latin America is much more than just Brazil. That country may be the biggest Latin American economy but has very specific features: it is a very large and comparatively closed economy, with important industrial and services sectors and a diversified primary sector. Most Latin American economies tend to be smaller, more open and sectorally concentrated than Brazil, with typically one or two important primary sectors. Chile, located in the Pacific coast of South America, is an example of that, and is also a country that is usually considered a reference in Latin America concerning macroeconomic management (it also joined the Organization for Economic Co-operation and Development—OECD—in 2010, the second Latin American country to do so, after Mexico in 1996) (Table 4.4).

After the first oil price shock (Chile is largely dependent on energy imports), there was pronounced macro instability in Chile and even a hyperinflation episode, with prices increasing by 400% and the budget deficit reaching a staggering 23% of GDP in 1973—the same year the country suffered a military coup, and by a further 600% the next year. A slow stabilization afterward ended in another economic crisis in 1982–1983, after the second oil price shock, and Chile was forced into two back-to-back IMF programs during 1984–1989, which led to the implementation of a managed exchange rate regime and of tighter fiscal policies, including the creation in 1987 of a "Sovereign Wealth Fund" (SWF—an "off balance sheet" entity commonly used to save surpluses from commodities boom to avoid "Dutch disease" types of dynamics).

The first democratic government after the end of military dictatorship in 1990 opted to continue following an "orthodox" mix of macro policies, while opening-up further the Chilean economy to international

Table 4.4 Brazil and Chile compared

	GDP (nominal $, 2022)	Trade (% of GDP, 2022)	Machinery & transport equip. (% manufacturing value added, 2019)
Brazil	1920.1	39.3	17.1
Chile	301.0	75.1	5.0

Source: Author

trade.[30] Those policies included following an *implicit* fiscal rule, and as a result, from 1990 to 1997 there was an average budget surplus of 2% of GDP. However, a terms of trade shock related to the Asian financial crisis (Asia was already a major market for Chilean exports back then) led to a recession in 1999, and to an overhaul of the macroeconomic policy regime. A new government in 2000 introduced a more formal fiscal rule based on a structural balance surplus equivalent to 1% of GDP, to shelter the economy from international copper price variations (copper is by far the main Chilean export and a very relevant part of government revenues), and in 2006 the existing SWF was replaced by two different ones, an Economic and Social Stabilization Fund (ESSF) and Pension Reserve Fund (PRF), with the ESSF performing the traditional macro stabilization function of SWFs.[31]

On the monetary side, the Central Bank of Chile had become independent in 1989—one of the earliest in the region, with a primary mandate to achieve price stability while following an exchange rate policy based on a crawling band. Equally as an effect of the 1999 crisis, in 2000 the Central Bank of Chile introduced an inflation target regime and a fully floating exchange rate, scrapping capital controls in 2001.[32]

The above are very important institutional developments, especially in the regional context. However, it terms of *actual* macroeconomic stabilization (after the period of Brazilian hyperinflation), the long-term differences in terms of basic macro variables between these two countries is not as large as one would assume, and it does not necessarily always favor Chile (Fig. 4.7): for instance, the Brazilian fiscal performance is considerably better, with an average surplus of around 1% of GDP *pa*, their current account deficits since 1996 are roughly similar, while, on the other hand, the Brazilian average inflation is 2–3% higher *pa* (Brazil also had on average higher *real* interest rates than Chile).

* * *

---

[30] Caputo, R. and Saravia, D. (2018), "The Monetary and Fiscal History of Chile: 1960-2016", University of Chicago, Becker Friedman Institute for Economics Working Paper No. 2018-62.
[31] Solimano, A. and Calderón Guajardo, D., (2017), "The Copper Sector, Fiscal Rules, and Stabilization Funds in Chile: Scope and Limits", WIDER Working Paper 2017/5.
[32] Medina, J., Toni, E. and Valdes, R., (2023), "The Art and Science of Monetary and Fiscal Policies in Chile", MPRA Paper 117,198, University Library of Munich, Germany.

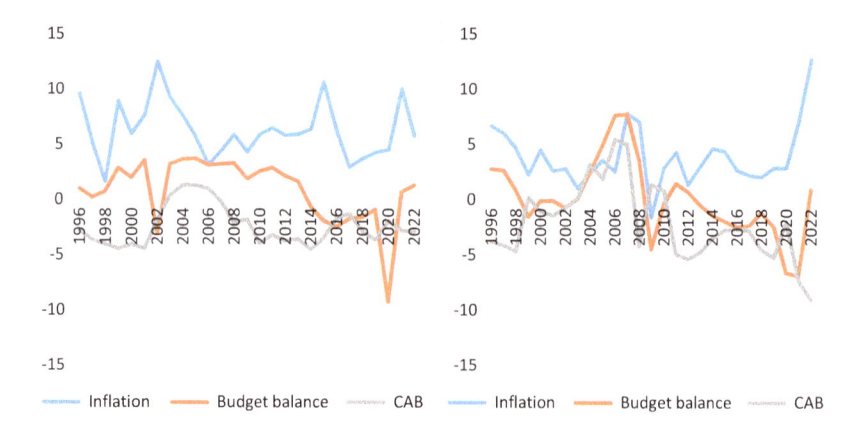

Fig. 4.7 Brazil (left) & Chile (right) compared: II. (Source: IMF)

This likely reflects the fact that not only both countries were exposed to fundamentally similar shocks, but also the (more belated than Chile's) improvements of the Brazilian fiscal and monetary frameworks since the hyperinflation period, which was described in the previous section, and equally the fundamentally greater sensitivity of Chile to shocks, given its far higher level of openness and much more concentrated (and therefore exposed to external shocks) productive structure.

Annex 4.A: Economic Models Incorporating Expectations

As has been said several times in this book, expectations are a core matter when dealing with inflation dynamics. Since the expectations modelling breakthroughs in the late 1960s (see Phelps 1967, ibid. and Friedman 1968, ibid.) provided the analytical tools to deal with the price dynamics of the "Great Inflation" and overtook the previous vintage of Keynesian models, variations of so-called Full Information Rational Expectations models arguably became the dominant approach for modeling the formation of expectations, especially after Calvo's 1983[33] seminal microfounded model with overlapping "vintages" of firms' pricing decisions based on their future inflation expectations.

---

[33] Calvo, G. (1983), "Staggered Prices in a Utility-Maximizing Framework", Journal of Monetary Economics, 12(3):383–398.

Two of the key assumptions in this class of models are that economic agents have a complete (perfect) information set and that their forecasts of future variables are rational, given this perfect information. However, empirical observations have rejected some of the underlying assumptions of these types of models: the main likely reason for this is that economic agents **do not actually operate under full or perfect information and are not fully rational** (see Lucas 1977, classic piece on business cycles, for a formalization: these conclusions will not be surprising ones for non-economists).[34]

A way to model less than perfect information are frameworks incorporating so-called information frictions, which can be either **sticky** or **noisy information**. Sticky information models assume that in each period a "Calvo-like" random fraction of firms obtains new (and perfect) information about the state of the economy, while the probability in each period that a given firm does not get new information determines the amount of "information friction" in the model. In contrast, noisy information models reflect the assumption that agents update their information in every period t but each individual i observes an *imperfect* signal S_t^i of the (true) information set, as given by Eq. (4.1):

$$S_t^i = X_t + W_t^i \tag{4.1}$$

where X_t is the true unobserved information set and W_t^i are independent and identically distributed (i.i.d.) error terms. As a result, in each period, agents update their estimate of the true unobserved information state by combining an old estimate with their new private signal, following Eq. (4.2):

$$F_t^i(X_t) = G_t \cdot S_t^i + (1 + G_t) \cdot F_t - 1_i(X_t) \tag{4.2}$$

where F_t^i is the individual's updated estimate and $F_t - 1_i$ is the individual's prior estimate. The updated estimate is a weighted average of these two signals, with weights G_t determined by the information content of the individual's signal. If the information content is low, then G is small, and the agent puts very little weight on this signal. If the information content is high, then G is large, and the opposite happens. Therefore, the weight

---

[34] Lucas, R. (1977), "Understanding Business Cycles", Carnegie-Rochester Conference Series on Public Policy, 5(1):7–29.

that an economic agent puts on its previous estimate of the state today, $(1 + G_t)$, measures the amount of information friction in the model (available empirical measures of expectations formation tend to support more "noisy information" models than "sticky" ones).

Importantly, **in both sticky information and noisy information models, agents are still assumed to be fully rational**, implying there is no correlation between the *ex post* errors resulting from an individual's forecasts and the *ex ante* revisions made by that same individual. There are different modeling approaches to also relaxing this rationality assumption, via, for example, agents whose rationality is "bounded" by the fact that they are optimizing according to a biased understanding of reality, or, alternatively, by assuming that economic agents are constantly updating their understanding of how each variable evolves as they "learn" from its latest observed value.

In the end, incorporating both informational frictions, biases and staggered learning processes in the expectations-formation process of different agents (and thereby making then less than fully rational agents operating with less than perfect information) improves the predictive performance of economic models, by making those more reality-like.

References

Calvo, G. 1983. Staggered Prices in a Utility-Maximizing Framework. *Journal of Monetary Economics* 12 (3): 383–398.

Cardoso, E. 1989. Hyperinflation in Latin America. *Challenge* 32 (1): 11–19.

Clarida, R., J. Gali, and M. Gertler. 2000. Monetary Policy Rules and Macroeconomic Stability: Evidence and Some Theory. *Quarterly Journal of Economics* 115 (1): 147–180.

Friedman, M. 1968. The Role of Monetary Policy. *American Economic Review* 58 (1): 1–17.

Friedman, M., and A. Schwartz. 1963. *A Monetary History of the United States, 1867–1960.* Princeton University Press.

Johnston, L., and S. Williamson. 2023. What Was the U.S. GDP Then? MeasuringWorth.

Kehoe, T., and J. Nicolini, eds. 2021. *A Monetary and Fiscal History of Latin America, 1960–2017.* University of Minnesota Press.

Langhammer, R., and L. Vinhas Souza, eds. 2005. *Monetary Policy and Macroeconomic Stabilization in Latin America.* Springer.

Lucas, R. 1977. Understanding Business Cycles. *Carnegie-Rochester Conference Series on Public Policy* 5 (1): 7–29.

Phelps, E. 1967. Phillips Curves, Expectations of Inflation and Optimal Unemployment Over Time. *Economica* 34 (135): 254–281.

Romer, C., and D. Romer. 2002. *The Evolution of Economic Understanding and Postwar Stabilization Policy.* NBER Working Paper 9274.

Secretaria do Tesouro Nacional, Brazil. 2009. Dívida Pública: A Experiência Brasileira.

Sims, C., and T. Zha. 2006. Were There Regime Switches in U.S. Monetary Policy? *American Economic Review* 96 (1): 54–81.

Stock, J., and M. Watson. 2003. *Has the Business Cycle Changed? Evidence and Explanations.* Federal Reserve Bank of Kansas City.

CHAPTER 5

Houses Built on Sand: The "Global Financial Crisis"

5.1 From Humble Beginnings: How It All Started

The "Great Moderation" had many implications, some intended, some unintended, some positive, some less so. One of those was a greater appetite for financial risk (e.g., for returns) in different asset classes, caused by stable low rates and parallel to and enabled by greater financial deregulation and innovation.

On the deregulation side, the progressive dismantling of the "Great Depression" era Glass–Steagall Act of 1933, notably of its separation (and geographical sheltering) of commercial banking from investment banking and market trading—a restriction aiming to reduce the potential for financial market speculation and contagion, and the existence of interest rate caps (the infamous "Regulation Q", only repealed in 2011), via the 1994 Riegle–Neal Interstate Banking and Branching Efficiency Act and the 1999 Financial Services Modernization Act, allowed the creation of US-wide bank holding corporations.

Following this deregulation, a bubble—a self-reinforcing cycle of non-fundamentals-based asset price increases[1]—progressively formed in housing markets as real estate prices across the US increased continuously from 1997 to 2005 (Fig. 5.1). Like traditional asset price bubbles (see Annex

[1] Minsky, H. (1992), "The Financial Instability Hypothesis", The Jerome Levy Economic Institute of Bard College, Working Paper n. 74.

© The Author(s), under exclusive license to Springer Nature Switzerland AG 2024
L. Vinhas de Souza, *A Century of Global Economic Crises*, https://doi.org/10.1007/978-3-031-53460-7_5

Fig. 5.1 Purchase-only house price index, US, yearly change. (Source: FRED)

5.A), expectations of future price increases developed and were a significant factor in inflating house prices.[2] From 2000 onward, a rapid rise of lending to so-called subprime borrowers (e.g., borrowers that would not qualify for prime mortgages due to their lower credit scores, which implied great risk of nonrepayment) helped to further inflate the housing price bubble.

This happened parallel to the development of financial innovations—positive developments, as are technological innovations in general, from Adjustable Rate Mortgages to new processes of "securitizing" mortgages—for example, the pooling of mortgages into packages of so-called asset-backed securities or ABS (which frequently also included other types of loans—for example, auto and student loans, credit card debts—beyond mortgages). The securities backed by those "packages" of assets would be sold to investors, who would then receive revenue flows from the borrowers' (expected) repayment of their loans.

---

[2] This real estate bubble dynamics were also observed in other parts of the world, see Green, R. and Wachter. S. (2007), "The Housing Finance Revolution", paper presented at the Federal Reserve Bank of Kansas City Symposium.

The two main US government-sponsored enterprises (GES) devoted to mortgage lending, Fannie Mae and Freddie Mac,[3] developed this disintermediation financing technique from the 1970s onward, adding their guarantees to a particular type of ABS, so-called mortgage-backed securities (MBS) to enhance their market attractiveness. The GESs largely confined their guarantees to "prime" borrowers with "conforming" loans—for example, loans with a principal below a certain dollar threshold—and to borrowers with a credit score above a certain limit.

Naturally, the private financial sector eventually started using these innovations—partially as a consequence of the late 1980s "Savings and Loans" crisis that decimated the class of more traditional *private* and regionally specific financial institutions that previously dominated the US mortgage sector[4]—and further developed them toward MBS backed by "non-conforming loans"—for example, loans for borrowers with low credit scores, and by *further* packaging those into "Collateralized Debt Obligations" (CDOs, which therefore "re-securitized" the same assets pooled under a MBS or ABS), and then dividing the cash flows of those into different "tranches" to appeal to different classes of investors with different risk tolerances.[5]

---

[3] The Federal Home Loan Mortgage Corporation (commonly known as Freddie Mac) was originally created to encourage homeownership by supporting mortgage markets, while the Federal National Mortgage Association (a.k.a. Fannie Mae, another "Great Depression" era body, created in 1938) was created to increase the flow and reduce the costs of mortgage credit. Both are so-called Government-Sponsored Enterprises (GSEs), entities created by the US Congress that are nevertheless privately held organizations (albeit perceived by market as being endowed with implicit government support, which effectively reduced their market funding costs). As the crisis intensified, they were eventually nationalized in September 2008.

[4] This was the biggest US banking crisis since the "Great Depression" half a century earlier. 1043 Savings and Loans (S&L) institutions—roughly half of all such firms—holding $519 billion in assets were ultimately closed during this crisis, which was partially caused by the Federal Reserve interest rate increases during the Volcker era: see Curry, T. and Shibut, L. (2000), "The Cost of the Savings and Loan Crisis: Truth and Consequences", FDIC Banking Review 13(2).

[5] By ordering the rights to the cash flows, the issuers of CDOs could get AAA (Triple A) ratings from credit rating agencies to the securities in the highest tranche (those with the lowest associated default risk). These CDO holders, on the other hand, were insured via "mono-line" insurance companies that would collaterize those liabilities through the then unsupervised selling of "credit default swaps", or CDS (financial instruments with limited capital collateral): this effectively worked as an additional "credit rating enhancer" technique, for example, it enabled credit rating agencies to rate these financial instruments at higher rating brackets. See Ashcraft, A. and Schuerman, T. (2008), "Understanding the Securitization of Subrpime Mortgage Credit", Staff Report n. 318, Federal Reserve Bank of New York.

This process seems convoluted, but at its core this is actually a rather traditional financial technique of distributing the risks and leverage of an asset among different economic agents to reduce its costs and increase its returns. This said, these innovations did make the asset structure underlying those instruments considerably more complex and much more leveraged (e.g., more reliant on—eventually short-term—debt), and therefore more difficult to evaluate the associated risks of those instruments.

Such financial innovations and expansion of mortgage financing were also enabled by an environment of easier monetary policy by the Fed (the Fed policy rate was cut by a total of 550 basis points between 2001 and 2004, hitting the 1% mark in May 2004, partially to cushion the downturn in the US caused by the bursting of the "dot-com" stock market bubble in 2000: Fig. 5.2) and by a very complex, and at the same time also fragmented, overlapping and incomplete regulatory and oversight framework.[6]

As an example of the effects of a such regulatory framework, many financial corporations created off-balance sheet entities—for example, Structured Investment Vehicles (SIVs)—to purchase MBS, as those SIVs were not subject to standard regulatory capital requirements, and also significantly expanded the usage of short-term repurchase agreements for

[6] At the federal level, the several financial regulators in the US (also mostly Great-Depression era creations) can be divided in four types (see Congressional Research Services (2020), "Who Regulates Whom? An Overview of the U.S. Financial Regulatory Framework", Washington, DC):

- **Depository regulators:** Office of the Comptroller of the Currency (OCC), Federal Deposit Insurance Corporation (FDIC), and Federal Reserve for banks, plus the National Credit Union Administration (NCUA) for credit unions;
- **Securities markets regulators:** Securities and Exchange Commission (SEC) and Commodity Futures Trading Commission (CFTC);
- **Government-sponsored enterprise (GSE) regulators:** Federal Housing Finance Agency (FHFA) and the Farm Credit Administration (FCA);
- **Consumer protection regulator:** Consumer Financial Protection Bureau (CFPB), which was created by the 2010 Dodd-Frank Act.

Additionally, 50-state banking departments charter and regulate state banks. Only with the passage of the 2010 so-called "Dodd-Frank Act" the Federal Reserve was finally made responsible for the consolidated supervision of bank and nonbank financial holdings companies in the US. This act also created the Financial Stability Oversight Council, an "umbrella" organization chaired by the Treasury Department, tasked with in principle identifying threats that could destabilize the US financial system (but without a regulatory mandate in how to address those).

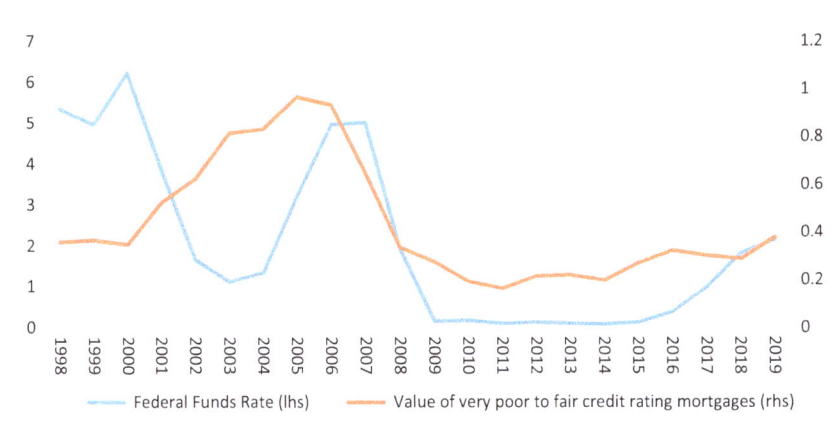

5 HOUSES BUILT ON SAND: THE "GLOBAL FINANCIAL CRISIS" 71

Fig. 5.2 Federal funds rate (in %) and "subprime" mortgages (in $ trillion). (Sources: FRED and Federal Housing Financing Agency)

the financing of those (remarkably, by 2006 US investment banks were *reportedly rolling over a quarter of their balance sheet on average every night* via "repo loans", highlighting not only an extreme vulnerability to short-term movements but a dangerous level of systemic interconnectedness).[7] This amounted to using a **parallel "shadow banking" system** (i.e., entities that perform banking functions but are not classified and regulated as such) to finance the bubble.

All bubbles eventually burst: suddenly reversing course in mid2004, the Fed began a very sharp tightening cycle (in fact, the sharpest since the Volcker tightening over 20 years earlier), with the Fed policy rate peaking at 5.25% in the later summer of 2006. This started to unwind the mortgage asset bubble, as it became too costly to refinance the outstanding instruments: this process quickened after a Wall Street investment bank, Bear Stearns—highly exposed to collaterized instruments—was forced to close down two of its subprime mortgage funds, with huge losses for the company (Bear Stearns would be eventually sold to JPMorgan Chase in March 2008, after a complex and ultimately failed bailout attempt by the Federal Reserve, which at that time did not have the legal capacity to

---

[7] See Baily, M., Litan, R. and Johnson, M. (2008), "The Origins of the Financial Crisis", Brookings Institution.

directly support a non-deposit taking financial institution).[8] This happened because the sudden uncertainty over asset prices—current and future—caused lenders to refuse to rollover debts, and over-leveraged (e.g., over-indebted) banks like Bear Stearns found themselves exposed to falling asset prices *with* limited amounts of collateral capital (as an additional element its predicament, investment banks at that time were allowed lower capitals requirements than deposit-taking commercial banks).[9] In practical terms, this can be seen as an analogue to the series of bank runs during the "Great Depression", now originating in the "shadow banking" system but eventually spilling-over to the formal bank system.[10]

While one can *potentially* argue that US policies to increase home ownership may also have had some influence in this outcome,[11] one can *certainly* question how institutions along the securitization chain failed to properly perform an adequate risk assessment on these financial instruments, why the—admittedly fragmented and dispersed—US regulatory agencies did not take proper remedial action earlier, and why the Federal Reserve apparently failed to see (in 1929–1933, in 2004–2005 and again

---

[8] This failed attempt included the Fed's own piece of financial innovation, namely, the creation of an off-balance sheet "limited liability company", or LLC, called "Maiden Lane" (the name of street where the back entrance to the New York Fed headquarters in Manhattan is located), which the Fed and the Treasury Department would capitalize to support the planned transaction. Two extensions of "Maiden Lane LLC" (II and III, respectively) were subsequently created to support the bail-out of American International Group (or AIG) in 2008, whose government takeover was another traumatic episode of the GFC. The LLCs were all wound-up by 2018 (see here).

[9] Greenlaw, D., Hatzius, J., Kashyap, A. and Shin, H. (2008), "Leveraged Losses: Lessons from the Mortgage Market Meltdown" Paper prepared for the US Monetary Policy Forum, University of Chicago and the Rosenberg Institute for Global Finance at Brandeis University.

[10] Gorton, G. and Metrick, A. (2012), "Securitized Banking and The Run on Repo", Journal of Financial Economics, 104(3):425–451: these authors conclude that "the US banking system was effectively insolvent for the first time since the Great Depression".

[11] Wallison, P. (2011), "Dissent from the Majority Report of the Financial Crisis Inquiry Commission", American Enterprise Institute and Avery, R. and Brevoort, K. (2015), "The Subprime Crisis: Is Government Housing Policy to Blame?", The Review of Economics and Statistics, 97(2): 352–63.

in 2023, as we will see later in this book) the full implications of its policy rate moves (or non-moves) in the financial sector.[12]

However, a central point in this system-wide risk assessment failure was that each link of the securitization chain was plagued by asymmetric information (or, using the terminology introduced by the theoretical framework described in Annex 4.A, agents faced information frictions and demonstrated a biased and staggered learning process of the information around them, but were still, if you will, behaving rationally), which prevented traditional market-based adjustment mechanisms from working properly, leading to these inadequate risk-assessment efforts (and admittedly, this market failure was indeed compounded by what was eventually shown to be ineffective regulatory corrective mechanisms).

This was inherently linked to the incentive framework of the securitization model itself, which **by design** transferred risks to other agents further down the chain (risk transfer is, after all, one of the main functions of financial markets). However, the increased complexity—even opacity—of the new securitized instruments that were being used also meant that investors tended rely on third parties for their risk assessment, and notably on rating agencies.[13]

This US subprime mortgage crisis speedily became the deepest global financial crisis since the 1930s "Great Depression", worthy of its own "Global Financial Crisis" moniker and related acronym (GFC).

5.2 How It Spread

The collapse of another US investment bank, that of Lehman Brothers in (of all days) 9/11, 2008, is seen as the signal that the crisis had effectively become a global one (albeit over a year earlier, in August 2007, that same

---

[12] As an example, see McCarthy, J. and Peach, R. (2004), "Are Home Prices the Next Bubble?" Federal Reserve Bank of New York, Economic Policy Review, 10(3): 1–17: the authors' reply to their own question was *no*. This said and leaving aside the inherent uncertainty associated with accurately identifying asset bubbles, especially earlier in the cycle, it is important to recognize that US policy actions did not happen in vacuum (as during the "Gold Exchange Standard"): namely, low international interest rates and significant international capital inflows into the US imposed constraints to its actions in 2004 (as higher rates would have increased further inflows).

[13] This author was Managing Director and Sovereign Chief Economist at Moody's Investor Services (MIS), the second largest ratings agency in the world, between 2011 and 2015. The 2017 legal settlement between the US Justice Department and MIS related to alleged actions leading up to and during the GFC can be found here.

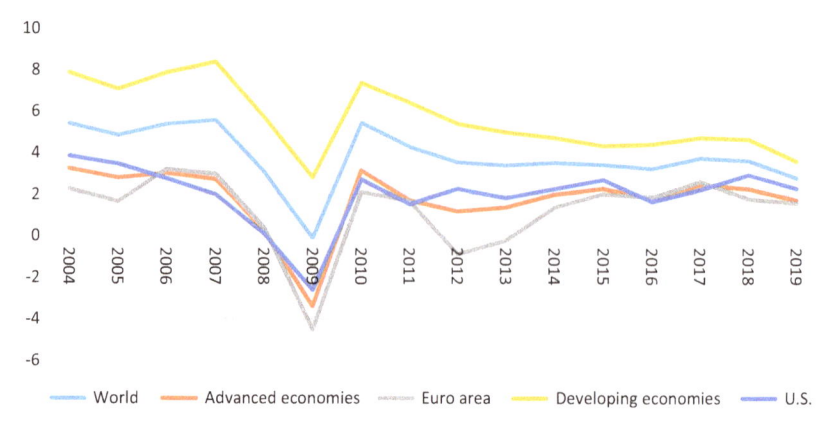

Fig. 5.3 Real GDP growth, yoy. (Source: IMF)

firm had already closed down its subprime-mortgage dedicated subsidiary). The resulting global losses can only be described as staggering (Fig. 5.3): global GDP growth went from 5.6% in 2007 to a slight contraction in 2009, and shrank by -3.4% among Developed economics that same year (-2.6% in the US, and a whopping -4.5% in the euro area: the reasons for the euro area dismal performance will be explored in the Chap. 6), the first such fall since World War II.

It is very complex to estimate the overall losses associated with the GFC, but studies calculate cumulative effects of between 2% and 10% of GDP: when compared with a global nominal GDP of $58.5 trillion in 2007, this suggests losses between $1.2 and $5.9 trillion.[14] The global performance could have been much worse, if it were not by the fact that China's economy grew by above 11% *pa* throughout the worse GFC years (a simple growth decomposition exercise suggests that China alone added 126% to global growth in 2009, which implies that without it the global economy would have truly gone into a depression).

The spread of the crisis was inherently related to both the sheer size of US markets, but also to the degree of interconnectedness of global markets with it (Table 5.1: one should note that the figures for the EU and the

---

[14] Turner, D. and Ollivaud, P. (2018), "The output cost of the global financial crisis", OECD Economics Department. Their estimates are for developed OECD member countries, which, as is apparent from Fig. 5.3, were the ones most affected by the GFC.

Table 5.1 Shares of global financial markets, 2006 (in $ billion)

	Stock market capitalization	Debt securities	Bank assets	Bonds, equities, and bank assets	Share of global financial markets
World	50,826.6	68,734.4	70,860.5	190,421.5	
EU (then including the UK)	13,068.8	23,202.7	36,642.0	72,913.5	38.3
-of which, the euro area	8419.1	18,768.3	25,837.6	53,268.8	28.0
US	19,569.0	26,735.8	10,204.7	56,509.4	29.7
Japan	4795.8	8719.3	6415.4	19,930.5	10.5
Emerging markets	11,692.4	6056.4	11,271.3	29,020.1	15.2

Source: IMF, Global Financial Stability Report, October 2007, pp. 139

euro area are somewhat misleading when presented as single entities, as their financial markets, for a series of reasons, are still not fully integrated).

Hattori and Suda, 2007,[15] and Minoiu and Reyes, 2011[16] document discrete jumps in measures of cross-border financial interconnectedness in the run-up to the GFC (and, incidentally, in the run-un to other earlier crises too): in an environment where risk was reassessed and the normal flow of capital curtailed, financial linkages, which are in principle positive, can become a source of *contagion*. This strong and speedy global negative spillovers (e.g., "contagion") happened in several different phases and through various transmission mechanisms.[17]

The first phase was through **direct exposures**. This stage was largely limited to banks with direct exposures to the US market and affected a few specific financial markets. This was the case of some euro area banks, including German and French ones which were affected already in mid-2007. Also in the UK, with a similar real estate bubble as in the US, exposed banks were also affected, with an actual bank run on mortgage

---

[15] Hattori, M. and Suda, Y. (2007), "Developments in a Cross-Border Bank Exposure Network" Bank of Japan Working Paper no. 07-E-21.

[16] Minoiu, C. and Reyes, J. (2011), "A Networks Analysis of Global Banking: 1978–2009", IMF Working Paper 74, 11–41.

[17] Claessens, S., Dell''Ariccia, G., Deniz, I. and Laeven, L. (2010), "Lessons and Policy Implications From the Global Financial Crisis", IMF Working Papers 10/44.

lender Northern Rock (perhaps the last *physical* bank run in history). In the US, rating agencies belated downgrades led to sharply widening spreads on CDOs and liquidity disruptions in interbank and commercial paper markets. Interbank rates spiked and issuances of commercial paper contracted sharply.

A second phase took place via **asset markets**. This happened through liquidity shortages, freezing of credit markets, stock price declines and exchange rate instability. At this stage policy responses were speedy and large, with major central banks quickly making significant amounts of liquidity available to banks in their respective jurisdictions (more on that below). However, the effectiveness of those measures in stabilizing interbank markets was somewhat short-lived.

The third phase occurred after the collapse of Lehman Brothers, when **solvency concerns** about systemically important global financial institutions materialized, fueling a process of rapid deleveraging and fire asset sales, which led to further asset price declines, more fire asset sales, rising recapitalization needs and further loss of confidence. To top this up, resolution frameworks showed deficiencies, especially in the incompletely integrated financial markets of the euro area (for more on this, see Chap. 6).

Throughout those stages, as is frequently the case (not only from the historical narrative of the previous chapters, but as this author can personally attest to), the evolution of the crisis led to some policy responses that, with hindsight, were in some cases inappropriate, including the almost complete replacement of private markets by state (fiscal and monetary) financing—a feature that would prove to be very long lasting—and the (more temporary) "harboring" of liquidity in particular jurisdictions (in some cases due to *quasi*-legal "moral suasion" by national regulators, notably in the euro area).

Beyond the sheer level of interconnectedness, another significant difference in relation to the world of the "gold standard" presented in Chap. 2 is the larger multiplicity of relevant economic and sovereign actors during the GFC. After all, the world until the 1950s was still a world of colonial empires and economic systems' blocks. These largely European colonial empires were progressively dismantled between the late 1940s and the early 1970s—with help of the US, while the presumed alternative of state-led systems went down with the dismantling of the Soviet bloc (and ultimately of the Soviet Union) between 1989 and 1991 and the re-entry of those countries into the global monetary and financial system. A graphic example of this increase in complexity is the swelling of IMF membership: from 44 (overwhelming American and European) founding members, it ballooned to 190 countries currently, or an over 430% increase.[18] Those new sovereigns came in with their own individual financial systems (and monetary authorities and treasuries too), which made the evaluation of the impacts of the crisis very complex (and created a small cottage industry of "heat maps" and cross-exposures analysis that this author humbly contributed to).

5.3 What the Fed (and Others) Did: The Policy Response

Central banks duly and intensively used their traditional monetary policy tools, driving their policy rates into real negative territory (Fig. 5.4) and, in some cases, into **nominal negative territory, for instance, in Sweden and Switzerland.** Monetary policy around the "effective lower bound" (ELB) would remain the norm—with occasional, limited deviations—for over a decade.

With very limited inflationary pressures given the GDP contraction, the main aim of policy actions in response to the GFC was to allow financial markets to operate in face of the "sudden stop" brought about by the risk reassessment and the fears of contagion, and that was done largely by providing liquidity to banks and/or sovereigns in (very) large quantities, via the expansion of their balance sheets (Fig. 5.5), mainly via so-called quantitative easing, or QE.[19] Even the central banks of a few emerging markets also followed this policy, albeit in much smaller scales.[20] Additionally, some central banks also targeted the exchange rate, as the GFC also impacted

---

[18] See IMF, List of Members: only about 30 countries actually signed the IMF "Articles of Agreement" in 1945, and some of those would shortly leave the organization for the next half a century, due to the shifting political dynamics in Europe (e.g., the expansion of the Soviet block).

[19] QE is the *additional* buying up of government bonds in the secondary market, over and above normal operations a central bank might have with those instruments. These programs are as a rule financed by un-sterilized central bank monetary expansion (i.e., without offsetting policy actions by the central bank, like the tendering of fixed term deposits).

[20] Notably in South Korea and Israel: see Ishi, K., Stone, M. and Yehoue, E. (2009), "Unconventional Central Bank Measures for Emerging Economies", IMF Working Paper WP/09/226.

78   L. VINHAS DE SOUZA

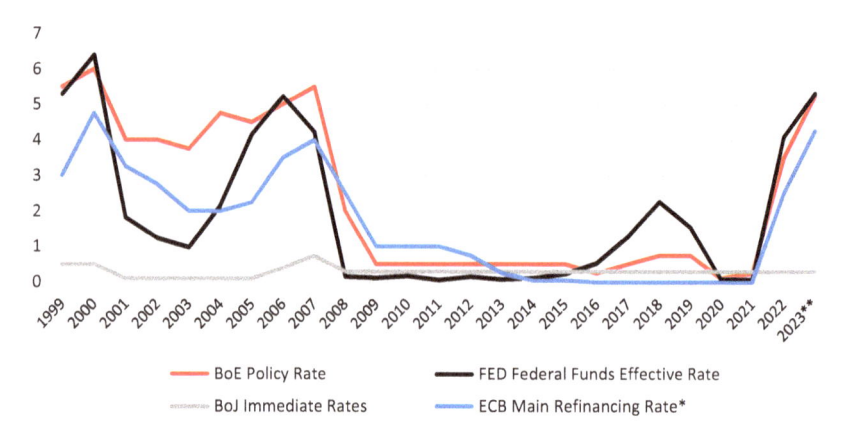

Fig. 5.4 Selected central banks' policy rates.** (Sources: FRED and ECB. *: The ECB policy rate is a splicing of the fixed and variable refinancing rate [the later for period from 2005 to 2007].** US Federal Reserve—Fed, European Central Bank—ECB, Bank of Japan—BoJ, Bank of England—BoE)

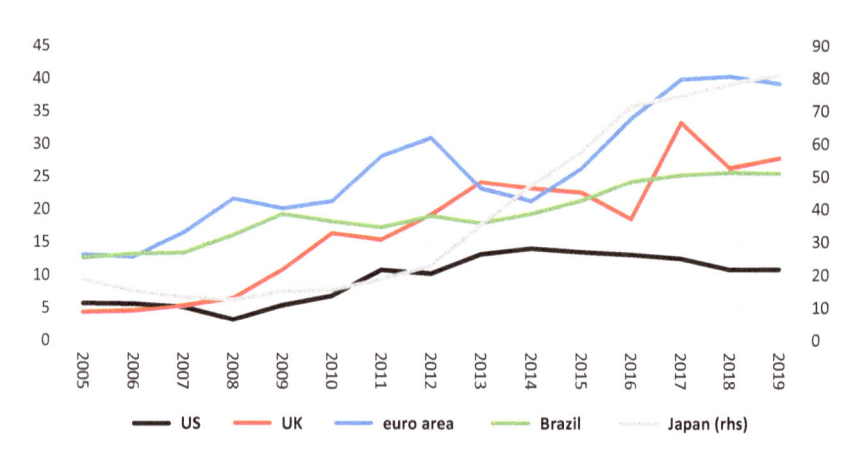

Fig. 5.5 Selected central banks' balance sheets, % of GDP. (Source: FRED)

countries through this channel (this was more typical of Developing countries, but the Swiss case demonstrates that it was not unique to those).[21]

Another way to think about those two different stages of the policy response is to look at this from the point of view of the balance sheet of a central bank. In the earlier phase of the crisis, the increase in central bank balance sheets could be seen as *liability-driven*, for example, demand for central bank liabilities had increased. However, once the ELB was reached, central banks switched from supporting interbank markets to *supporting economies* via asset purchases aimed at reducing longer-term interest rates (reducing "risk-free" reference rates and the spread between those and other rates). As these asset purchases were financed by reserve creation, central bank balance sheets continued to increase, but now the process was *asset-driven*.[22] Ultimately these operations were successful (in their own terms), as interbank yields fell, and eventually even to levels below those observed before the crisis (Fig. 5.6).

However, this (very) large increase in the balance sheets of these major central banks, doubling in percentage of GDP compared to the pre-crisis period by 2011,[23] was achieved largely via the further acquisition of government debt (with some exception and nuances: as examples, in the case of the Fed, emergency lending facilities were the largest item on the asset side of its balance sheet in 2008, while in 2009 the driver was the acquisition MBS; in the case of the ECB, only from 2009 onward the acquisition of euro area government paper progressively became a significant item in its balance sheet; some central banks used "off balance sheet" instruments

---

[21] The Swiss National Bank—SNB, also saw its balance sheet balloon from less than 25% to over 61% of GDP between 2007 and 2011, due to the increase in foreign currency assets in its balance sheet, as the SNB, issuer of an internationally accepted reserve currency, announced in 2010 a policy of *unlimited* buying of foreign currency to hold the value of the Swiss Franc fixed in relation to a given euro exchange rate. In other terms, it was *a reaction* to the capital flows generated by other central banks' policies of very low interest rates (this is a subject that will re-emerge in the section of this work that deals with Developing countries).

[22] Rule, G. (2015), "Understanding the Central Bank Balance Sheet", Bank of England Handbook, n. 32.

[23] Japan had a smaller increase, of around 40%, but it started from a considerably higher level.

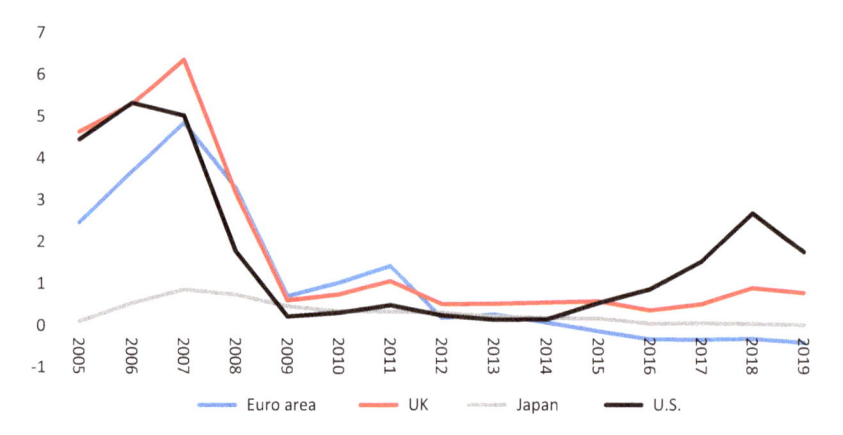

Fig. 5.6 Selected interbank rates (3-month or 90-day rates and yields). (Sources: FRED, OECD)

to implement this expansion).[24] This had the side effect of increasing the level of connection between governments, central banks, and the financial sector, and expanded "doom loop" type of linkages (and may even be seen in some contexts as "financial repression").[25] Below are more specific policy actions for the main global central banks in this stage of the GFC:

---

[24] For example, the BoE created a facility known as the Special Liquidity Scheme (or SLS, admittedly a far less poetic name than "Maiden Lane"). The SLS was designed to take mortgage-backed securities from commercial banks and swap them for UK treasury bonds. As these transactions were a collateral swap, they were not included in the BoE's balance sheet. This basic framework was later used in other BoE facilities.

[25] Financial repression may include (1) directed lending to the government by captive domestic agents (beyond the central bank, also domestic banks and pension funds), (2) explicit or implicit caps on interest rates, (3) restrictions to capital movements and the exchange rate, (4) a tighter connection between government and banks, either explicitly through public ownership, "bailed out" banks or through "moral suasion," (5) high reserve or liquidity requirements, (6) securities transaction taxes, and (7) forced placement of nonmarketable government debt (see Reinhart, C. and Sbrancia, M. (2011), "The Liquidation of Government Debt" NBER Working Paper 16,893): some of those elements—namely, high reserve or liquidity requirements—were integrated into the permanent global macroprudential regulation reforms arising from crisis (see Tarullo, D. (2019) "Financial Regulation: Still Unsettled a Decade after the Crisis", Journal of Economic Perspectives, 33(1): 61–80).

5.3.1 *Federal Reserve*

With prices marching toward deflationary territory (the US CPI would be -0.4% in 2009 and it would flirt again with deflation in 2015) and with its benchmark policy interest rate very close to zero, the Fed started its so-called large-scale asset purchases (LSAPs) in November 2008, announcing it would acquire $600 billion of debt and mortgage-backed securities of US federal housing agencies. In March 2009, it also decided to expand its purchases of agency and longer-term Treasury bonds by $1.75 trillion. In November 2010, the Fed announced a further round of QE, worth $600 billion in Treasury bonds. This was complemented a year later by "Operation Twist", that is, the exchanging of medium-term bonds in the Fed balance sheet for lower interest 10-year Treasuries, thereby also reducing market funding costs.[26] Finally, given the international importance of the US dollar, the Fed also established currency swap lines with several other major central banks.[27] Additionally, from 2013 onward, the Fed started performing capital assessment exercises of large US banks balance sheets, a two-pronged exercise consisting of the Dodd-Frank Act Stress Test and the Comprehensive Capital Analysis and Review (CCAR).

5.3.2 *BoE*

In January 2009 the Bank of England announced the launch of the Asset Purchase Facility (APF) and in March 2009 the terms of the APF were altered to facilitate the purchase of assets through the direct creation of reserves. The target amount for asset purchases increased to £375 billion (almost $700 billion) by late 2012. As a result of these, the BoE's balance sheet became dominated by asset purchases and new reserves.[28]

---

[26] Kohn, D. (2010), "The Federal Reserve's Policy Actions during the Financial Crisis and Lessons for the Future", Remarks at Carleton University, Ottawa, Canada.

[27] Fleming, M. and Klagge, N. (2010), "The Federal Reserve's Foreign Exchange Swap Lines", Current Issues in Economics and Finance, Federal Reserve Bank of New York, 16(4).

[28] These purchased assets are also held off the balance sheet of the BoE, in a subsidiary called the Bank of England Asset Purchase Facility Fund (BOEAPFF). What appears on the BoE's balance sheet is a loan to BOEAPFF on the asset side under the "Other Assets" item.

5.3.3 BoJ

Reflecting the bursting of Japan's own financial (and real estate) bubble in the 1990s, the BoJ has the longest running QE program among major central banks (it is still operational, as a matter of fact). Its first large increase in government bonds purchase was in 2001, reaching ¥35 trillion (around $270 billion) by the mid-2000s. With the GFC, the BoJ increased those further, reaching a total of ¥56 trillion (around $730 billion) by the end of 2011.[29] BoJ's GFC policies were later integrated as the so-called Abenomics,[30] a three-pronged policy announced in December 2012 and developed under the (correct) assumption that there were significant synergies between the different parts of the program, more precisely between fiscal stimulus (the first "arrow", adopted in February 2013, which led to a comparatively modest fiscal support of 2% of GDP), monetary stimulus (the second "arrow", introduced in April 2013 and dubbed "qualitative and quantitative monetary easing", or QE^2) and structural reform, the third and last "arrow", focused on the liberalization of trade, labor and product markets with the aim of increasing the economy's long-term sustainable growth rate (this arrow arguably misfired).

5.3.4 ECB

The euro area's central bank created its own limited government bond purchase program, the Securities Market Program (SMP) in May 2010, during the beginning of the euro area act of the GFC (see Chap. 6), with the stated objective of supporting the proper functioning of financial markets to enable the transmission of monetary policy, and *not* to provide additional liquidity or funding. This reflected differences in the ECB institutional set-up when compared to other central banks: the ECB has (or at least had) much stricter institutional limits concerning direct financing to sovereigns than the other monetary authorities,[31] while its "ownership"

---

[29] "The Bank of Japan's Policy Measures during the Financial Crisis", Bank of Japan, 2010.

[30] Vinhas de Souza (2014) "Japan's Abenomics: Answers to Frequently Asked Questions about Progress 1.5 Years On", Moody's. This policy set was named after Shinzo Abe, then Japanese Prime Minister, murdered in 2022 (I had the honor of later working with PM Abe and his team during my time with the President of the European Commission, Jean-Claude Juncker).

[31] Known as the "no bail out clause", this prohibits ECB monetary financing to euro area governments, and is in Article 104 of the so-called Maastricht Treaty, one of the EU legal texts.

structure means it has no direct "fiscal principal".[32] As a result, the direct ECB sovereign exposure via the SMP at the beginning of the GFC was just 8% of its balance sheet, or 2% of the euro area GDP, an order of magnitude below that of the monetary authorities described above.[33] However, this would speedily change with the expansion of the crisis to other euro area members, which led to the two three-year loan long-term liquidity operations (LTRO) provided by the ECB in late 2011/early 2012, resulting in a combined extension of credit to euro area banks of around €500 billion. As those relied on an increase of the eligible collateral list to lower-rated bonds issued by stressed euro area sovereigns held by banks, it increased the ECB *indirect* exposure to sovereigns (nevertheless, banks remained the holders of the sovereign debt).

There is a legitimate policy debate about how to classify such policies,[34] what should be the "steady state" or optimal size of the balance sheet of a central bank (to say nothing about its composition),[35] but one must recognize that even independent monetary authorities cannot avoid fiscal consequences for their actions (as, after all, central banks, as state bodies, do share a unified budget constraint with the rest of the Government): more than that, a case can be made these aspects *should not be avoided*, and especially during a crisis, due to the importance of a fiscally sustainable sovereign for both monetary and financial stability, the core tasks of central banks.[36]

---

[32] The "owners" of the ECB capital are not the national treasuries, as is usually the case, but the national central banks of the euro area: therefore, contrary to traditional national central banks, there is no single, *direct* link to a Ministry of Finance or Treasury that could lead to a push for government debt monetization.

[33] Some authors also mention the particular nature of the ECB Governing Council (namely, its size and heterogeneity) for this delayed response (arguably a somewhat similar dynamics to the Fed Board during the "Great Depression"), while also recognizing that the voting patterns have evolved as the ECB matured as an institution: see Rieder, K. (2022), "Monetary Policy Decision-Making by Committee: Why, When and How it Can Work", European Journal of Political Economy, Vol. 72 and Claeys, G. and Linta, T. (2019), "The Evolution of the ECB Governing Council's Decision-Making", Bruegel.

[34] Borio, C. and Disyatat, P. (2009), "Unconventional Monetary Policies: an Appraisal", BIS Working Papers n. 292.

[35] Goodhart, C. (2017), "A Central Bank's Optimal Balance Sheet Size?", CEPR Discussion Paper n. 12,272. Goodhart's conclusion can be summarized as "not as big as it is now".

[36] Orphanides, A. (2018), "Independent Central Banks and the Interplay between Monetary and Fiscal Policy", International Journal of Central Banking, International Journal of Central Banking, 14(3): 447–470.

This said, even if successful in terms of their stated aims, these policies not only increased exposures and vulnerabilities in the economies in which they were enacted (see Annex 5.B), but they "exported" those to other economies, especially Developing ones. Namely, the massive additional liquidity and associated negative real interest rates generated capital flows looking for yield, which led those on the receiving end of these flows into potentially suboptimal policy actions of their own, beyond any GFC-specific effects they might have experienced.

5.4 More Granularity on the Regulatory Response

On the US side, the 2010 Dodd–Frank Act was the main GFC-linked reform legislation. While it was a complex collection of enhancements related to financial stability and systemic risk measures, it did not imply the comprehensive regulatory solutions of the type enacted during the "Great Depression" era, remaining mostly at a more general level and largely leaving decisions and discretion on practical implementation to the (multiple) US regulatory bodies. In general terms, its actions concentrated on reinforced bank regulation calibrated to the size of the institution,[37] on measures aiming toward greater financial resiliency for financial institutions[38] and on defining a framework for the orderly resolution of failing banks.[39] These reform efforts were naturally incomplete, with gaps going from the regulation of the "shadow banking system" to the role of macro prudential measures.[40]

---

[37] Those were partially rolled back by the "Economic Growth, Regulatory Relief and Consumer Protection Act" of 2018, which may have had some role in the bank stresses of early 2023, see Annex 5.B.

[38] Addressing (1) the quality and quantity of capital required and kept by banks (e.g., minimum capital requirements, (2) the greater stability of funding sources for banks (e.g., Liquidity Coverage Ratio, or LCR) and (3) the risk management capacities and practices of banks (assessed via periodic "stress tests").

[39] Informally known as "living wills": "living wills" or not, there remains many doubts of the practical "resolvability" of large, systemically important financial institutions (see Tarullo 2019, ibid.).

[40] See Tarullo (2019), ibid.

Many of those US measures were also reflected in the global regulatory response, the 2010 so-called **Basel III rules**[41]: the name is a reference to the "Basel Committee on Banking Supervision" (BCBS), the international body that negotiated those and which is housed within the Bank for International Settlements (BIS), an institution headquartered in Basel, Switzerland. Basel III are a set of reforms of global banking regulation that aim to bring stricter capital and liquidity requirements to banks around the globe in the aftermath of the GFC: they are still in the process of implementation. These rules also bring more stringent stress testing procedures to assess the adequacy of those liquidity levels.[42]

Their ultimate goal was to bolster both micro-prudential (by increasing the resilience of individual banking institutions) and macroprudential regulations (by reducing risks that systemically affect the banking system as whole) of the global banking system,[43] building on the three-pillar structure of the earlier international regulatory framework, known as "Basel II", by strengthening rules in each of its "pillars". This said, its key elements are new additions to Pillar I: the Enhanced Minimum Capital and New Liquidity and Leverage standards. Elements of Pillar II and Pillar III such as supervision, risk management, governance, transparency, and disclosure have also been strengthened (see Fig. 5.7).

Concerning Pillar I, Basel III defines capital more narrowly, requiring higher quality of capital and more transparency in the calculation of it: namely, the so-called core "Tier 1" capital must be composed predominately from common equity and retained earnings, while the different and less liquid Tier 2 capital types were harmonized, and Tier 3 capital discontinued.

---

[41] See Vinhas de Souza, L. (2013), "Limited GDP Benefits of Basel III Expected for Developing Economies", Moody's.

[42] Since December 2017, the BCBS has agreed to what is informally referred to as **Basel IV, a partial enhancement of Basel III**. It includes changes to the capital treatment of credit risk, operational risk and the credit valuation adjustment, the imposition of an "output floor" (which sets a lower limit—a "floor"—on the capital requirements—an "output"—that banks calculate when using their own internal risk models: the "floor" is set at 72.5% of the Basel III standardized approach: this was a major point of contention between US and non-US banks), revisions to the definition of the leverage ratio and the application of the leverage ratio to global systemically important banks (a revised market risk framework had already been agreed in 2016).

[43] Ghosh, S., Sugawara, N. and Zalduendo, J. (2011), "Bank Flows and Basel III—Determinants and Regional Differences in Emerging Markets" Economic Premise, n. 56, World Bank.

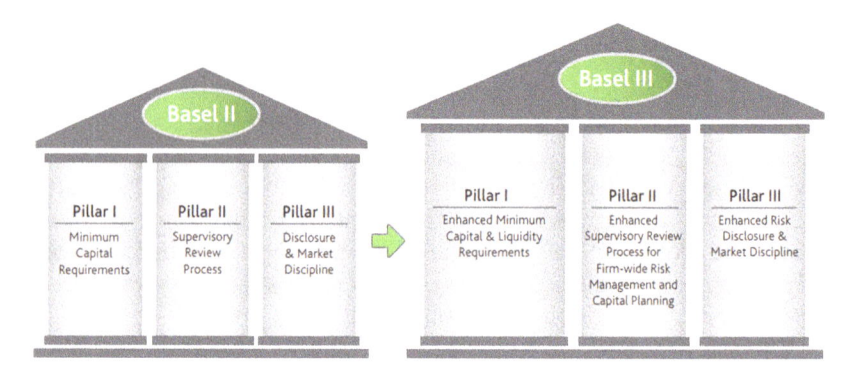

Fig. 5.7 The pillars of Basel II and III. (Source: Basel III New Capital and Liquidity Standards—FAQs, Moody's Analytics)

Under Basel III, the core Tier 1 (common equity tier, or CET 1) capital ratio increases to 4.5% and the Tier 1 ratio to 6.0%, while maintaining the total capital ratio at 8%. It also introduces two additional capital surcharges: a "capital conservation buffer" of 2.5% and a "countercyclical buffer" of 0–2.5%, set by individual jurisdictions depending on macroeconomic circumstances. Systemically important financial institutions (so, particularly large and interconnected banks) will be required to hold an additional buffer of between 1% and 2.5% of risk-weighted assets (RWA), potentially reaching 3.5%.

In addition to capital buffers, Basel III introduces liquidity and leverage standards: the purpose of the Liquidity Coverage Ratio (LCR) is to ensure that banks have sufficiently highly liquid assets to face stress scenarios lasting for up to 30 days. The ratio of high-quality liquid assets to total net liquidity outflows over a 30-day period needs to be equal or greater than 1, while a Net Stable Funding Ratio (NSFR) incentivizes banks to seek more stable sources of funding over a longer period, namely, one year (the ratio of available stable funding to that of required stable funding should be equal or greater than 1). Basel III also adds a 3% non-risk-based leverage ratio to prevent leverage buildup on a bank's balance sheet.

5.5 Effects in and Policy Actions of Developing Countries

So, how did some Developing economies act to prevent potential negative effects (e.g., inflationary pressures, currency appreciation, asset price bubbles, and risks of sudden withdrawals or sudden stops) of the large capital inflows created by the advanced economies GFC-induced monetary policy? Via a tighter regulation on their domestic financial systems and of capital inflows, and also via policies that effectively generate interest rates of levels similar to those in Developed economies (Table 5.2 provides

Table 5.2 GFC-related policies in selected developing countries[a]

	Interest rate ceilings, capital controls and/or reserve requirements
Bolivia	Tightened reserve requirements.
Brazil	Several financial transactions taxes on Investments in capital markets, bonds (2010), derivatives (2011), foreign loans, consumer loans (2011), portfolio inflows (2008–2010) introduced.
	Short-term dollar positions reserve requirements introduced (2011)
Colombia	Liquidity requirements (2008)
India	The Reserve Bank of India regulated interest rates on savings deposit accounts in commercial banks (until October 2011), yielding negative real returns
Indonesia	Limit of foreign currency bank accounts introduced (2010)
	Minimum holding periods on capital inflows introduced (2009, 2010).
Peru	Reserve requirements introduced (2009, 2011)
	Managed exchange rate (2010)
	Foreign investment restrictions introduced (2010)
Philippines	Limits on foreign capital inflows introduced (2010)
Thailand	Tax on foreign bond revenues introduced (2010)
Türkiye	Central bank cut borrowing interest rate as the economy experienced large capital inflows.
	Raised reserve requirements

Sources: IMF and Carvajal et al. (2012); Carvajal, M., Tudela, M. and Vinhas de Souza, L. (2012), "Counter-cyclical Central Banking Policies and their Longer-Term Implications", Moody's

[a]Argentina and Venezuela also have capital and foreign exchange rate control, but these policies were not GFC-related, but rather reflect their long-standing (persisting even to the time of the writing of this book) economic and financial instability. See McCandless (2005) and Pesce and Feldman (2023), ibid., for Argentina

examples of these policies for selected Developing countries).[44] In the end, many Developing countries were actually able to implement reasonably effective countercyclical fiscal and monetary policy during the GFC, even weathering the Fed eventual policy reversals as the GFC "faded away".[45]

Developing countries could do that because they had accumulated sizable policy buffers during a precedent period of stronger and more balanced growth that left them with more sustainable external and fiscal positions and with more moderate inflation than before (and that was true even for Latin America, as demonstrated by the sections on Brazil and Chile earlier in this book). Importantly, one additional reason for this better performance was that emerging markets had developed more robust policy frameworks, from fiscal rules enshrined in law to inflation targeting regimes administered by independent monetary authorities, and more strict supervisory regimes of their financial sectors, reinforcing the earlier conclusion that good (monetary) polices do matter.[46] As we will also see later, those will also allow Developing countries to weather better the next global crises.

However, the next act of the GFC saga will begin in the spring of 2010, and what prolonged that particular crisis did not come about from either US policies or from Developing countries' vulnerabilities. Rather, it reflected the inherent shortcomings of the European common currency project, the euro: this will be addressed in Chap. 6.

Annex 5.A: Spotting a Bubble[47]

Assuming that you could do that, how do you determine that a bubble has happened (which is, of course, a different thing from forecasting one)? Let's start by defining the fundamental value of any asset, and initially one that yields a known and fixed stream of dividends.

---

[44] They did that because of the traditional aim of forcing captive domestic agents (private and public) to absorb government debt and to limit the interest rate differential with Developed economies and hence limit destabilizing capital inflows.

[45] Vinhas de Souza, L. (2014), "QE Tapering: Impact Differs Amongst Emerging Markets", Moody's.

[46] Kose, A. and Ohnsorge, F. (eds), 2020. "A Decade after the Global Recession: Lessons and Challenges for Emerging and Developing Economies", World Bank.

[47] Barlevy, G. (2007), "Economic Theory and Asset Bubbles", Economic Perspectives 31(3): 44–59.

5 HOUSES BUILT ON SAND: THE "GLOBAL FINANCIAL CRISIS"

So, let d_t denote this stream paid out by the asset at date t, where t runs from 0 to infinity. To value the future revenue stream, let's further assume there are markets in which any investor could buy and sell bonds that pay at any specified date. Let q_t denote the current price of a bond that pays off at date t. If all those who trade in the asset could also access this bond market, each would equally value the payment at date t and q_t today. Hence, the value an investor attaches to the revenue stream from this asset is given by

$$F = \sum_{t=0}^{\infty} q_t d_t \qquad (5.1)$$

where F denotes the fundamental value of the asset. **An asset bubble is an asset whose price P is not equal to its fundamental value**, which is given by (Eq. 5.1), that is, $P \neq F$.

Next, consider the case where dividends are uncertain. That is, suppose that at date t, the realized state of the world can be one of the states in set Ω_t, which defines the set of all possible outcomes at that date, and let $\omega_t \in \Omega_t$ refer to a particular state of the world at date t, which investors believe will occur with probability $Prob(\omega_t)$. The state of the world determines the value of the dividend at that date t, that is, $d_t = d(\omega_t)$. Let $q_t = q(\omega_t)$ denote the value individuals assign today to revenue they will receive at date t in that particular state of the world ω_t. To link this to the price of a bond as in the case where dividends are known with certainty, note that if there were a market for state-contingent bonds that paid at date t in a particular state, and this market were available to all investors, then $q(\omega_t)$ would be the price of this bond. The fundamental value investors assign to the asset here is given by

$$F = E\left[\sum_{t=0}^{\infty} q(\omega)_t d(\omega)_t\right] = \sum_{t=0}^{\infty} \sum_{\omega_t \in \Omega = 0_t} Prob(\omega)_t q(\omega)_t d(\omega)_t \qquad (5.2)$$

where the expectation is taken with respect to the distribution over all states of the world in Ω_t. Here, an asset would also be considered a bubble if its price $P \neq F$, as defined in (Eq. 5.2).

Of course, the actual process is *much* more complex and uncertain than what is described above: to start with, the fundamental value of an asset is a nonobservable variable, and deviations from it, as a rule, are assessed only *ex post*.[48] Beyond that, even if one has accurately spotted a bubble, what should one do, as a policy maker? The timing of "pricking a bubble" is very tricky, and mistakes can be very costly.

Additionally, q_t and d_t above are assumed as exogenous, while they should actually be seen **as endogenous to policy actions** (just ask the Fed or the ECB…). This has nontrivial implications for how to address even that rare animal, a properly identified bubble, as should be apparent from Chap. 4 and the following chapters in this book.

ANNEX 5.B: CREATING FUTURE VULNERABILITIES WHILE DEALING WITH A CRISIS[49]

It is important to stress again that the (still-partial) separation of central banks from national treasuries is a recent phenomenon: well into the twentieth century, beyond the issuing of currency, the domestic financing of national governments (e.g., being their "fiscal agent") was among the core functions of a monetary authority.[50] The links with fiscal authorities is made clear by their accrual of the profits from central banking activities: a monetary authority will typically generate profits from "seigniorage" (the monopoly or quasi monopoly rights to issue legal tender, which itself is derived from and upheld via government legal acts),[51] which are then

---

[48] Brunnermeir, M. (2020), chapter "Bubbles", in *The New Palgrave Dictionary of Economics*, Palgrave.

[49] This section partially follows Carvajal et al. (2012), ibid.

[50] An example of that is provided by the BoE. It was created in the seventeenth century, initially as a private institution with a royal regulatory charter (for which it also had to pay the Exchequer—the Ministry of Finance—for its periodic renewal): that charter enabled it to, among other things, provide loans to the British sovereign. During the following centuries, it enabled the UK to finance the Napoleonic War and two world wars. The BoE was nationalized in 1946, and monetary policy operational independence was granted by the Exchequer only in 1997.

[51] While seigniorage is historically the greatest source of central bank's profits, other elements include obligatory reserves—non-remunerated or remunerated at below market rates, the management of foreign exchange reserves and operations linked to the provision of liquidity to the financial system (fees from activities like bank supervision are another revenue source).

transferred to the national treasury,[52] the entity usually responsible for the paid-in capital of the monetary authority.[53]

This underlying relationship means that there are several historical precedents in which a national monetary authority was directly and openly used as a tool to deal with the fiscal matters of a country. For instance, in the US, the Fed deliberately held interest rates below inflation for a decade between the 1940s and 1950s, so pursuing a "financial repression" strategy.[54] Partially due to this, the stock of public debt to GDP in the US fell by a remarkable *50%* of GDP between 1946 and 1952 (Fig. 5.8). An obvious potential problem with this strategy is that it may affect future inflation expectations: if the monetary authority is perceived as not prioritizing price stability, it may unanchor expectations leading to an inflationary spiral (as demonstrated in several chapters in this book).

---

[52] For instance, in 2011 the US Fed transferred to the US Treasury Department profits in the amount of $77.4 billion (of course, losses may and do also occur, including recently). As another example, the Deustche Bundesbank, the German central bank (in the euro area, the participating national central banks—NCBs, albeit integrated into the ECB structure, still survive as separate legal entities—as do the Fed's 12 Districts, separately incorporated "Reserve Banks") transferred in 2011 around €0.6 billion in profits to the German Federal Ministry of Finance (as the Bundesbank has the statutory obligation of transferring 80% of its profits to the German Government up to a value of €2.5 billion, via its Ministry of Finance, all its 2011 profits were transferred to the German Government). Belhocine et al. (2023), estimate that, due to expansion of the ECB balance sheet during the GFC and the Pandemic period, plus the increase in interest rates since 2022, the ECB will face meaningful medium-term losses, but that those are not materially relevant to pursuing of its mandate, given the particular nature of monetary authorities (see Belhocine, N., Bhatia, A., Frie, J.M., "Raising Rates with a Large Balance Sheet: The Eurosystem's Net Income and its Fiscal Implications", IMF Working Paper WP/23/145).

[53] There are several exceptions to this pattern. For example, in the case of the Fed, "participating member banks", that, all nationally chartered banks and, depending on some criteria, state-chartered banks, own a share of the Federal Reserve System capital (and are paid a 6% dividend on this, after which deduction profits are transferred to the Treasury). As described earlier, in the case of the ECB, the NCBs are the entities responsible for its paid-in capital (while, on their turn, their respective national Ministries of Finance hold their own paid-in capital on the NCBs on behalf of their respective sovereigns). As another example, the Swiss National Bank is partially owned by private investors and even list shares at the Swiss Stock Exchange (as is the National Bank of Belgium, or NBB, a monetary authority that is part of the euro area and which is also a public listed company).

[54] From March 1942, the FOMC formally instructed all regional Reserve Banks to buy all Treasury bills offered at 3/8 per cent: a similar policy was followed for Treasury bonds (but without a formal instruction) at 2.5%. This situation remained largely unchanged until the 1951 "Treasury-Fed Accord" (the one that would later eventually lead to the Fed's "even keel" policy mentioned earlier).

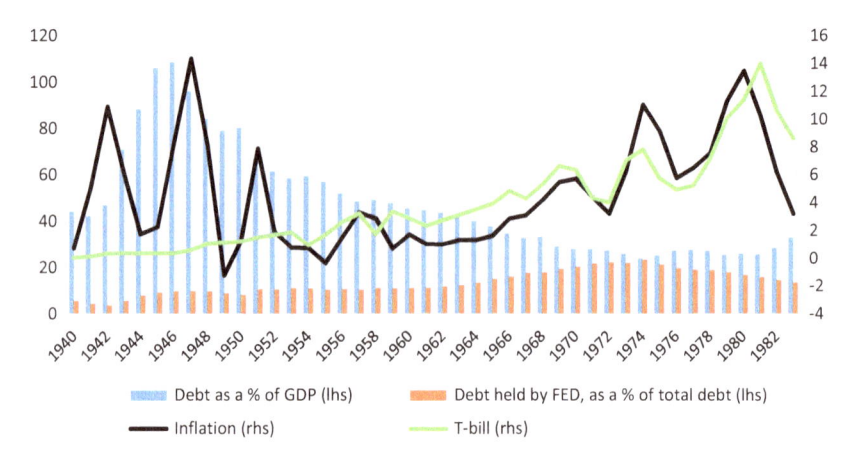

Fig. 5.8 Using monetary policy to reduce accumulated fiscal imbalances in the US. (Sources: BEA, U.S. Bureau of Labor Statistics (BLS), FRED and OMB)

Leaving aside the desirability (to say nothing of the feasibility) of pursuing such "financial repression" policies under current circumstances, it is not clear that evidence supports their overall effectiveness in terms of debt reductions strategies (Table 5.3): a quarter to a third of debt reduction achieved in the post–World War II period was attributable **to primary surpluses, not financial repression** (the perceived importance of financial repression may be linked to another "original sin"[55] in economics, namely, overemphasizing the representativeness of US data and experiences, see Arslanalp and Eichengreen 2023[56]).

Importantly, beyond macro-level vulnerabilities, such low interest rates policies also cause *microeconomic distortions in the broader banking system*. While very low interest rates may also help at first to recapitalize the banking system by supporting a greater net interest margin (NIM),[57] as banks can borrow more cheaply while still collecting higher interest on loans

---

[55] The original "original sin" (in macroeconomics literature) refers to the limited capacity of Developing countries to use their domestic currency to borrow abroad, or even to borrow long term domestically: see Eichengreen, B. and Hausmann, R. (1999). "Exchange Rates and Financial Fragility", National Bureau of Economic Research Working Papers n. 7418.

[56] Arslanalp, S. and Eichengreen, B. (2023), "Living with High Public Debt", Federal Reserve Jackson Hole Symposium.

[57] The difference between interest expenses a bank pays (so, the costs of its funds) and interest income a bank receives on the loans it makes.

Table 5.3 Decomposition of post–WWII large[a] debt reductions in advanced economies (1945–1975)[b]

	Debt/GDP ratio			Decomposition (in pp)		
	Start	End	Decrease	Primary balance	r-g differential	Stock-flow adjustment
Simple average	95.5	22.4	73.1	22.6	82.6	-32.2
Weighted average	112	26.2	85.8	33.3	80.2	-27.7
Weighted average (contribution to debt reduction, % of total)				38.8	93.6	-32.4

Source: Eichengreen et al. (2021)
[a] Large means at least 10 pp of GDP
[b] Sample includes 19 advanced economies, period covered varies by country, as peak-to-trough years vary

made earlier, however, as old loans mature, low interest rates lead to a compression of NIMs, the longer the low rates environment persist. The lengthy period of low rates the GFC unleashed made it harder for banks to earn a real positive rate of return, leading banks to reduce rates on saving and deposit accounts, increasing fees and also to look for investment in assets with higher yields: this "search for yield" was not only restricted to banks but happened in other financial institutions like insurers and pension funds.

Also, while low policy rates and higher long-term rates may increase banks' profits by borrowing short term and lending long term (so-called maturity transformation), an unexpected rise in policy rates accompanied by a similar increase in bond yields will result in a fall in bond prices, imposing considerable losses on banks: as a result of that, banks can face difficulties in rolling over their short-term debt, setting off fire asset sales and a further price declines that may ultimately lead to insolvency (cue to the bank stresses in the US in early 2023).[58] In summary, GFC-related policies ultimately also created riskier portfolios for financial institutions.

---

[58] This section was written before First Republic, Signature Bank and Silicon Valley Bank had to be resolved by US Federal regulators in May and March 2023, respectively. These banks were exempted from the Fed's CCAR since the "Economic Growth, Regulatory Relief and Consumer Protection Act" of May 2018 reclassified midsize banks with assets between $50 billion and $250 billion as "systemically unimportant" (this does not necessarily imply that if those banks were covered by the CCAR their balance sheet vulnerabilities would have been discovered and acted upon).

Importantly, this overall point of unintended (but frequently foreseeable) micro and macro negative consequences of (mostly) well-meaning and (even arguably) necessary policies runs throughout this book.

References

Arslanalp, S., and B. Eichengreen. 2023. *Living with High Public Debt*. Federal Reserve Jackson Hole Symposium.

Belhocine, N., A. Bhatia, and J.M. Frie. 2023. *Raising Rates with a Large Balance Sheet: The Eurosystem's Net Income and Its Fiscal Implications*. IMF Working Paper WP/23/145.

Carvajal, M., M. Tudela, and L. Vinhas de Souza. 2012. *Counter-cyclical Central Banking Policies and their Longer-Term Implications*. Moody's.

Eichengreen, B., A. El-Ganainy, R. Esteves, and K. Mitchener. 2021. *In Defense of Public Debt*. Oxford University Press.

Hattori, M., and Y. Suda. 2007. *Developments in a Cross-Border Bank Exposure Network*. Bank of Japan Working Paper no. 07-E-21.

McCandless, G. 2005. Argentina: Monetary Policy by Default. In *Monetary Policy and Macroeconomic Stabilization in Latin America*, ed. R. Langhammer and L. Vinhas Souza, 87–112. Springer.

Minoiu, C., and J. Reyes. 2011. A Networks Analysis of Global Banking: 1978–2009. *IMF Working Paper* 74: 11–41.

Pesce, M., and G. Feldman. 2023. Monetary Policy Challenges over Two Decades: A View from Argentina. In *Central Banking in the Americas: Lessons from Two Decades*, 21–39. Basel: BIS.

Tarullo, D. 2019. Financial Regulation: Still Unsettled a Decade after the Crisis. *Journal of Economic Perspectives* 33 (1): 61–80.

CHAPTER 6

Trojan Horses: The Long Shadow of the Euro Area Sovereign Crisis

6.1 The Very Progressive Take-Off of the European Bumblebee

The creation of the euro is truly a remarkable and historical achievement—this author, in a piece cowritten with a former colleague (and dear friend), even compared it to a bumblebee (e.g., as something that should not fly and yet somehow does),[1] but it has also been an undeniably very complex and lengthy process, started by a crisis (namely, the final collapse of the Bretton Woods system described earlier)[2] and punctuated by several additional ones.

It is far beyond the scope of this chapter to tell the story of this long and winding road toward the European Common Currency—from the 1970 'Werner Report' and the creation in 1972 of the 'Monetary Snake', the subsequent 1979 'European Monetary System' and its Exchange Rate

---

[1] Gill, I. and Vinhas de Souza, L. (2013), "The Flight of the European Bumblebee", Project Syndicate and Politico.

[2] The so-called October 1970 "Werner Report" (named after the Prime Minister and Minister of Finance of Luxembourg, Pierre Werner, who chaired the study group that produced the report) was a reaction to Bretton Woods stresses. It proposed the establishment of an economic and monetary union that would involve significant transfers of responsibility from Member States to the European Commission (EC) in the field of monetary policy. It was adopted in 1971.

© The Author(s), under exclusive license to Springer Nature Switzerland AG 2024
L. Vinhas de Souza, *A Century of Global Economic Crises*,
https://doi.org/10.1007/978-3-031-53460-7_6

Mechanism I (and II), followed by the 1989 'Delors Report',[3] which led to the creation of the European Monetary Institute in 1994 and of the ECB in 1998, the body that under its first president, Wim Duisenberg, managed the final 'fixing' of the conversion rates of the founding euro national currencies in January 1999 and the **final physical introduction of the euro** in January 2002. However, there are several works that address the many dimensions of this ongoing saga in great detail.[4]

6.2 Why Did It Happen?

The years that preceded the crisis were promising ones, as convergence (nominal and real) between euro area members seemed to be progressing as planned: sigma-convergence (a measure of the reduction of dispersion) of interbank rates for euro area countries were speedily moving toward zero,[5] while GDP grew by a brisk (by euro area standards) average of 2.2% *pa* between 1999 and 2007. Reflecting that benevolent environment, the ECB's Systemic Stress Composite Indicator, or SSCI, averaged a paltry 0.13 (conversely, GDP performance during the 2008–2013 crisis years was an abysmal -0.2% *pa* and the SSCI increased almost threefold and interest rates diverged explosively).

This apparent calm and policy successes may have lulled both policy makers and market participants into a misleading sense of control (see Buti et al. 2010, ibid.), while imbalances were building under the surface and risks were correspondingly being underpriced. Eventually, the same "gradually, then suddenly" dynamics described earlier concerning the Bretton Woods system manifested itself.

The starting shot of the euro area-centric extension of the GFC was the announcement by a newly elected Greek government of very large

---

[3] Named after Jacques Delors, then EC president, who chaired the committee that wrote it: European Commission (1989), "Delors Report".

[4] A few examples are Buti, M., Deroose, S., Gaspar, V., and Nogueira Martins, J. (eds), (2010), *The Euro: The First Decade*, Cambridge University Press (a massive, over 1000-page long work, timely published at just about the same moments as the first Greek bailout) to De Grauwe, P. (2009), *Economics of the Monetary Union*, Oxford University Press, UK (*the* "go to" book for graduate and undergraduate student on the EU's monetary union), and Vinhas de Souza, L. and van Aarle, B. (ed) (2004), *The Euroarea and the New EU Member States*, Palgrave Macmillan, UK (which looks at the expansion of the euro area to Eastern Europe).

[5] Vinhas de Souza, L. and Tudela, M. (2014), "Voltar a Empezar: Crisis and the Renationalization of the Iberian Financial Systems", Comparative Economic Studies, 56(3): 337–350.

revisions (from 6% to eventually *15% of GDP*) of its public deficit in November 2009: market pressures speedily led Greece to become the first euro area country to ask for a support package, and the country was duly granted €110 billion by the EU and the IMF in mid-May 2010 (this program was cancelled before full disbursement and replaced by a €130 billion one in March 2012, and a third program eventually became necessary in August 2015—when Greece defaulted on its debt to the IMF, after another newly elected government took power, this last package worth €130).[6]

The first Greek program was followed by a €85 billion package for Ireland already in November 2010, and in May 2011 by a €78 billion one for Portugal. Spain was granted in June 2012 a (up to) €100 billion in a bank sector-specific program with euro area resources only—which would not be fully used, and finally Cyprus (largely due its direct exposures to the Greek bank system and sovereign) was subject to an EU-IMF program worth €10 billion in April 2013.

Those developments led to the euro area GDP additional contractions in 2012–2013, after the 2009 GFC-related one (which was duly dubbed a "two-dip recession", like the US during the Great Depression), but those later contractions were avoided by other, non-EU economies.[7]

Again, risk had been mispriced by markets (albeit for different reasons than in the earlier US case). The degree of convergence among the bond

---

[6] In total, Greece received an astounding €243.7 billion from the EU, the EFSF/ESM and EU member states, plus €32.1 billion from the IMF, or well over 100% of its GDP. As an aside, my personal evaluation is that a major factor preventing a Greek exit from the euro in 2015–2016 after its IMF default was the personal and far-sighted commitment of European Commission President Jean-Claude Juncker (another prime Minister and Minister of Finance of Luxembourg, and who was then my boss) to the integrity of the euro area.

[7] In general terms, the global effects of the euro area part of the GFC were far less acute than those of its US-centric period: see Chen, Q., Lombardi, M, Ross, A. and Zhu, F. (2017), "Global Impact of US and Euro Area Unconventional Monetary Policies: A Comparison", BIS Working Paper No. 610. This is the case even for the subset of Developing countries more closely linked to the EU, notably in Eastern Europe and the former Soviet Union (and contrary to initial expectations, see for Instance Vinhas de Souza, L. (2012) "CEE and CIS Countries Could be affected by Possible Euro Area Economic Shocks, Albeit to Varying Degrees", Moody's). Namely, GDP growth in the World Bank's developing "Europe and Central Asia" region was −5.7% in 2009, but a robust 4% in 2013. The main reason for that was the "sudden stop" in capital flows to this region (see EBRD, "Transition Report", 2008 and 2009) that was observed during the GFC was largely absent during the euro area sovereign crisis, even if *real linkages* via trade and FDI were actually more significant than in the case with the US.

yields of euro area Sovereigns was nothing short of remarkable (Fig. 6.1): at its lowest point in mid-2007, their standard deviation was 0.08, implying that with the creation of the euro area *they were effectively being priced by markets as financial assets that were perfect substitutes.*[8] On the other hand, in early March 2012—when the first Greek program collapsed, standard deviation reached 15.8. And it was not only governments: while euro area sovereigns were experiencing those financial stresses, the financial institutions of several euro area members (and notably in Italy) also came under market pressure (Fig. 6.2).

Banks experienced an even larger degree of risk mispricing (the standard deviation of spreads in Fig. 6.2 goes from **a minimum of 1.6 to a maximum of 154.5**): underlying this was the *apparent* logical implication that joining a monetary union should imply a convergence of interest rates toward, if not a single one, to at least a lower one (for some euro area member states at least). When stresses hit, the resulting (re) fragmentation was reinforced by the type of integration that happened among banks in

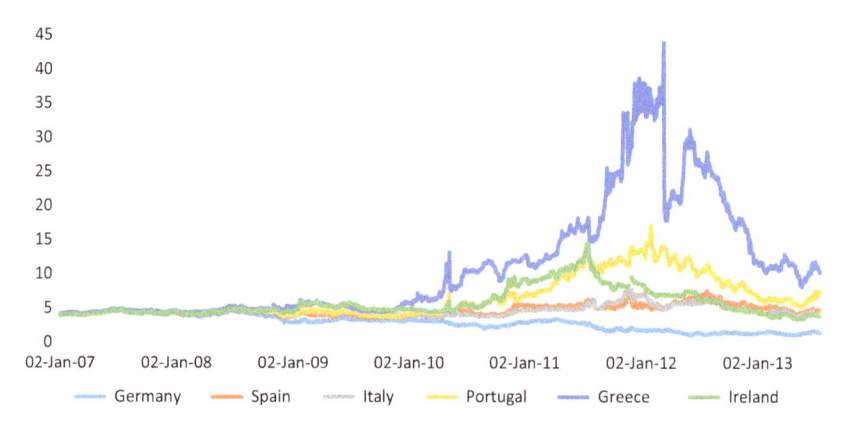

Fig. 6.1 Sovereigns 10-year benchmark government bond yield (% p.a., daily data). (Source: Datastream)

---

[8] In a summit at the French city of Deauville in October 2010, the then French President, Nicolas Sarkozy, and the then German Chancellor, Angela Merkel, reached an agreement that future EU sovereign bailouts would require that losses be imposed *on private creditors* (this was however never implemented). Some analysts suggest that part of the spike in yields and CDS spreads was related to that announcement, but the data does not see to actually back this interpretation up (see Mody, A., 2014, "The Ghost of Deauville", CEPR).

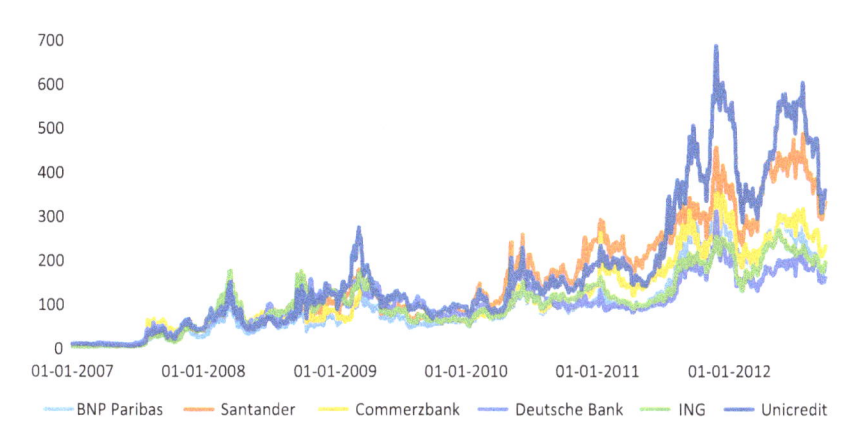

Fig. 6.2 Banks 5-years CDS spreads (daily data). (Source: Datastream)

the different euro area members. Namely, the earlier financial integration was not *equity-based* (so, banks acquiring capital shares in banks in other EU MS), but rather *debt-based* (e.g., relying on short-term loans between banks) and therefore inherently more fragile. To this day, euro area member states are still largely served by mostly "national banks", with limited true cross-euro area banks: there are no analogues to Citibank or Bank of America in the euro area.[9]

This highlights the key role of the private sector stresses, as was the case in the earlier, US-centric stage of the GFC, but through a very different channel. The euro area channel was the persistent current account imbalances—reflecting the gap between domestic savings and expenditure, and divergences in competitiveness among different clusters of euro area' members (Fig. 6.3).

On the fiscal side, ahead of the creation of the euro area in January 1999 its (prospective) members had to reduce fiscal deficits as one of the pre-requisites for joining the framework. *Ex post* fiscal sustainability compliance was to be *theoretically* enforced with the help of an EU framework, the "Stability and Growth Pact" (SGP).[10] This happened to a degree, as

---

[9] Vinhas de Souza and Tudela (2014), ibid.

[10] The SGP, agreed in 1997, was the EU's answer for the euro area's unusual lack of a central fiscal capacity associated to it (Warin, T. (2008), Stability and Growth Pact, in *The New Palgrave Dictionary of Economics*, Palgrave Macmillan, London). Its implementation has been suspended since 2020, due to the Pandemic response effects in fiscal balances.

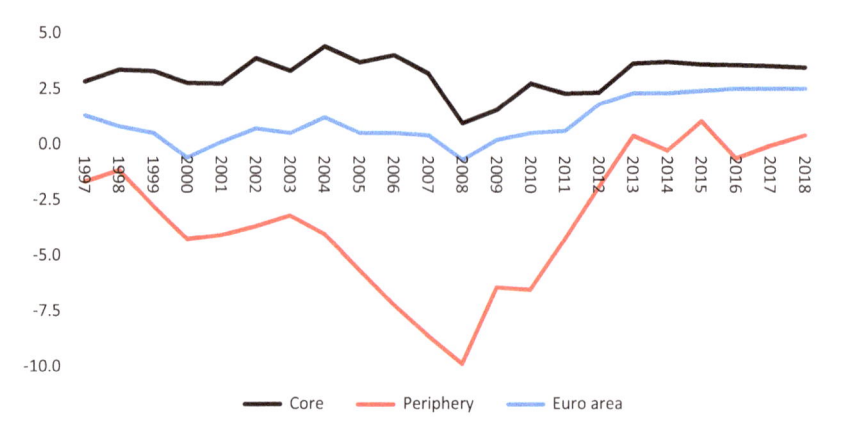

Fig. 6.3 Euro area, Core and Periphery current account dynamics. ("Core" includes Austria, Belgium, Germany, Finland and Luxembourg—largely, the euro area capital-exporting countries, while "periphery" includes Cyprus, Greece, Ireland, Italy, Portugal and Spain. The series are simple averages of the countries' current account balances. Source: IMF)

fiscal deficits were roughly steady until 2007, albeit this was likely due to largely benign external economic circumstances and the fall in interest rates experienced by euro area periphery countries than to the SGP[11]: the great exception of this picture was Greece—which actually fudged its own fiscal numbers to be able to enter the euro area and still needed a waiver for accession even after that, joining the euro area only in 2001 (Fig. 6.4).[12] In other terms, **net government savings had not *significantly* deteriorated ahead of the GFC** (a large deterioration did came *afterwards*, but it was largely across the board).[13]

---

[11] For a rather critical view on the effectiveness of the SGP, see Larch, M., Malzubris, J. and Santacroce, S. (2023), "Numerical Compliance with EU Fiscal Rules: Facts and Figures from a New Database", Intereconomics: Review of European Economic Policy, 58(1): 32–42 and Hukkinen, J. and Viren, M. (2023), "The Stability and Growth Pact Three Decades Later", SUERF Policy Brief, n. 564.

[12] For the Greek drama, see Dellas, H. and Tavlas, G. (2013), "The Gold Standard, the Euro, and the Origins of the Greek Sovereign Debt Crisis", Cato Journal, 33(3): 491–520. For a discussion of the "Maastricht Criteria", the set of exchange rate, fiscal and inflation numerical values and institutional requirements used to evaluate readiness for euro area accession, see Gaspar, V. and Buti, M. (2021), "Maastricht Values", CEPR.

[13] This section partially follows Vinhas de Souza, L., and Tudela, M. (2012), "Euro Area Periphery: Structural Reforms Have Significantly Improved External Imbalances, but Full Resolution May Still Take Years", Moody's. A similar analysis was echoed some years later in Giavazzi, F. and Baldwin, R. (eds), (2016), "The Eurozone crisis: A Consensus View of the Causes and a Few Possible Solutions", CEPR.

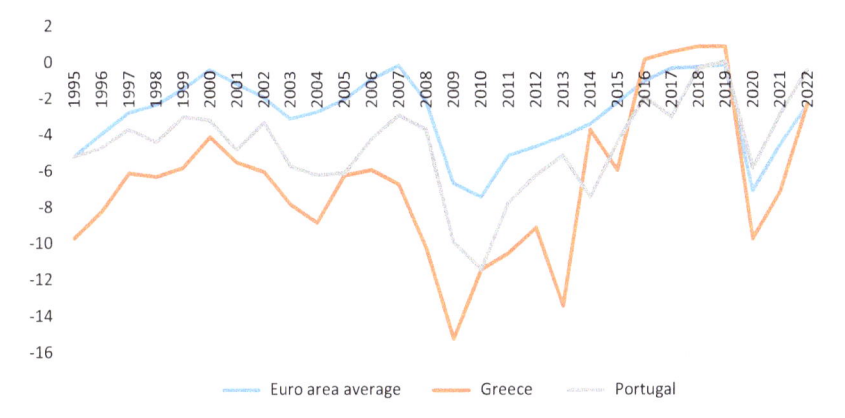

Fig. 6.4 Fiscal balances in the euro area, Greece and Portugal, percentage of GDP. (Source: *Eurostat*. (Eurostat—the EU's in *Understanding Financial Accounts*, van de Ven, P. and Fano, D. (eds), OECD].

However,[14] **the dynamics of net private savings was a different matter: it showed a large divergence between these so-called periphery and core countries**. In the core countries, net private savings as a percentage of GDP fell by 1.5 pp. between 1999 until the start of the GFC, while net private savings in the periphery countries deteriorated **three and half times more**. That is, most of the worsening in the periphery's current account was due to *private sector behavior* (Fig. 6.5).[15]

This increase in borrowing was facilitated by the fall in interest rates after the periphery countries joined the monetary union (again, an inherent consequence of joining a monetary union with a single monetary authority and policy rate) and also due to a reduction of perceived risk, as market participants (rationally but imperfectly forming expectations about

---

[14] Eurostat—the EU's official statistical agency—figures are used here as the data source because the definition of fiscal aggregates in the SGP's "Excessive Debt ProcedureExcessive Debt Procedure"—or EDP, the process through which the SGP assess if a euro area member complies with it—are different from those used, as an example, by the IMF, and the difference can be quite substantial for some years (see Dippelsman, R., Semeraro, G., Cadete de Matos, J., Catz, J., Quirós, G. and Lima, F. (2017), "Deficit and Debt of General Government and Public Sector ", in Understanding Financial Accounts, van de Ven, P. and Fano, D. (eds), OECD). Again, simple averages are used—the usage of median values would only yield significantly different values in 2010, almost cutting the euro areaEuro area budget deficit in half that year.

[15] Vinhas de Souza and Tudela (2012), ibid.

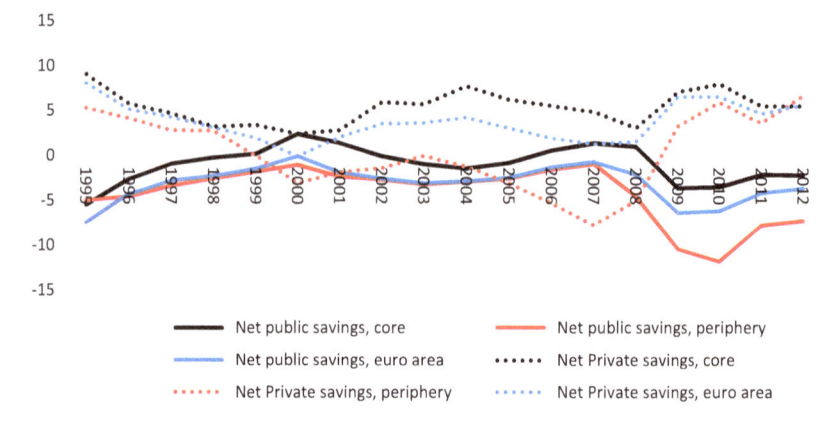

Fig. 6.5 Net public and private savings, euro area as a whole and core and periphery, % of GDP. (Source: Eurostat)

the future…) believed that those countries would no longer be vulnerable to (nominal) currency depreciation and high inflation.[16]

Those lower real interest rates duly boosted private consumption in Greece, Ireland, Portugal and Spain: Irish private consumption grew by 40% between 2000 and 2007, by around 30% in Greece and Spain and by 12% in Portugal (as a comparator, private consumption increased by a mere 3% in Germany during the same period). In Spain and Ireland, the share of private investment in GDP increased by 4.0 pp. and 2.2 pp., respectively, over the same period. In an echo of the US GFC experience, most of the new investment in Spain and Ireland helped finance a housing bubble. **Therefore, the fall in net private savings in the periphery financed a private consumption boom in Greece and Portugal and a housing bubble in Ireland and Spain**.

At the same time Greece, Ireland, Portugal and Spain (and also Italy) experienced rapid and significant losses in competitiveness, with the worsening trade balance for the periphery explained not by the weakening in exports but by increased imports due to domestic spending: namely, private consumption in the case of Greece and Portugal and construction in Spain and Ireland. Figure 6.6 illustrates that most of the persistent negative balance in the *average* current account for the euro area periphery between 1999 and 2007 was driven by the factor income balance: the

---

[16] Higgins, M. and Klitgaard, T. (2011), "Saving Imbalances and the Euro Area Sovereign Debt Crisis", Current Issues in Economics and Finance, 17(5), Federal Reserve Bank of New York.

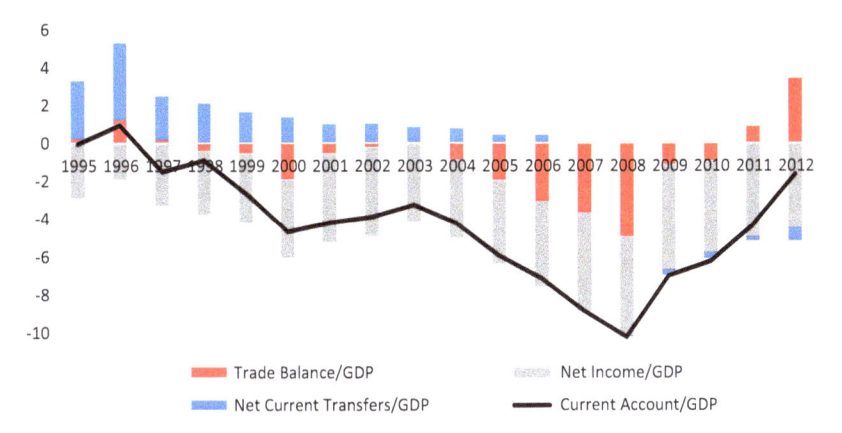

Fig. 6.6 Decomposition of the euro area Periphery Current Account Balance, percentage of GDP. (Source: Eurostat, updated from Vinhas de Souza and Tudela 2012)

periphery was using an increasing share of GDP to service larger debts owed to core creditors.[17]

Therefore, the main conclusion of this section is that the deterioration of the periphery external position was not rooted in dis-saving by the government but by *private sector* actions, namely using financing flows from core euro area economies to finance domestic spending[18]: the moniker "euro area Sovereign Crisis" is therefore incorrect, to the extent that **it mixes an effect with its causes**. This is important because a misinterpretation of a problem leads to inappropriate policy responses, as is demonstrated by the still incomplete nature of the EU's Banking and Capital Markets Unions (more on that later in this chapter). This section also illustrates another important insight that was largely unappreciated at that time, namely that the accumulated **euro area imbalances reflected area-wide processes, therefore inherently involving *both* its periphery and core economies.**[19]

This of course does not mean that the sovereign stresses shown at the beginning of this chapter did not imply significant policy problems,

---

[17] Holinski, N., Kool, C. and Muysken, J. (2012), "Persistent Macroeconomic Imbalances in the Euro Area: Causes and Consequences", Federal Reserve Bank of St. Louis Review, 94(1): 1–20.

[18] Vinhas de Souza and Tudela (2012), ibid.

[19] Vinhas de Souza and Tudela (2012), ibid.

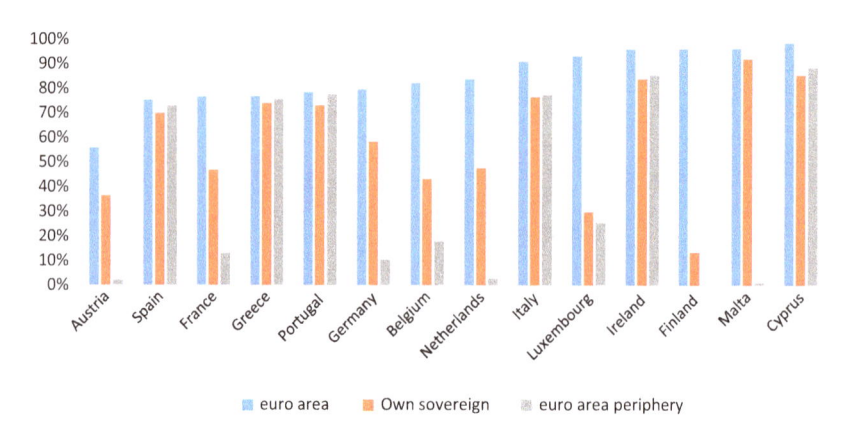

Fig. 6.7 Sovereign debt held by domestic banks, end 2013 (% of all government debt). (Source: European Banking Authority and BIS)

including monetary policy ones. Those arose in and of themselves and also through the effects of sovereign stresses in the overall economy—the national one, that of the euro area and of the EU itself, given the very high level of economic and financial interconnection between EU member states, and indirectly via the so-called doom loop[20] on the banking sector (Fig. 6.7: in some periphery countries, the exposure of bank Tier 1 capital to its own sovereign *was over 90% of the whole exposure to euro area sovereigns*). **Again, to properly understand the crisis' causality chain is necessary for the effective design of a policy response.**

6.3 What the ECB (and Others) Did: The Policy Response

So, what did the ECB do? The ECB initial policy actions and institutional mandate were introduced in the Chap. 5, and the rationale for its actions, given those institutional constraints, was that the tensions in the financial *and* sovereign markets had the potential to impair the transmission of monetary policy decisions (the rationale certainly was not inflation, as inflation undershot its target consistently throughout this period). Like in the US earlier in the crisis, it used both standard measures, for example, policy rates, and non-standard measures, for example, liquidity and

---

[20] Vinhas de Souza, L., and Frie, J.M. (2015),"Severing the 'Doom Loop': Further Risk Reduction in the Banking Union", EPSC, European Commission, Brussels.

refinancing operations. Most of the actions concerning policy rates measures happened in the earlier, US-centric part of the GFC (Fig. 6.8), but, on the other hand, ECB asset-driven policy actions were clearly more related to the euro area stage of this crisis, to address increased market stresses as the crisis progressed (see a comparison of ECB and Fed actions in Table 6.1).

Long-term refinancing operations (or LTROs) and Targeted LTROs (or TLTROs) aimed at reassuring market participants about liquidity, *regardless of market conditions*.[21] The securities purchase programs (the Covered Bond Purchase Programs, CBPPs, and the Securities Market Program, SMP) was a reaction to the "sudden stop" in these market segments. The 2012 creation of the Outright Monetary Transactions (OMT) program allowed the ECB to potentially intervene in secondary sovereign bond markets,[22] and with the 2015 Public Sector Purchase Program (PSPP) the ECB could purchase government bonds (Table 6.1).[23]

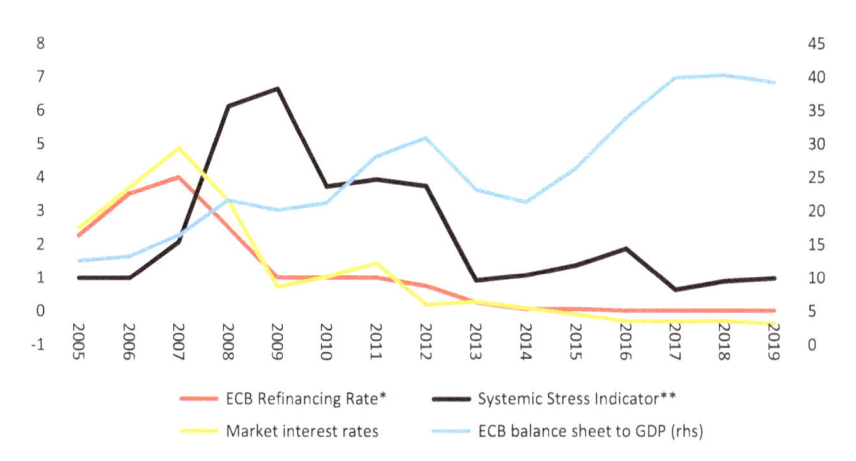

Fig. 6.8 ECB main policy rate (pp) and balance sheet to GDP (%), and effects in market stresses. (Source: ECB, FRED. *The ECB policy rate here is a splicing of the fixed and variable refinancing rate [the later for period from 2005 to 2007]. **Set to 1 in end-2005)

---

[21] These two distinct instruments had different aims: LTROs were designed to fund banks' balance sheets, while the TLTROs were a monetary authority tool of funding for lending.
[22] OMT were never actually used as an instrument, but its announcement was part of the strategy to convey to markets that the ECB would indeed do "whatever it takes".
[23] Hartmann, P. and Smets, F. (2018), "The first Twenty Years of the European Central Bank: Monetary Policy", Working Paper Series 2219, European Central Bank.

Table 6.1 An overview of the unconventional monetary policies of the ECB and the FED[a]

	Announcement	Termination	Assets purchased	Amount[1]
Federal Reserve's large-scale asset purchase (LSAP) programs				
LSAP1	Nov-08		Agency mortgage-backed securities (MBS) and agency debt	$600 billion
	Mar-09		Agency securities	$850 billion
		Mar-10	Longer-term US Treasury securities	$300 billion
LSAP2	Nov-10	Jun-11	Longer-term US Treasury securities	$300 billion
Maturity extension program (MEP)	Sep-11		Treasury securities with remaining maturities of six to 30 years	$400 billion
	Jun-12		Treasury securities with remaining maturities of six to 30 years	$40 billion per month[2]
LSAP3	Sep-12	Oct-14	Agency MBS	
	Dec-12	Oct-14	Longer-term US Treasury securities	$45 billion per month[2]
ECB main non-standard measures				
	Announcement	Termination	Assets purchased	Amount[3]
LTRO1	Oct-08	Mar-09	Enhanced longer-term refinancing operations, three- and six-month; fixed-rate full allotment	€300 billion
	Jun-09	Dec-09	12-month fixed-rate full-allotment	€442 billion
CBPP1	Jun-09	Jun-10	Covered bond purchase program	€60 billion
SMP	May-10	Sep-12	Securities markets program, sterilized	>€200 billion
CBPP2	Nov-11	Oct-12	Covered bond purchase program	€16.4 billion

(*continued*)

Table 6.1 (continued)

	Announcement	Termination	Assets purchased	Amount[1]
LTRO2	Oct & Dec 2011Dec 2011; Feb 2012		12- & 13-month LTROs; Three-year fixed-rate full allotment	€529 billion
OMT	Sep-12		Outright monetary transactions, government bonds of one to three years	Open-ended[4]
TLTRO	Sep-14	Jun-16	Targeted longer-term refinancing operations	
EAPP	Sep-16		Expanded asset purchase program	€60 billion per month[4]
CBPP3	Oct-14	At least 2 years	Covered bond purchase program	€131.14 billion
ABSPP	Nov-14	At least 2 years	Longer-term US Treasury securities	€14.58 billion
PSPP	Mar-15	Sep-16	Public sector purchase program	€393,64 billion

[a]Chen et al., ibid.

(1) Initially announced amount of asset purchases for each program or program expansion. In US dollars. (2) The purchases were open-ended when they were announced. The Federal Reserve started to taper the asset purchases in January 2014, and eventually halted the purchases altogether in October 2014. (3) Amount for each program or program expansion. In euros. For CBPP3, ABSPP and PSPP, amount outstanding on October 30, 2015. (4) The purchases were supposed to be open-ended and unlimited in size when they were announced, but the facility was never used

Eventually, and just like in the US, as described in Chap. 5, ECB asset and liquidity operations had their desired policy effects: namely, constraining market interest rates and progressively lessening stresses in euro area financial markets. On the other hand, the correction of mis-incentives for the faulty (private and public) risk assessment that underlined the crisis was achieved by joint euro area and global regulatory actions, coordinated with ECB monetary actions.[24] Importantly, the regulatory-wise incompleteness of the euro area (like the fragmentation of it in the US) needed also to be addressed.

[24] Kok, C., Mongelli, F. and Hobelsberger, K. (2022), "A Tale of Three Crises: Synergies between ECB Tasks", ECB Occasional Paper No. 2022/305.

6.4 The Incompleteness of EMU

As indicated in Chap. 5, part of the reason behind the GFC in the U.S was a fragmented institutional, supervisory and regulatory framework. In the euro area—which, like the EU itself, is a *process*,[25] even after the ECB was created, these other frameworks had effectively still to be built. The incompleteness of the EU's monetary and financial space has several dimensions that in different degrees were associated with the crisis' start, depth and duration: first, its regulatory/institutional framework was—and is—incomplete; second, its financial markets were—and are—segmented, and finally, it lacked—and still lacks—an associated single fiscal authority.[26] This incompleteness begot and interacted with market expectations, reinforcing those in a negative loop (see Annex 6.B).[27]

On the first dimension, an initial action was the speedy creation on May 9 ("Europe Day" itself) 2010 of the European Financial Stability Facility (EFSF), a special purpose vehicle (yes, another one) financed only by members of the euro area and which would provide the first bailout loans.[28] With the deepening and lengthening of the crisis, this was followed by the creation in September 2012 of the European Stability

---

[25] Even in a physical sense, as since the beginning of the GFC, eight countries joined it (four of which since the euro-area stage of the GFC began).

[26] My work for European Commission President Jean-Claude Juncker was intimately related to designing ways to ameliorate the incompleteness of the common currency framework. See "The Five Presidents' Report: Completing Europe's Economic and Monetary Union", 2015, European Commission, Brussels (this followed the 2012 "Four Presidents Report: Towards a Genuine Economic and Monetary Union": I would tell my staff back then that part of our job was to help prevent that a "Six Presidents Report" would ever be necessary).

[27] It is also likely that less than adroit policy decisions–for instance, the ECB rate hikes in April and July 2011 due to alleged price pressures (ECB, "Jean-Claude Trichet, President of the ECB, Vítor Constâncio, Vice-President of the ECB, Frankfurt am Main, 7 July 2011"), or the initial decision to impose a levy on *all bank deposits* in Cyprus in March 2013, regardless of their insured or uninsured status (Demetriades, P. (2017), *A Diary of the euro crisis in Cyprus: Lessons for Bank Recovery and Resolution*, Palgrave Macmillan, UK)—also helped to prolong the euro-area crisis (on the latter, and without getting into details, due to my work at Moody's I can personally attest to the significant market implications of those discussions).

[28] The capital of the EFSF came from guarantees of the euro-area members in proportion to their share of ECB capital.

Mechanism (ESM).[29] The EFSF and the ESM (the EFSF was subsumed into the ESM structure) became the two main sources of EU/euro area sovereign financing during the crisis (the ECB was the main source of market liquidity provision, albeit indirectly—and later directly with the PSPP—it performed this role also for sovereigns). The ESM toolbox has been progressively expanded, to include so-called Precautionary Conditions Credit Line (PCCL), an Enhanced Conditions Credit Line (ECCL) and loans for recapitalization of financial institutions.

In parallel, the euro area macro-prudential supervisory framework was reinforced through the establishment of the European Systemic Risk Board (ESRB) in December 2010, which, operating under the ECB structure, issues warnings and macro-prudential recommendations whenever deemed necessary[30]—in a way similar to the US Financial Stability Oversight Council, and via the so-called six-pack set of regulations, which reinforced the SGP's EDP and that entered into force in December 2011. An agency—the European Banking Authority (EBA)—was also created in 2011 to implement a standard set of rules to regulate and supervise banking sectors across all EU countries. The EBA, with its EU-wide mandate, is also the body responsible for implementing bank stress test in the EU (and not the ECB, which does not cover all EU member states).[31]

To further address the **fragmentation of EU/euro-area markets**, a series of initiatives under the umbrella of the 2014 so-called **Banking Union** was also introduced. These initiatives focused initially on designing stronger prudential requirements for banks, improved depositor protection and rules for managing failing banks, via the so-called "Single

---

[29] The ESM is not an EU institution, but rather an intergovernmental organization with a capital structure made up of (paid-in and callable) capital from euro-area members only. It has not engaged in any new operations since the 2015 third Greek support package, and now largely concentrates on economic and financial surveillance tasks and on the management of the (large) legacy loan portfolios from its series of 2010–2015 bailouts. For a blow-by-blow description of its short but eventful history, see ESM (2019), "Safeguarding the Euro in Times of Crisis: The Inside Story of the ESM", Luxembourg. During its first ten eventful years of existence, the ESM was led by another of my former bosses, the formidable Klaus Regling.

[30] Further details can be found at http://ec.europa.eu/internal_market/finances/committees/index_en.htm.

[31] EBA (2020), "On the Future Changes to the EU-wide Stress Test", Discussion Paper EBA/DP/2020/01, Paris (with the UK leaving the EU, the EBA, originally located in London, was relocated to Paris in 2019).

rulebook"[32] regulating all financial actors in the EU (in a way largely consistent with Basel III reforms). Institutionally, the Banking Union led to the creation of two fully operational "pillars", namely the Single Supervisory Mechanism (SSM) and the Single Resolution Mechanism (SRM), both of which apply to euro area countries only but are open for all EU Member States to opt in.[33] The SSM—which, like the ESRB, "sits" within the ECB structure—sets the framework for bank supervision, making the ECB the sole supervisor of all large banks in the euro area, while the SRM established the "Single Resolution Board" as the bank resolution authority for the euro area, which can tap into an industry-financed Single Resolution Fund[34] and enforces the so-called "Bank Recovery and Resolution Directive", or (BRRD), the legal framework for bank resolution in the euro area.[35]

From a financial stability perspective, the SSM and the SRM respectively perform complementary supervision and resolution roles. However, the so-called "third pillar" of the Banking Union, a common euro area deposit guarantee scheme (as opposed to the patchwork of currently existing national ones) is still needed to complete the fully-fledged Banking Union as planned, as the so-called European Deposit Insurance Scheme (EDIS) has effectively not advanced since its initial proposal in 2015.[36]

While the primary objective of the Banking Union is to increase resilience of the EU single market and of the euro area, the 2015 **Capital Markets Union** (CMU) is a set of initiatives aimed at deepening the EU single market by reducing barriers to cross border flows of capital and

---

[32] Valia, B. (2018), "The Single Rulebook and the European Banking Authority", University of Cambridge Faculty of Law Research Paper n. 45/2018.

[33] So far, the only non-euro area member of the SRM is Bulgaria.

[34] Vinhas de Souza, L, and Frie, J.M. (2015), "Strengthening the EU's Financial System: Bridge Financing Options for the Single Resolution Fund", European Commission, Brussels. One should note that the SRM effectiveness has not yet been tested by a truly systemic EU banking crisis.

[35] Two other EU/euro area financial regulatory and supervisory agencies were created during this period, the European Insurance and Occupational Pensions Authority (EIOPA) and the European Securities and Markets Authority (ESMA).

[36] Vinhas de Souza, L, and Frie, J.M. (2015), "Regaining Citizens' Trust, Safeguarding Banks' Stability: Towards a European Deposit Insurance Scheme", European Commission, Brussels. This continuing failure to implement EDIS is the single largest professional regret from my time working for the Juncker administration (and not only because of the, let's say, harsh words personally addressed to me by some of the members of the banking associations of a few large euro area MSs…).

financial services (given their still limited level of integration): initially designed for an EU with the United Kingdom as its largest financial center, the CMU had to be adjusted when the UK voted to leave the EU in 2016 (the effective date of the UK's EU exit was January 2020). **However, both the BU and CMU are still only partially completed initiatives, and the shallow, concentrated and fragmented nature of the EU's financial system is still a concern, as it was during the euro area crisis.**

On the final missing element, one of the most fundamental insights of the so-called "optimum currency area theory" is that in a currency union, given the absence of the nominal exchange rate adjustment mechanism, countries have to rely on some other policy tools to help counter shocks.[37] In principle, adjustment could take place through labor and capital mobility and through price and wages changes. However, the degree of labor mobility between countries in the euro area (and in many cases even within countries) is too low to serve as a cushion in an event of an idiosyncratic shock (and is too costly and slow in any case),[38] while price and wage differences among euro area member states are also 'sticky', adjusting in a rather slow and partial fashion. Finally, as the GFC demonstrated, capital flows are prone to abrupt swings and sudden stops that can endanger the financial stability of not only a country, but of the whole euro area (implying a systemic tool would still be needed).[39]

Therefore, policy and academic discussions have tended to conclude that a stabilization function against the effects of an asymmetric shock (which could become a source of systemic stresses) would be carried out more effectively by some sort of common euro area fiscal capacity, by both mitigating individual fiscal constraints and by pooling a larger amount of resources. A euro-area-level fiscal policy would also **be a more effective counterpart to the ECB pan-euro area monetary policy and to a euro-area-wide economic and financial**

---

[37] Mundell, R. (1961), "A Theory of Optimum Currency Areas", American Economic Review 53: 657–65.

[38] Decressin, J., Espinoza, R., Halikias, I., Leigh, D., Loungani, P., Medas, P., Mursula, S., Schindler, M., Spilimbergo, A., and Xu, T. (2015), "Wage Moderation in Crises: Policy Considerations and Applications to the Euro Area", IMF Staff Discussion Note. Interestingly, physical geographical labor mobility has also been decreasing in the U.S., and most notably since the Pandemic. This may be partially related to the technological developments that enable remote work, which also have several positive implications.

[39] Lane, P. (2013), "Capital Flows in the Euro Area", European Commission, DG ECFIN, Economic Papers 497.

regulatory space, allowing for a better policy mix than the mere SGP-led *attempts* at fiscal policy coordination.

Already the so-called MacDougall report of 1977[40] discussed the role of fiscal policy in the process of European integration and pointed out to the need for some sort of common fiscal stabilization function. Nevertheless, the principle of fiscal stabilization *only* at the national level was enshrined in the EU's Maastricht Treaty of 1992, even if it was subsequently complemented by the EU-wide coordination approach described earlier, the SGP. The underlying assumption of this principle was that financial markets would provide sufficient (and effective…) risk-sharing (and risk-pricing…) and that the "Maastricht" limits of 3% of GDP for national fiscal deficits and a 60% for national debt stock would constitute an adequate fiscal space for automatic stabilizers to operate at the country level. However, as the GFC showed, markets did not price risk accurately, acting instead as risk amplifiers, and on the fiscal side, even countries with a headline budget surplus and a low debt to GDP level *prior* to the crisis (like Ireland and Spain) were not able to cushion the shock within the Maastricht limits. This generated both national and euro-area-wide financial stresses (Fig. 6.9).

A euro area fiscal capacity would therefore address not only national asymmetric shocks, but also those area-wide, systemic shocks. While it is true that the euro area already has a body whose role is to provide support to countries hit by a crisis—namely, the ESM, this institution was designed more as a risk-sharing mechanism, and therefore it does not have a wider stabilization function.[41] To correct for that, a common euro area fiscal capacity should ideally be a more regular insurance tool, based on predefined rules, prerequisite criteria and trigger indicators.[42] Taking all this into account, there are many strong reasons why the current EU model of fiscal rules (regardless of the continued debate about their reform even after the changes introduced in February 2024,

---

[40] "Report of the Study Group on the Role of Public Finance in European Integration", Commission of the European Communities, 1977.

[41] To some degree different funds within the Multiannual Financial Framework (MFF), the EU's €1.2 trillion, 7-years long budget, also provide public fiscal goods on a pan-European level, however their scope of operation is mostly restricted to redistribution toward those EU member states and regions that are poorer than the EU average. The MFF is also not a euro-area-specific tool.

[42] Pisani-Ferry, J., Vihriala, E. and Wolff, G. (2013), "Options for Euro-Area Fiscal Capacity", Bruegel.

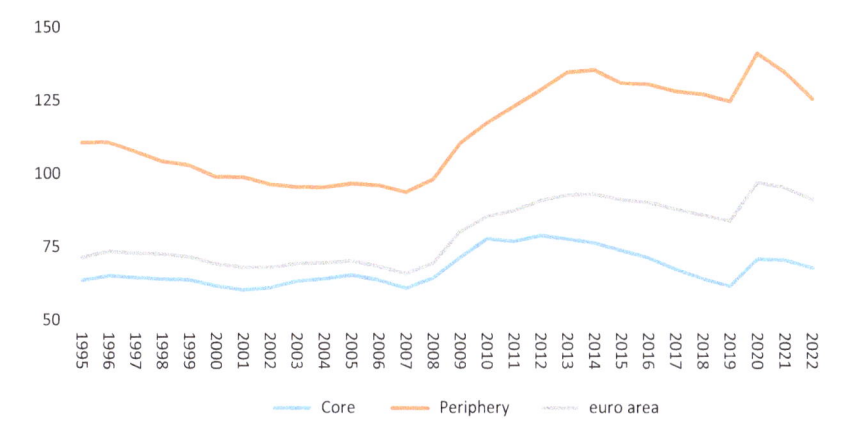

Fig. 6.9 Public debt stock, euro area, core and periphery, percentage of GDP. (Source: Eurostat)

and the end of the suspension in their use) should be further complemented with some type of wider fiscal stabilization function, at least for the euro area.

Nevertheless, such euro area fiscal capacity—much like the BU and the CMU—is still an ongoing, non-resolved discussion, albeit, as we will see in Chap. 7, an unexpected event led to some developments in this front.

As a conclusion, the GFC, after its US, euro area and global chapters, left behind central banks with much larger balance sheets and negative (in real terms) policy rates for a prolonged period, considerably more used to enacting nonorthodox interest rates and assets-based policies and, last but not least, a greatly expanded micro- and macro-prudential supervisory and regulatory footprint that helped *ameliorate* (not eliminate, as to fully eliminate risk is both impossible and undesirable) some of the faulty private sector risk assessments and incentives that underlined the crisis (albeit those policies also created newer vulnerabilities or enhanced preexisting ones). The GFC and this euro area stage of it, like old soldiers, almost simply "faded away" progressively (bar the occasional, mostly Greek-related hiccups) after the ECB President Mario Draghi's "whatever it takes" speech of July 23, 2012.[43]

Until it was replaced by the next crisis, that is.

---

[43] "Speech by Mario Draghi, President of the European Central Bank at the Global Investment Conference in London 26 July 2012", ECB.

Annex 6.A: Let's Talk a Little More about Sovereign Ratings

What are those mysterious and sometimes controversial instruments? Sovereign ratings, in short, are a *relative* measure of the creditworthiness of debt instruments issued by governments (a.k.a. "Sovereigns"): they therefore provide a *comparative* measure of the risk associated with investing in those, and by helping to ameliorate an asymmetric information problem between lenders and debtors, they allow rated sovereigns (even those with relatively lower, e.g., "speculative" sovereign ratings) better access to a deeper and wider set of funding opportunities under less costly terms.

For fundamental reasons (their greater levels of wealth, more robust institutions, etc.), historically Developed economies—like those in the euro area—have been associated with higher average Sovereign ratings (i.e., are assumed as less risky from a debt-repayment point of view) than, say, Developing ones.

6.A.1. First Things First: A Brief History of Sovereign Ratings

The first know publication of what can be called a Sovereign risk report is John Moody's 1900 "Manual of Industrial and Miscellaneous Securities", published during the tail end of the first globalization era under the classic "Gold Standard".[44] This publication had a list of sovereign bonds and also provided related public finance data for those Sovereigns, but did not had any *actual* Sovereign ratings.[45] Ratings proper will only appear in 1909, also a Moody's primer, in its "Analyses of Railroad Investments", but initially for *private* corporate debt instruments only (Sylla 2002).[46] Moody's started rating non-US government bonds in March 1918, becoming the

---

[44] Moody, J. (1900), "Manual of Industrial and Miscellaneous Securities", New York, O.C. Lewis Co. I had the opportunity to see the original publication at Moody's headquarters in New York during my work there: it reminded me of the Gutenberg Bible at the Library of Congress in Washington, DC.

[45] Beyond the US, the other sovereigns with listed debt instruments in that publication were Argentina, Austria, Belgium, Brazil, Canada, Denmark, Germany, Mexico, the Netherlands and the UK (Moody, J., 1900).

[46] Sylla, R. (2002), "An Historical Primer on the Business of Credit Rating", in Levich, R., Majnoni, G. and Reinhart, C. (eds.), *Ratings, Rating Agencies and the Global Financial System*, Kluwer Academic Publishers, Boston.

first company in the world to engage in this activity. Its "Moody's Analyses of Investments—Government and Municipal Securities of 1918" contained data on around 30,000 government bonds, 85% of which from US issuers (Sovereign and Sub-Sovereign, e.g., federal states, municipalities, etc.). The remaining 15% were obligations issued by foreign government entities from ten non-US issuers (Table 6.2).

The global economic recovery and a wave of financial innovation immediately after World War I led to a fast, albeit brief, expansion of the Sovereign ratings activity: by the late 1920s, Moody's rated around 60% of the then existing Sovereigns.[47] However, the "Great Depression" (leading to a wave of Sovereign defaults in the early 1930s: almost a full third

Table 6.2 Early Sovereign ratings[a]

Country	Date of issue of first rated Sovereign bond	Rating
Argentina	1915	A
Canada	1916	Aaa
Cuba[b]	1904	Aa
Dominican Republic	1908	A
France	1915	Aaa
Japan	1905	Aa
Norway	1916	A
Panama[c]	1914	Aa
Switzerland	1915	A
UK	1916	Aaa

[a]The Sovereign rating system back then had much less "granularity" than now: in the interwar period, the number of Moody's rating categories was 9, compared to the current 21 (most of which are further refined by three "outlook" qualifiers: negative, stable and positive). Also, a formal division between "investment" and "speculative" grades will not be introduced by Moody's until 1931

Source: Moody's. [b]Cuba, a colony of the US after its victory in the 1898 Spanish-American war, became formally independent from the US in 1902, but under a constitution that granted the US significant intervention and supervision powers. [c]Panama became independent in 1903, after a secession war from Colombia with US support, and under a treaty that granted US Sovereign rights upon part of the Panamanian territory, a situation that lasted until 1999. Also, since 1903 Panama runs a hard-peg currency regime toward the US dollar

[47] This percentage will only be reached again in the late 2000s, albeit by then the number of existing Sovereigns, as an effect of de-colonization and the breakup of large Sovereign entities like the Soviet Union made the number of existing Sovereigns much bigger than in the 1930s, increasing both diversity and complexity in the Sovereign ratings space.

of all countries were then classified in default, see Reinhart and Rogoff 2009, ibid.), financial re-regulation and later World War II caused international Sovereign issuances to stop: as a reflection of that, by the 1940s several of the then existing rating agencies had shut down their Sovereign ratings departments.[48] As recently as 1975, Moody's rated just *half a dozen* Sovereigns, including the US itself, and only with the (re)liberalization of global capital flows (after the end of the Bretton Woods system of fixed exchange rates *and* restricted global capital flows described earlier in this book) would international Sovereign debt issuance expand again, and with it the need for Sovereign ratings.

The 1990s witnessed a remarkable expansion of the universe of rated Sovereigns: between 1990 and 2000, their number *trembles*, increasing from around 30 to around 100 (Fig. 6.10). The collapse of communism and the breakup of the Soviet Union, Federal Republic of Yugoslavia and Czechoslovakia both increase further the sheer number of Sovereigns and free those economies to access international debt markets, at a moment in which international capital markets were expanding, making the

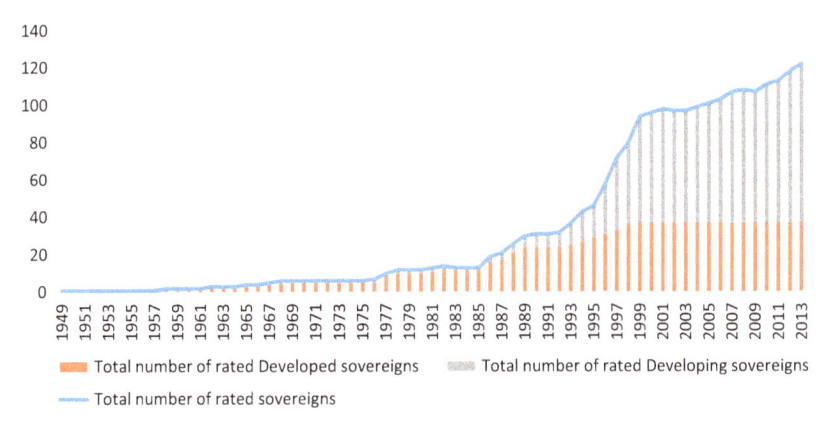

Fig. 6.10 Total number of Sovereigns, developed and developing, rated, 1949–2013. (Source: Moody's)

---

[48] Of the three major international Sovereign ratings agencies (a.k.a. "the Big Three", S&P, Moody's and Fitch), Moody's was the only one that continued to publish regularly analytical reports covering Sovereigns (even if those were largely not rated during that period).

advantages of having a Sovereign rating more apparent (so apparent that, even after the large stresses of the GFC, no Sovereign asked for their ratings to be withdrawn).[49]

6.A.2. Euro Area Periphery Ratings

It is in this benign environment that many euro area members start to be rated: among those in its' periphery, Portugal and Italy began to be rated by Moody's in 1986, Ireland in 1987, Spain in 1988, Greece in 1996 and finally Cyprus in 1998.

These Sovereigns experienced an upward ratings trend between their original rating, the entry into the euro area and the beginning of the euro area crisis, bunching around the upper levels of Sovereign ratings and some even reaching the coveted "triple A" status (another instance of the mispricing of risk shown earlier in this book). In another similarity, namely the sudden repricing of risk observed in other asset classes, this trajectory was replaced by a series of repeated and fast downgrades during the 2010–2013 euro area crisis, with some of these Sovereigns falling all the way down to the "default" category.[50] Even with their progressive recovery since, **none of them has yet achieved their pre-euro area crisis Sovereign rating level** (Fig. 6.11),[51] which implies that the analytical underpinnings of the earlier ratings compression have been adjusted.[52]

---

[49] Iran (in 2002) and Russian (in 2022) did have their ratings withdrawn, but for somewhat different reasons.

[50] Albeit no *systemically important euro area sovereign* ever fell into the "speculative grade" territory, some came pretty close to that during particularly stressful episodes I experienced throughout my tenure as Moody's Chief Economist.

[51] Scope Ratings, a leading European credit rating agency, which is nevertheless not among the "Big Three", finally brought Greece back to investment grade territory in **August 2023**: see Scope Ratings (2023), "Scope upgrades Greece's long-term credit ratings to BBB and changes the Outlook to Stable", Berlin. Scope was also recently added to the very exclusive list of credit rating agencies in the ECB's "Eurosystem Credit Assessment Framework", the framework it uses to assess the credit risk of collateral used in monetary policy operations, in November 2023: see "ECB accepts Scope Ratings within Eurosystem Credit Assessment Framework".

[52] The latest methodology that Moody's uses as *part* of its rating process is described at Moody's (2022), "Rating Methodology Sovereigns", New York (Moody's previously revised its Sovereign rating methodology in 2013, 2018 and 2019: this author was involved in the 2013 revision). Importantly, the "methodology" is all but one of the tools used in the rating process. Namely, the actual rating of any given Sovereign is always decided within the setting of "rating committee" discussions, which uses the insights of the methodology as one of the inputs that informs these discussions.

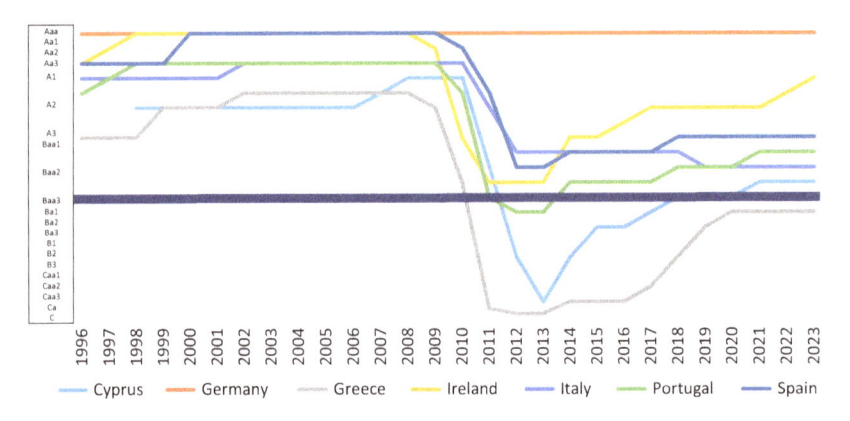

Fig. 6.11 Moody's rating of selected euro area Sovereigns. (Source: Moody's*: Baa3 is the dividing line between an "investment" and a "speculative" grade rating)

Annex 6.B: Modeling the Euro Area Crisis Using Expectations

This book has again and again stressed the important role that expectations play in economic behavior: this was also true for euro area stresses. While there were large accumulated real vulnerabilities—albeit not necessarily, or at least not in the beginning, at the government level, as shown earlier, it seems clear that negative self-fulfilling market expectations had a role to play in the euro area crisis.

This self-fulfilling component would appear when investors, fearing default—perhaps triggered by inconsistent policy decisions, behave in such a way that *leads to that default becoming more likely*. In an incomplete monetary union as the euro area, this mechanism is akin to a "sudden stop" dynamics in Developing economies, when capital inflows suddenly dry-up, leading to a liquidity, and ultimately, an external sustainability crisis (Calvo 1988).[53] This process is also similar to the one in bank runs like those experienced in the US during the "Great Depression", where a "bad equilibrium" (e.g., a state of reality among the set of possible outcomes with a lower aggregate welfare associated to it) can be avoided by a monetary authority credibly committing to provide liquidity if and when

---

[53] Calvo, G. (1988), "Servicing the Public Debt: The Role of Expectations", American Economic Review, 78(4): 647–661.

needed (so, Draghi's 2012 "whatever it takes" speech can be understood as a central bank signaling to markets that it will *really* perform its traditional "lender of last resort" function).

Formalizing those insights by following De Grauwe and Ji (2013),[54] Eq. (6.1), where I_{it} is the interest rate spread of country i in period t, which is dependent on CA_{it}, the current account deficit to GDP of country i in period t,, $Debt_{it}$ is the government debt to GDP in country i in period t, REE_{it} is the real effective exchange rate, $Growth_{it}$ is GDP growth rate, while α is the constant term and α_i is country i's fixed effects, and u_{it} is a residual term (independent and identically distributed, or i.i.d.) that measures the individual features of a country that affect its spread. The term γ_2 shows that there is a nonlinear relationship between the spread and the debt to GDP ratio (e.g., as the debt to GDP ratio increases, investors realize that they are coming closer and closer to a potential default episode, so they react in stronger fashion to additional increases in the debt to GDP ratio).

$$I_{it} = \alpha + \zeta \times CA_{it} + \gamma_1 \times Debt_{it} + \mu \times REE_{it} \\ + \delta \times Growth_{it} + \gamma_2 \times \left(Debt_{it}\right)^2 + \alpha_i + u_{it} \quad (6.1)$$

Such self-fulfilling expectations can be tested by adding a time dummy variable for movements in the spreads *that are unrelated to the fundamental variables of the model*. This is represented by β_t in Eq. (6.2) below:

$$I_{it} = \alpha + \zeta \times CA_{it} + \gamma_1 \times Debt_{it} + \mu \times REE_{it} \\ + \delta \times Growth_{it} + \gamma_2 \times \left(Debt_{it}\right)^2 + \alpha_i + \beta_t + u_{it} \quad (6.2)$$

If β_t is significant for a country or group of countries (say, the euro area periphery set of Sovereigns), this means a mispricing of risk *not accounted for by fundamentals is present*: as it turns out, De Grauwe and Ji (ibid.) do find that this term is significant for those countries (but only *after* the euro area crisis), implying market self-fulfilling expectations contributed to that outcome.

---

[54] De Grauwe, P., and Ji, Y. (2013), "Self-fulfilling Crises in the Eurozone: An Empirical Test", Journal of International Money and Finance, 34:15–36. Note that this formulation does not add direct measures for risk or ratings, as these are endogenous.

References

Buti, M., S. Deroose, V. Gaspar, and J. Nogueira Martins, eds. 2010. *The Euro: The First Decade*. Cambridge University Press.

Calvo, G. 1988. Servicing the Public Debt: The Role of Expectations. *American Economic Review* 78 (4): 647–661.

Commission of the European Communities. 1977. *Report of the Study Group on the Role of Public Finance in European Integration*. Brussels: Commission of the European Communities.

De Grauwe, P., and Y. Ji. 2013. Self-fulfilling Crises in the Eurozone: An Empirical Test. *Journal of International Money and Finance* 34: 15–36.

EBA. 2020. *On the Future Changes to the EU-wide Stress Test*. Discussion Paper EBA/DP/2020/01, Paris.

ESM. 2019. *Safeguarding the Euro in Times of Crisis: The Inside Story of the ESM*. Luxembourg: ESM.

European Commission. 1989. *Delors Report*. Brussels: European Commission.

Moody, J. 1900. *Manual of Industrial and Miscellaneous Securities*. New York: O.C. Lewis Co.

Moody's. 2022. *Rating Methodology Sovereigns*. New York: Moody's.

Reinhart, C., and K. Rogoff. 2009. *This Time Is Different: Eight Centuries of Financial Folly*. Princeton University Press.

Scope Ratings. 2023. *Scope Upgrades Greece's Long-Term Credit Ratings to BBB—And Changes the Outlook to Stable*. Berlin: Scope Ratings.

Sylla, R. 2002. An Historical Primer on the Business of Credit Rating. In *Ratings, Rating Agencies and the Global Financial System*, ed. R. Levich, G. Majnoni, and C. Reinhart. Boston: Kluwer Academic Publishers.

Vinhas de Souza, L., and M. Tudela. 2012. *Euro Area Periphery: Structural Reforms Have Significantly Improved External Imbalances, but Full Resolution May Still Take Years*. Moody's.

———. 2014. Voltar a Empezar: Crisis and the Renationalization of the Iberian Financial Systems. *Comparative Economic Studies* 56 (3): 337–350.

CHAPTER 7

COVID-19: The Fiscal and Monetary Responses to a Global Pandemic

7.1 Faster Than a Speeding Train: The "Light Switch" Recession

The story is still (sadly) fresh in our minds, but let's start with a brief recap. A fast-spreading global pandemic (COVID-19, a type of respiratory illness) started in late 2019 in a large, populous country that is also a key link for the global economy, the People's Republic of China. From there, it reached the whole planet in a few months. On January 30, 2020, the World Health Organization declared COVID-19 to be a public health emergency and, on March 11, upgraded the threat to "pandemic" (e.g., a disease outbreak that spreads across countries or continents) status.

Massive and speedy policy responses to deal with a new and contagious disease of uncertain mortality levels and for which no vaccine was initially available were taken worldwide, first and foremost a comprehensive government-mandated curtailing of physical interactions (e.g., "lockdowns"), which inevitably led to very significant economic effects and to

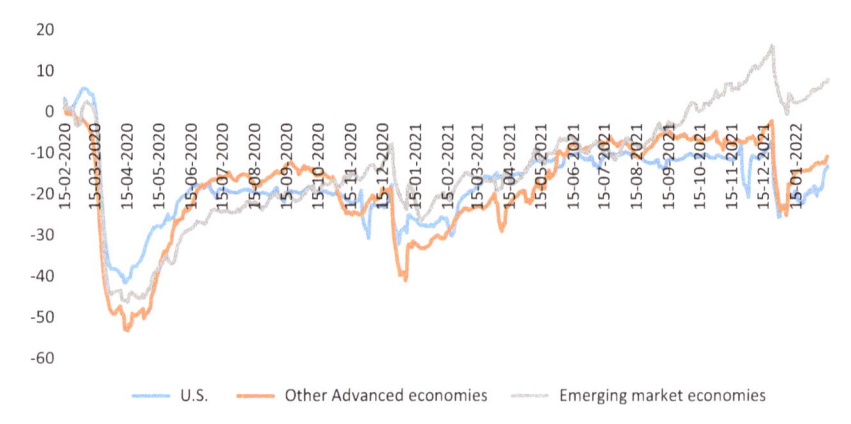

Fig. 7.1 Google mobility data (index)
(The mobility index is a simple average of Google's grocery, workplace, retail, recreation, and transportation mobility. Other advanced economies are Canada, France, Germany, Italy, Japan, Spain and the UK, while emerging markets are Argentina, Brazil, Chile, Colombia, Hong Kong, Korea, Indonesia, Malaysia, Philippines, Singapore, Taiwan and Thailand. Series ends on March 26, 2022. Source: Google, FED. 0 is the pre-pandemic level of mobility)

a remarkable and global reduction of the levels of human mobility, which, by some measures, *more than halved* in about a month (Fig. 7.1).[1]

The speed through which this policy shock spread was astounding: between early February 2020 and early April, 2020, the global economy experienced *double digit contractions in a matter of a few weeks* (Fig. 7.2).

---

[1] Bearing in mind the elevated uncertainty at the time they were introduced, a proper evaluation of the effectiveness of the level of strictness of those lockdowns, comparing not only their stated objectives (e.g., to reduce the loss of human lives) but also assessing the relative costs they imposed toward that aim (in GDP, education losses, unemployment, and, last but not least, inflation and disruption of supply chains, etc.) is still to be made. Given that there are intuitive empirical counterfactuals readily available (e.g., the different types and levels of lockdowns through time within the same country and between countries, say, the US and Brazil or India, Sweden and the EU/euro area, or Florida and New York), this seems a complex but worthwhile and achievable analytical undertaking (of course, properly taking into account differences in terms of overall level of development, comprehensiveness of health system, demographics—notably the share of elderly in total population, etc.: one may here refer to the saga concerning Herby, J., Jonung, L. and Hanke, S. (2022), "A Literature Review and Meta-Analysis of the Effects of Lockdowns on Covid-19 Mortality—II", version two, and Herby, J., Jonung, L. and Hanke, S. (2022), "A Literature Review and Meta-Analysis of the Effects of Lockdowns on Covid-19 Mortality", version one).

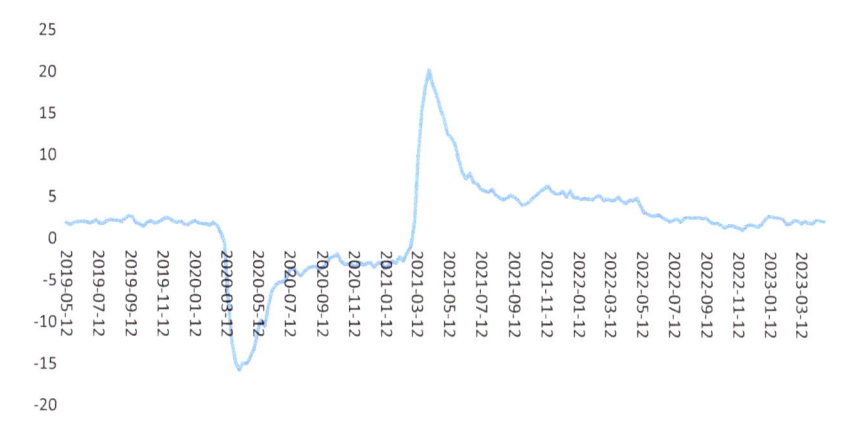

Fig. 7.2 "Weekly Tracker", GDP growth proxy. (See source and the explanation of how this series is constructed at OECD, Tracking GDP growth in real time, Paris. Source: OECD)

This truly was a global "light switch" recession, as would naturally be the case given the nature of the hurried-up (not to say panicked) and similar policy actions that were undertaken around the globe: in total, the global economy contracted by -2.8% in 2020 (-4.5% in Advanced economies, while Emerging markets suffered a much shallower contraction, at -1.7%, even with the large stresses faced by the Chinese economy). Some of those actions (the lockdowns and the related fiscal/monetary support) will also have medium-term, direct implications concerning the global inflationary spike that will be examined in Chap. 8.

This made the COVID recession more synchronized (and sharper) than the GFC itself—albeit far briefer (Fig. 7.3), as it was a shock shared by both Developed and Developing countries and largely simultaneously (an inherent implication of it having started in a Developing country, and a particularly central one from the point of view of the global economy, and of the type of policy responses).

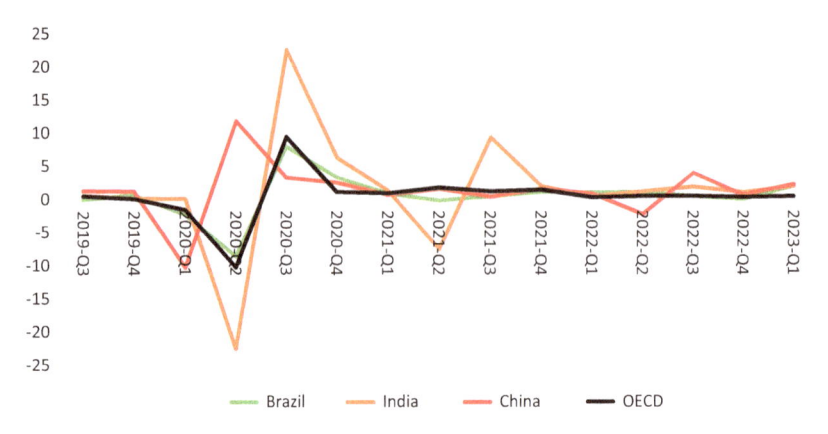

Fig. 7.3 Quarterly GDP in selected economies (percentage change, previous period). (Source: OECD)

7.2 The Policy Reaction: There We Go Again (But Now with Even More Fiscal Support)

The situation described above had significant and clear implications in terms of both price dynamics and the stability of the financial sector, the core mandates of a monetary authority, and therefore when the global pandemic hit, those institutions duly acted, applying measures similar to the ones they used during the GFC (which, as a reminder, can be largely described as an endogenous financial shock): however, as this time the global economy faced what can be best described as an *exogenous real shock*, the size and comprehensiveness of the fiscal measures was much larger than before (even if in many cases tilted toward guarantees, see Fig. 7.4). This *a priori* justifiable policy set would later complicate further the medium-term challenges monetary authorities were already facing.[2]

Following the structure used earlier in this book, it will now zoom in on the measures deployed by some of the largest economies in the world.

---

[2] Beyond the economic and financial aspects, the technological and medical policy response was also historically unique: already by December 2020 the first effective vaccines had been developed, and by the spring of 2021 over a billion doses had been administered (this figure had reached **13 billion** by the fall of 2022: see Mathieu, E., Ritchie, H., Rodés-Guirao, L., Appel, C., Giattino, C., Hasell, J., Macdonald, B., Dattani, S., Beltekian, D., Ortiz-Ospina, E. and Roser, M. (2020), "Coronavirus Pandemic (COVID-19)", published online at OurWorldInData.org.

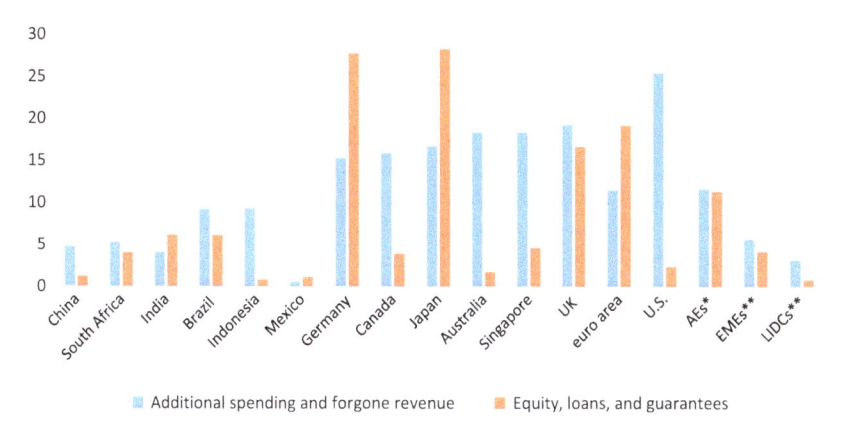

Fig. 7.4 Scale of fiscal measures in response to the Pandemic (% of GDP). (The IMF has a very comprehensive policy tracker of the economic measures applied by each individual country during the Pandemic: see, IMF, Policy Responses to COVID-19, Washington, DC. Source: IMF, data as of October 2021, modified by the author.*AEs: Advanced economies; **EMEs: Emerging market economies; ***LIDCs: Low income Developing countries)

7.2.1 The US Policy Response

The US Fed had started a rather slow "normalization" of its policies already in late 2015. There were eight small but successive interest rate increases of 0.25% between December 2016 and December 2018 (a 0.25% increase had been decided already in December 2015). The reduction of the size of its balance sheet was even slower, as it stayed around its GFC high mark of $4.4 trillion from mid-2014 till early 2018, picking up some speed from that point onward and thereby falling to $3.7 trillion (or over four times the pre-GFC size) by the fall of 2019. However, between 2019 and 2020, this partial "normalization" was not only fully reversed, but these policy levers were pushed far beyond their GFC levels: CPI prices halved between 2018 and 2020, falling to slight more than 1%, but Fed policy rates had reached zero by March 2020, and the Fed balance sheet was back to $4.4 trillion (it would surpass $7 trillion by the summer of the same year, and reach almost $9 trillion by March 2022, *or over twice its GFC high mark and an order of magnitude higher than the pre-GFC one*).

The Fed policy actions can be grouped into four broad categories. First, the tried and tested interest rates and balance sheet operations; second, measures to provide liquidity and funding to money markets (including outside the US, via the reinforcement of the swap lines created during the GFC); third, facilities to support the flow of credit to multiple public and private economic agents and fourth, temporary regulatory and supervisory relief to incentivize banks to continue issuing credit.[3] This blueprint would be largely followed worldwide.

While several of these Fed actions effectively revived facilities created during the GFC, expanding and tweaking those (for instance, in its renewed QE operations, it now purchased securities of different maturities), several tools were new, and went considerably beyond the scope of the previous frameworks, by, for instance, purchasing loans of nonfinancial businesses and the debt of US federal states and municipalities. Also building on the Fed's GFC experience, many of these facilities were structured as SPVs or LLCs, allowing the pooling of Fed and Treasury[4] funds (as was the case with the "Maiden Lane" LLC described earlier), while avoiding restrictions on the purchase of assets that are ineligible under the Federal Reserve Act, such as corporate debt.[5]

As the current Fed Chairman Jerome Powell said in 2020, "the Fed has lending powers, not spending powers".[6] Therefore, upon initiative of the US Government and Congress, not only the monetary, but also the fiscal policy response in the US was truly unprecedented in scale, scope and speed: over **$5.1 trillion in fiscal support was provided to the US economy, or a staggering 25% of its GDP** (Table 7.1). As a comparator, the amount of fiscal support during the GFC (i.e., the Troubled Asset Relief Program—TARP—of October 2008, and the American Recovery and Reinvestment Act—ARRA—of February 2009) altogether provided federal economic stimulus totaling "just" about $1 trillion, or around 7%

---

[3] Clarida, R., Duygan-Bump, B. and Scotti, C. (2021), "The COVID-19 Crisis and the Federal Reserve's Policy Response", Finance and Economics Discussion Series 20,221–035, Federal Reserve Board, Washington, DC.

[4] The 2020 CARES act appropriated up to $500 billion to the US Department of Treasury's Exchange Stabilization Fund (ESF) to support several of the emergency lending facilities created by the Fed in response to the COVID-19 pandemic.

[5] Labonte, M. (2021), "The Federal Reserve's Response to COVID-19: Policy Issues", Congressional Research Service, R46411, Washington, DC.

[6] Powell, J. (2020) "Current Economic Issues", Federal Reserve Board, Washington, DC. Jerome Powell, incidentally, renewed the pre-Burns tradition of non-economist heading the Fed (he is a lawyer, just like, incidentally, Christine Lagarde, the current head of the ECB).

Table 7.1 Pandemic-related fiscal support in the US

Pandemic-related bills	Date of enactment	Total ($ billion)
Coronavirus Preparedness and Response Supplemental Appropriations Act (CPRSAA)	March 6,2020	8.00
The Families First Coronavirus Response Act (FFCRA)	March 18,2020	192.00
The Coronavirus Aid, Relief, and Economic Security Act (CARES)	March 27,2020	1721.00
The Paycheck Protection Program and Health Care Enhancement Act (PPHCEA)	April 24,2020	483.00
Coronavirus Response and Relief Supplemental Appropriations Act (Response and Relief, or CRRSAA), a component of the Consolidated Appropriations Act	December 27,2020	868.00
The American Rescue Plan Act (ARPA)	March 6,2021	1844.00
Total		5116.00

Source: CRS (2021), "The COVID-19-Related Fiscal Response: Recent Actions and Future Options", CRS Insight IN11734

of US GDP, and the average COVID-19 fiscal response for Advanced economies in Fig. 7.4 is 11.7% of GDP.[7]

7.2.2 The Policy Response of a (Less Fragmented) Euro Area

The ECB (and the EU) reacted in a much faster, bigger and more coordinated way than to the previous crisis, to no small measure because of the several institutional reforms implemented to address the shortcomings of the euro area described in Sect. 6.4 (and the sheer experience acquired in addressing a deep crisis by all European institutions involved). Also, by far and large, the fragmentation pressures that were the hallmark of the euro area part of the GFC were now absent.

On the fiscal side, the EU created several temporary fiscal facilities, the largest of which was the "Next Generation EU", or NGEU, instrument, worth € 750 billion. The bulk of NGEU funds (€ 724 billion) were for financing the so-called Recovery and Resilience Facility (RRF), a

---

[7] CRS (2008) "Cost Estimate - Economic Stimulus Act of 2008", Washington, DC, and CRS (2014), "Estimated Impact of the American Recovery and Reinvestment Act on Employment and Economic Output in 2014" Washington, DC.

framework designed to finance investments (and some structural reforms) identified at each individual EU member state, via so-called National Recovery and Resilience Plans, or RRPs: € 386 billion of the RRF funds were in the form of loans, and € 338 billion as grants.[8] In addition, the EU created a € 100 billion fund to finance short-term work schemes under the so-called Support to Mitigate Unemployment Risks (leading to the imaginative acronym of SURE). The ESM also created a Pandemic Crisis Support (PCS) instrument, with a maximum envelope of € 240 billion in loans (all euro area countries were eligible for this for amounts up to 2% of their respective GDPs). Finally, the European Investment Bank (or EIB, the EU's development bank, somewhat akin to the World Bank, but with the crucial difference that it overwhelmingly operates in the Developed economies of the EU) set up a € 25 billion Pan-European Guarantee Fund (EGF) to support EU companies affected by the pandemic. These instruments together amount to around € 1.2 trillion (however, while the NGEU, SURE and EIB facilities where effectively all fully used, there was no demand for the ESM's PCS funds, which brings the actual amount of EU-level fiscal support down to around € 1 trillion).

In total, and besides the ECB, the EU collectively (so, EU plus EU member states, or EU MS) mobilized about € 3.4 trillion. This is equivalent to almost 25% of the EU's GDP, and was the largest (and fastest) EU response to a crisis ever.[9] However, these € 3.4 trillion were mostly *liquidity measures* without a direct fiscal impact, and were also very heterogeneously distributed between EU MS (naturally, MS with more "fiscal space" like Germany could afford both more stimulus in general and more stimulus of a fiscal nature). Additionally, a very significant flexibilization of several EU policy frameworks was adopted (notably of the SGP, whose application of its excessive deficit procedure component was effectively suspended, and remains so to this date), to allow the individual EU member states to pursue both stimulus and liquidity measures. For the euro area, the IMF estimates an actual net fiscal impulse of around 11.5% of

[8] In another difference in relation to the US, the actual distribution of NGEU funds during the pandemic shocks was actually quite limited (they can be used until 2026).

[9] As a comparison, the EU fiscal response to the euro area sovereign crisis, the so-called European Economic Recovery Plan (EERP) was estimated at about 1.8% of EU GDP (or up to 4%, if adding the estimated effects of automatic stabilizers—that is, increases in spending and/or decreases in taxes when the economy slows down that happen without the need for discretionary policy action). Support to bank sectors (mostly via guarantees from EU member states) would add another 12.6% to this figure.

GDP (an impressive figure, but two and half times smaller than in the US), plus another 19% of GDP in guarantees. This fiscal impulse was not only smaller, but also considerably more targeted than in the US (no "check is in the mail" for individual households).

The ECB exceptional measures in response to the pandemic include the March 2022 expansion of its existing Asset Purchase Program and the launching of a Pandemic Emergency Purchase Program (PEPP) for both public and private sector securities, initially with a volume of € 750 billion but subsequently increased in two steps to € 1.85 trillion.[10] The ECB also continued to provide liquidity through additional LTROs, and in May 2020 it launched non-targeted so-called Pandemic Emergency Longer-Term Refinancing Operations (or PELTROs). Like the Fed, it also engaged in temporary regulatory and supervisory relief, by allowing financial institutions to operate with lower capital requirements, adding an estimated €120 billion to banks' CET1 capital that could be used to provide more loans to the private sector (the ECB also forced all euro area banks to suspend dividend payments and equity buybacks, to prevent these resources from being distributed to shareholders), and other macroprudential authorities across the euro area released or reduced an additional €20 billion via lower capital buffer requirements. Regarding the provision of euro liquidity to non-euro-area central banks, the ECB reactivated existing swap lines and repo arrangements and established new ones with non-euro-area central banks.[11]

7.3 The (Short-Term) Effectiveness of Policy Measures

GDP in the US and the euro area contracted by, respectively, -2.8 and -6.1% in 2020, but growth returned already by the next year (with increases of 6.0% and 5.3%): this macro trajectory picture is similar in other Developed economies. These massive (budget deficits reached 14% and 7% of GDP in those two economic areas in 2020, increasing by factors of 3 and 10, respectively) and fast measures were effective in not only cushioning the economic and social fallout of the pandemic and associated lockdown policies, but also in containing financial stresses: stress

---

[10] The PEPP was a temporary program, terminated in March 2022.
[11] Kok, C., Mongelli, F. and Hobelsberger, K. (2022), "A Tale of Three Crises: Synergies between ECB Tasks", ECB Occasional Paper n. 2022/305.

indicators duly went up, **but far off from 2007–2008 levels, and only briefly** (Fig. 7.5). The regulatory and institutional changes brought about by the previous crisis also helped to achieve this outcome.

These fast and large responses can also be observed in the balance sheet of the monetary authorities (Fig. 7.6): the speed and the scale in the

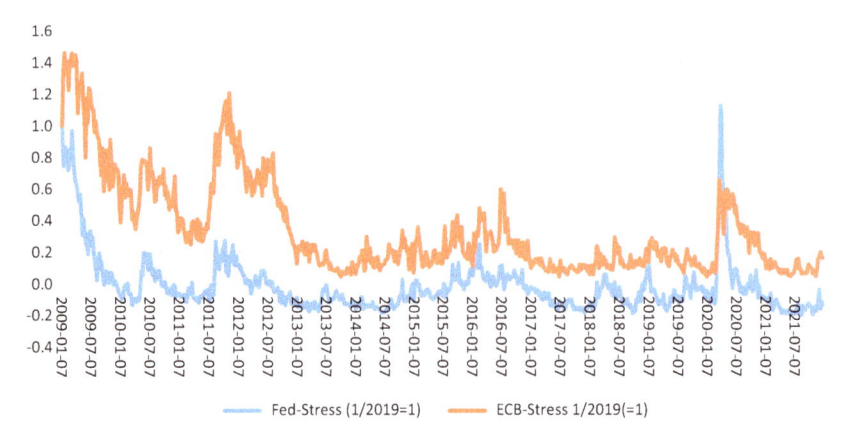

Fig. 7.5 Fed and ECB systemic stress indicators (January 2009 set to 1). (Sources: FRED and ECB)

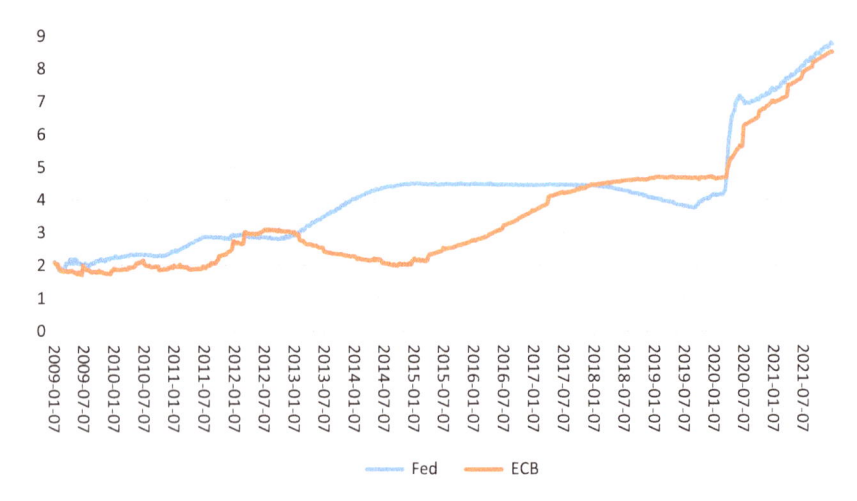

Fig. 7.6 Fed and ECB balance sheets ($ and € trillion). (Sources: FRED and ECB)

increases is strikingly similar for the Fed and the ECB (suggesting a much greater degree of coordination—even if informal—than before). As a result, by the end of 2021, the size of the Fed balance sheet to US GDP was around 38%, while in the euro area this was just shy of 70% (as a comparator, the balance sheet of the BoE almost doubled, from around £ 600 billion to around £ 1.1 trillion, while that of the BoJ grew by 30%, from ¥5.7 to ¥7.4 trillion, between January 2020 and March 2022).

So, from a short-term point of view, these policy measures achieved their stabilization objectives. However, distortions were *again* created that will lead to instability later on (see Chap. 8).

7.4 The Pandemic Policy Response in Developing Economies

How about the less developed economies? An analysis of the policy responses reveals (a) a much larger scale of support than in preceding crises, (b) a broad similarity with measures undertook in Developed economies (naturally bearing in mind specific constraints, like a more limited fiscal space and structural features, notably shallower financial markets) and (c) a high level of coordination between fiscal and monetary measures. By far and large those measures also achieved their intended aims and most countries (bar some low-income Developing economies, mostly in Africa) were largely spared the "sudden stop" of capital inflows episodes common to emerging markets in earlier moments of stress. This will be illustrated with the examples of two systemically important large emerging markets,[12] India and Brazil.

7.4.1 *India*

India imposed a nationwide lockdown on March 25, 2020, which lasted only until the end of May 2020 and was then lifted in a phased fashion. The country suffered a brief but severe economic contraction, with GDP estimated to have fallen by 24% in Q1 FY[13] 2021, and by 7.3% in FY 2020–2021 as a whole (the 2020 calendar year contraction was -5.8%, but

---

[12] "Emerging markets" is a higher-income category of Developing country, officially used by the IMF in its documents and analysis.

[13] FY stands for fiscal year, which in India starts on April 1 and ends on March 31 of the following year.

GDP in 2021 increased by over 9%). The policy response to the economic impact of both the pandemic and the subsequent brief lockdown was an effectively coordinated mix of fiscal, monetary, financial and regulatory measures.[14] Total fiscal stimulus was estimated by the IMF at about 4% of GDP (additional spending plus foregone revenue: this was smaller than the emerging markets average of 5.7% calculated by the IMF), with an additional 6.2% in guarantees (4.2% for emerging markets): the budget deficit reached almost 13% in 2020, and almost 10% in 2021 (from almost 8% in 2019).

The Reserve Bank of India (RBI, the country's central bank and a self-described "flexible inflation targeter")[15] cut its policy rate from 5.15% to 4%. Among other measures, the RBI lowered the banks' reserve ratio to provide additional liquidity to the banking system, a measure worth about 0.7% of GDP, and LTROs-like operations worth a similar share of GDP were made, as were asset purchases of government securities in the secondary market amounting to 1.5% of GDP (or about 30% of all central government's total net market borrowings), and it also created special refinancing facilities for different market segments and institutions: in total, RBI support amounted to around 7% of India's GDP.[16] Similarly to other jurisdictions, the RBI also engaged in temporary "regulatory forbearance" measures.

7.4.2 Brazil

Brazil, another inflation targeter (see Annex 7.A), by far and large did not impose lockdown measures at national level (albeit some federal states and even municipalities imposed some localized measures, of different types, strictness and duration). The first and second quarters of 2020 saw GDP contractions of around -10%,[17] but the total year average was -3.3%, and

---

[14] Chakraborty, L. and Harikrishnan, S. (2022), "COVID-19 and Fiscal-Monetary Policy Coordination: Empirical Evidence from India", Levy Economics Institute, Working Papers Series 1002.

[15] Reserve Bank of India, "Monetary and Fiscal Policy Interactions in the Wake of the Pandemic", BIS Papers n. 122: 149–157.

[16] Mohan, R. (2021), "The Response of the Reserve Bank of India to Covid-19: Do whatever it Takes", Centre for Social and Economic Progress, Working Paper 8, New Delhi.

[17] Morceiro, P., Tessarin, M. and Pereira, H. (2022), "Políticas Macroeconômicas Adotadas no Brasil em Resposta à Pandemia de COVID-19 em 2020", Textos de Economia, Florianópolis, 25(1):1–23, Universidade Federal de Santa Catarina.

the country grew by 5% the following year. Total fiscal stimulus was estimated by the IMF at about 9.3% of GDP (almost double the emerging markets' average), with an additional 6.2% in guarantees. The budget deficit reached 13.3% of GDP in 2020 (over twice the 2019 figure) but fell back to around 4% in 2021. The most noticeable element in the Brazilian fiscal response were the large direct income transfer programs, worth over 5% of GDP and which reached an estimated 66 million people: 40% of households, representing over 50% of the Brazilian population, benefited from some sort of assistance.[18]

Temporary waivers from the legal provisions concerning the recently adopted fiscal rules framework and the CBB mandate were approved (including the capacity for the CBB to buy public and private bonds in secondary markets: this in the end was not necessary, as the *signaling* was enough to help calm markets, similarly to the case of the ECB's OMT),[19] allowing the monetary authority to provide liquidity support and capital relief to the banking sector in more flexible ways (liquidity and capital relief measures totaled around 17% of GDP *each*). The CBB also lowered its policy rate from 4.5% to 2% between January and August 2020.

However, while the measures were similar in nature, Figs. 7.7 and 7.8 show that the CBB adjusted both the size of its balance and its policy rate in a more flexible way than the RBI, speedily adjusting downward the size of its balance sheet when markets stabilized, and quickly increasing interest rates as inflation started going up in early 2021.

Albeit this is a largely encouraging story about emerging markets (where, additionally, newly flexible exchange rates adjusted downward—reflecting the looser fiscal and monetary policies—and thereby supporting external sustainability), lower income Developing countries showed a notably smaller capacity for implement polices to cushion the pandemic shock: while Developed economies managed to provided fiscal support worth 11.7% of GDP (plus 11.4%% in guarantees), and "emerging markets" 5.7% and 4.2%, respectively, lower-income Developing countries could only muster on average 3.2% of fiscal support (around a quarter of the Developed countries figure) and an order of magnitude less in guarantees (0.9%). Additionally, some would experience "sudden stops" and

---

[18] Comisión Económica para América Latina y el Caribe, (2021), "Preliminary Overview of the Economies of Latin America and the Caribbean 2020", Santiago.

[19] Nechio, F. and Fernandes, B. "Brazil: Covid-19 and the Road to Recovery", BIS Papers n. 122: 39–55.

Fig. 7.7 Balance sheet, RBI and CBB (₹ & R$)

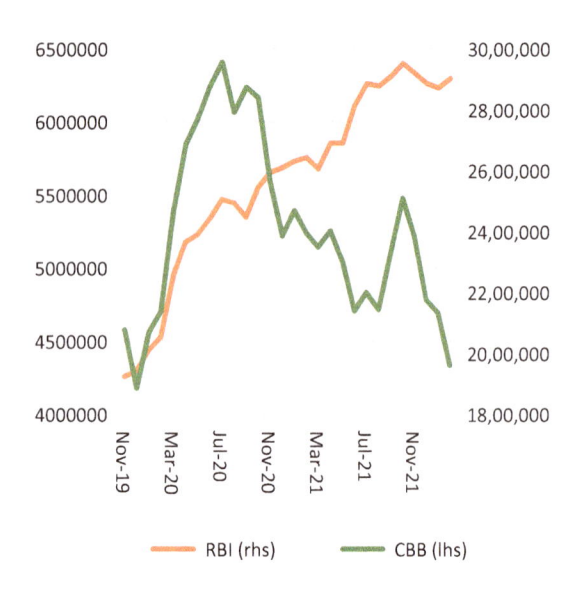

Fig. 7.8 Policy rates, RBI and CBB. (Sources: RBI, CBB and FRED)

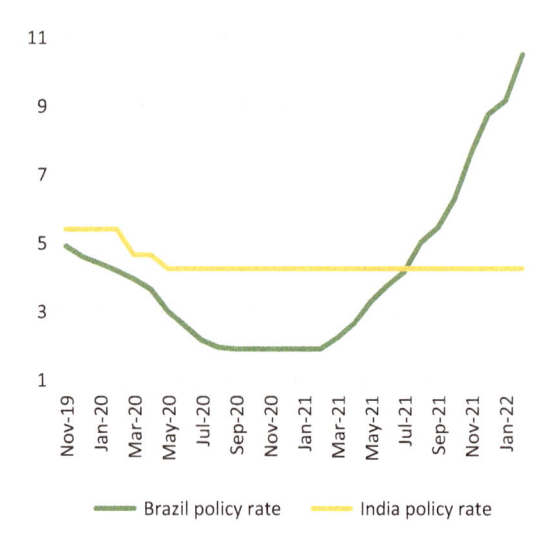

external sustainability crises (but this time, those crises were fundamentals-driven, not expectations-driven, ones).

Another less positive point is that the policies used during the pandemic sowed the seeds of a worldwide inflationary spike not seen since the "Great Inflation" 40 years before: this will be addressed in Chap. 8.

Annex 7.A: What Is Inflation Targeting after All?

Inflation targeting is currently the monetary framework of choice for central banks around the world, easily replacing the alternative of German-style monetary targeting (largely due to the increased unreliability of the relation between monetary aggregates and inflation, linked to financial innovation and changes in economic agents' behavior). Inflation targeting (or, in Svensson 1996[20] words, inflation *forecast* targeting) is a monetary policy framework with an explicit commitment to price stability as a goal, providing an anchor for inflation expectations while making the central bank more transparent and accountable. Following Leiderman and Svensson (1995),[21] inflation *forecast* targeting regimes have as essential characteristics (a) an explicit quantitative inflation target (in the form of either single points or bands, symmetric or asymmetric) for a specific price measure at a specific date in the future (b) no intermediate monetary aggregate or exchange rate target (the exchange rate was a common one among Developing countries), (c) an explicit policy decision framework to achieve the stated objectives and (d) a high degree of transparency concerning the course of action planned by the central bank to achieve its aims. Implicitly, the monetary authority capable of delivering on those characteristics would be an *independent* one.

Since these requirements do not guarantee that monetary policy achieves price stability, it is important to elaborate on what inflation (forecast) targeting means. To understand the rationale behind it, it is useful to think of it as a three-pronged strategy to improve the performance of monetary policy (Bernanke et al. 1999).[22] First, price stability is defined as the *primary goal* for monetary policy. Second, the central bank should

---

[20] Svensson, L. (1996), "Inflation Forecast Targeting: Implementing and Monitoring Inflation Targets", National Bureau of Economic Research Working Paper n. 5797.

[21] Leiderman, L. and L. Svensson, L. (eds) (1995), *Inflation Targets*, Centre for Economic Policy Research.

[22] Bernanke, B., Laubach, T., Mishkin, F. and Posen, A. (1999), *Inflation Targeting*, Princeton University Press.

have the *flexibility* to choose the means for achieving the goal. Third, through *transparency* on the implementation of monetary policy, the central bank is accountable for achieving the goal.

These elements, following Bernanke and Mishkin (1997),[23] define it as a *framework* that allows monetary policy to be implemented within a "constrained discretion" setting. *Transparency* is what effectively constrains monetary authorities since the central bank is accountable to the general public *and* to its principals for achieving that goal. On the other hand, *flexibility* is what allows the central bank to respond to short-term macroeconomic fluctuations as needed, since there is no pre-commitment to an intermediate target. Therefore, the key issue for inflation forecast targeting framework is to find the right balance between *transparency* and *flexibility within the constraints of the framework*.

Annex 2.A showed how gold provided the price anchor during the "Gold Standard". In inflation targeting regimes, a framework that speedily became the standard for the implementation of monetary policy, **the short-term nominal interest rate, i_t, provides this anchor**.[24] A related important difference is that this anchor is an exogenous one, and that it only guarantees a stable equilibrium under particular conditions (as a reminder, in Annex 2.A, the equilibrium is endogenous, unique and stable).

Given the context of Emerging markets, a "flexible inflation forecast targeting" can formally be operationalized as a Taylor rule, as given by (Eq. 7.1):

$$i_t = \bar{i} + \gamma\left(\pi_t - \bar{\pi}\right) + \lambda\left(y_t - \bar{y}_t\right) \qquad (7.1)$$

On the left-hand side of (Eq. 7.1) we have the **short-term nominal interest rate** (the exogenous "anchor"), i_t, which depends on $\bar{i}$, the equilibrium interest rate, as well as on deviations of the inflation rate, π_t, and output, y_t, from their target values $\bar{\pi}$ and $\bar{y}_t$, respectively. $\bar{\pi}$ is **chosen by the monetary authority as to stabilize prices**, $\bar{y}_t$ is potential output and, hence, $\left(y_t - \bar{y}_t\right)$ is the output gap.

---

[23] Bernanke, B. and Mishkin, F. (1997), "Inflation Targeting: A New Framework for Monetary Policy?", National Bureau of Economic Research Working Paper n. 5893.

[24] For the inflation targeting experience of emerging markets in general and of Latin America in particular (namely, Argentina, Brazil, Chile and Mexico), see Langhammer and Vinhas Souza (2005), ibid.

An open economy version of it would add terms for the real exchange rate, q_t, and for and exchange rate target level, $\bar{q}_t$, as in (Eq. 7.2) below:

$$i_t = \bar{i} + \gamma\left(\pi_t - \bar{\pi}\right) + \lambda\left(y_t - \bar{y}_t\right) + \delta\left(q_t - \bar{q}_t\right) \tag{7.2}$$

Therefore, an emerging market monetary authority may choose to use an inflation forecast target that is actually an extended, open economy Taylor rule.[25]

From its origins in a country with the worst OECD inflation track record between 1970 and 1984—namely, New Zealand—in 1989, the increase in inflation targeting frameworks use among Developing countries has been truly remarkable: by 2021, these countries housed around 72% of all 109 monetary authorities that followed this framework (Fig. 7.9).

This expansion among emerging markets (EMs) was for a long time concentrated in Latin America, starting in the late 1990s, as inflation targeting was the framework of choice for the stabilization of those economies after the hyperinflationary period,[26] with developing Asia and the Middle East and North Africa regions catching up only from the mid-2010s onward (Fig. 7.10). Sub-Saharan Africa lags in terms of adoption, due to the structural constraints of implementing more sophisticated monetary policy frameworks like inflation targeting (e.g., shallow domestic financial markets, faulty transmission mechanism) in such mostly low income Developing countries.[27]

---

[25] Clarida, R., Galí, J. and Gertler, M. (1997), "Monetary Policy Rules in Practice: Some International Evidence", National Bureau of Economic Research Working Paper n. 6254.

[26] Mariscal, R., Powell, A. and Tavella, P. (2014), "On the Credibility of Inflation Targeting Regimes in Latin America", IDB Working Paper Series, n. IDB-WP-504, Washington. This was of course not a universal tendency in the region, as Argentina's late 2023 proposals for dollarization (and abolishing of its Central Bank) shows. For Argentina's earlier travails, see McCandless (2005) and Pesce and Feldman (2023), ibid.

[27] Morozumi, A., Bleaney, M. and Mumuni, Z. (2020),"Inflation targeting in low-income countries: Does IT work?", Review of Development Economics.

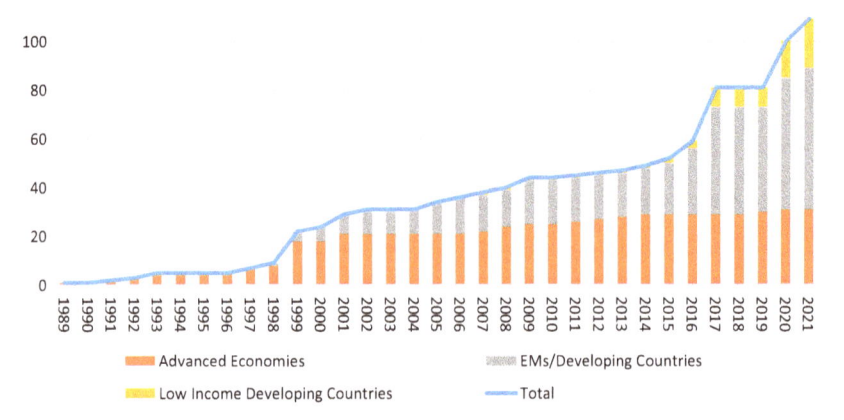

Fig. 7.9 Growth in the number of inflation targeting monetary authorities (Members of EU common currency are classified as inflation targeters from the moment they join the euro area; however, as the requirements of ERM participation imply an exchange rate pegging, they are not classified as such before joining. The same procedure is used for the countries that are members of the Eastern Caribbean Central Bank [ECCB], and Central Bank of the West African States and the Bank of the Central African States [BCEAO and BEAC, respectively], as the ECCB manages a peg to the US dollar, and the BCCEAO and the BEAC manage a peg to the euro. Source: Author, based on IMF)

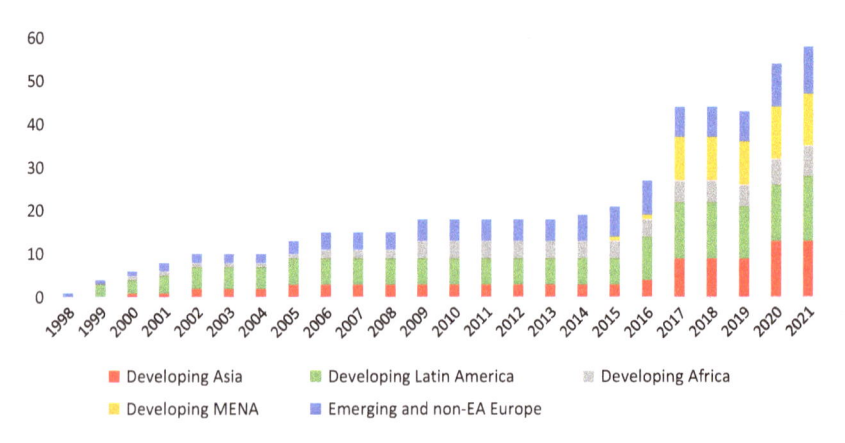

Fig. 7.10 Expansion of inflation targeting in developing regions. (Source: Author, based on IMF)

Annex 7.B: China's Limited Role in Global Financial Crises

The Chinese experience had a somewhat limited coverage in this book, compared with other smaller emerging markets like Brazil or India. The reason for that is simple: **the differentiated patterns of China's real and financial (re) integration into the global economy, and that country's different role as concerning global real and financial shocks** (Miranda-Agrippino and Rey 2021),[28] which is linked to the more reduced level of financial integration of China compared with other large Emerging markets. I will elaborate on that below.

The return of China as a systemically important part of the global economy is by now a well-established fact: with an average real annual GDP growth of 9% since 1980, its economy grew from a paltry 1.7% of the global nominal GDP as recently as 1991 to an estimated 17% of that total in 2023 (a figure that, incidentally, shows a fall from the 18.5% registered in 2021). However, its growth has sharply decelerated since the highs of the late 2010s, from an average of over 10% *p.a.* between 1990 and 2010 to around 6.5% in the period since. This has led to a reduction of the speed of its sharp trajectory of convergence to the US level of GDP per capita, which has recently plateaued at around 15% of the US nominal GDP per capita.[29]

This slowdown aside, and even with increased doubts about the future growth rates of China, that country is and will remain a major economic factor globally. However, its importance concerning global economic and financial cycles has been restricted, largely due to its limited level of financial integration, where it clearly "punches below its weight".

While China (ex-Hong Kong) was responsible for 18% of global exports and 13% in global imports in 2022 (ex-intra EU trade, which is a free-trade area)—both figures are around three times their pre-WTO accession level, the international financial role of China is quite limited: based on SWIFT data, the use of China's currency, the renminbi (RMB), is minimal, accounting for 3.7% of all global cross-border payments by September

---

[28] Miranda-Agrippino, S. and Rey, H (2021), "The Global Financial Cycle", NBER Working Paper Series n. 29327, Boston.

[29] Not a uniquely Chinese phenomenon by any means: the convergence of the EU as an aggregate has stalled at around 55% of the US per capita GDP since the 1970s.

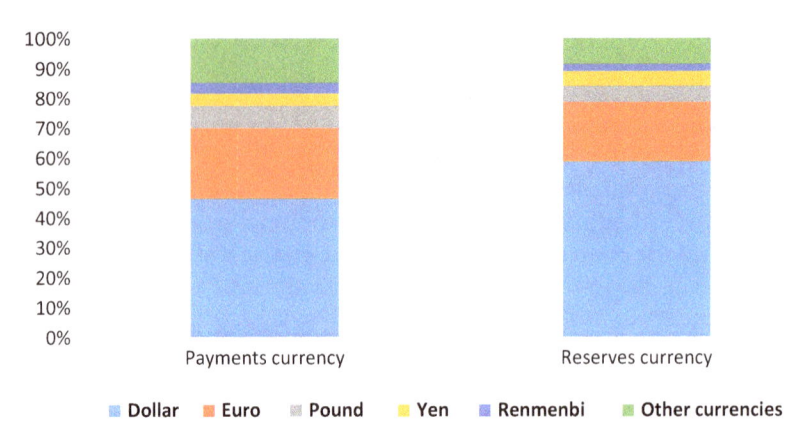

[Chart showing shares of main currencies in Payments currency and Reserves currency, with legend: Dollar, Euro, Pound, Yen, Renmenbi, Other currencies]

Fig. 7.11 Shares of main currencies in payments (September 2023) and reserves (Q2 2023). (Source: SWIFT and IMF)

2023[30]—compared with over 70% for the US dollar and the euro combined, and around 2.5% of global *allocated*[31] central bank reserve assets by mid-2023—compared with almost 70% for the US Dollar and the euro (Fig. 7.11).

The channels of global transmission of Chinese shocks identified by Miranda-Agrippino and Rey (ibid.), are also very different from those they estimate for the US and the EU. Global financial variables are largely unaffected by Chinese shocks, with world financial conditions, the VIX, and the global factors in asset prices and capital flows not responding to those in any significant way, **while world production does**, due to the effects of Chinese domestic demand contractions on world trade and commodity prices. Hence, the main channel of the international transmission of Chinese monetary and financial shocks is its large relative weight in world GDP, and therefore the Chinese monetary policy seems to affect mainly international trade and commodity markets but not the "Global Financial Cycle". Miranda-Agrippino and Rey (ibid.) conclude that while the Fed

---

[30] SWIFT is the "Society for Worldwide Interbank Financial Telecommunication", a body that provides services related to the execution of financial transactions and payments between most global banks. One should note that this latest figure for China shows an over sevenfold increase when compared to the September 2012 share of 0.51%.

[31] Using IMF data, around $900 billion, or 8% of total, global central bank hard currency reserves have no reported currency denomination linked to them.

plays an important role in the Global Financial Cycle, the PBOC (and, incidentally, the ECB) plays an important role for international trade, output and commodity prices, driving what the call a "Global Trade and Commodity Cycle".

Notwithstanding the above and the significant capital account restrictions, the PBOC began promoting RMB internationalization, notably after the GFC (see Perez-Saiz and Zhang 2023)[32]: in 2009, the PBOC began permitting cross-border settlements in RMB, initially in selected Chinese provinces, and nationwide since 2011, and it has also introduced bilateral swap lines (most recently used by Argentina) and offshore clearing banks to facilitate the cross-border use of RMB (which joined in 2015 the basket of IMF's Special Drawing Rights). Additionally, Zhang (2023)[33] concludes that, based on the experience of comparator economies, an open capital account could lead to a significant expansion of China's global financial footprints, while Barcelona et al. (2022)[34] estimate that using an expanded definition of "shock" that takes into account the second-round effects of Chinese real shocks on domestic and external financial variables (and also using an alternative series for Chinese GDP), China's role as a source of global financial shocks may be already somewhat larger than that estimated by Miranda-Agrippino and Rey (2021). Therefore, a greater consideration of China as a source of future financial crises in and of itself seems warranted.

---

[32] Perez-Saiz, H. and Zhang, L. (2023), "Renminbi Usage in Cross-Border Payments: Regional Patterns and the Role of Swaps Lines and Offshore Clearing Banks", IMF Working Papers Series WP/23/77.

[33] Zhang, L. (2023), "Capital Account Liberalization and China's Financial Integration", Harvard Kennedy School, Working Paper Series n. 196, Cambridge.

[34] Barcelona, W., Cascaldi-Garcia, D., Hoek, J. and Van Leemput, E. (2022), "What Happens in China Does Not Stay in China" International Finance Discussion Papers 1360, Board of Governors of the Federal Reserve System, Washington, DC.

CHAPTER 8

Shadows from the Past: Inflation and War

8.1 No Good Deed Ever Goes Unpunished

The basic story is rather simple and was already telegraphed in Chap. 7: the policy responses associated with the Pandemic, accommodated by monetary authorities until quite late on the game, created price pressures that led to the highest levels of inflation in almost two generations.

8.2 Fiscal Side Effects

Let's add granularity to this synthetic narrative, starting with the fiscal side, or more precisely, with its effects on personal income. Economies rebounded rather fast (already by the third and fourth quarter of 2020 double-digit growth rates were being observed), while at the same time the provision of very large amounts of fiscal (and monetary) support continued well into 2021. At the same time, the supply chains stresses caused by the Pandemic lockdowns period equally persisted through 2021, causing widespread goods shortages, while disposable income and savings skyrocketed: too much money was chasing too few goods, and on both sides of the Atlantic (albeit to *very* different degrees). Namely, between January and April 2020, US savings jump by an astonishing $5 trillion (a figure striking similar to the level of fiscal support provided), but the peak of disposable income will only be reached in March 2021—at the time of the ARPA package, see Table 7.1, reaching $22 trillion (also around $5

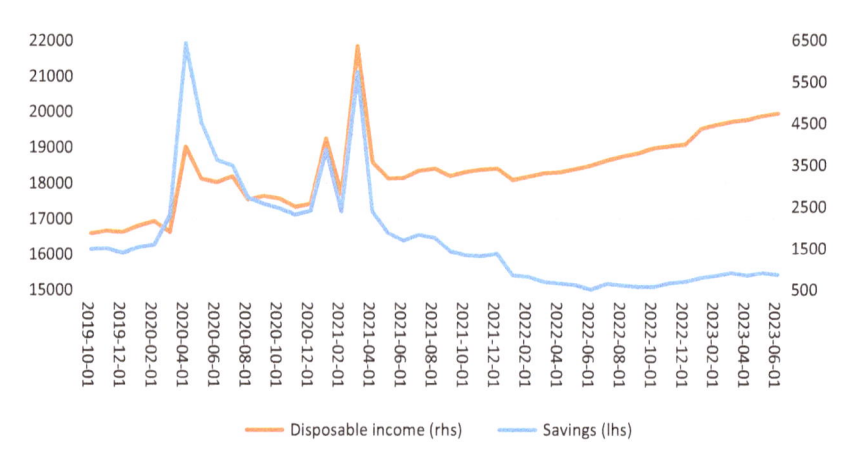

Fig. 8.1 Disposable income and savings ($ billions). (Source: FRED)

trillion above the January 2020 level: Fig. 8.1). The US personal savings rate *more than trembles*, from slightly more than 9% in January 2020 to almost 34% in April (there will duly be a second peak in March of 2021, when it climbs to over 26%).

Equivalent figures in the euro area are of a completely different order of magnitude, even if the direction is similar: gross savings of households will peak at below €540 billion in mid-2020—which is less than €300 above their end-2019 value, and the savings rate peaks at 25% in mid-2020, up from 13.5% in 2019.

At the same time this was happening, widespread goods shortages were being felt across multiple sectors from the moment lockdowns were imposed in early 2020, in items as diverse as semiconductors and wood planks, as these policies disrupted the global and intricate supply chains painstakingly built during this "Second Globalization" era. This dynamic is well captured by the Global Supply Chain Pressure Index (GSCPI) of the New York Federal Reserve (Fig. 8.2)[1]: this measure jumps from virtually zero to above three in a matter of weeks in early 2020.[2]

---

[1] The GSCPI tracks the state of global supply chains using data from the transportation and manufacturing sectors. For a full description of the methodology, see GSCPI, New York Federal Reserve.

[2] The actual historical record of this series is in the fall of 2021, due to the renewed lockdowns imposed in parts of China by its Government, which was them pursuing a so-called Zero Covid policy (this policy was suddenly abandoned only in *December of 2022*, after waves of protest in that country against it).

8 SHADOWS FROM THE PAST: INFLATION AND WAR   145

Fig. 8.2 Global Supply Chain Pressure Index. (Source: New York Federal Reserve)

Finally, the very sizable fiscal impulse described in Chap. 7 had rather limited supply effects (at least initially), so while it boosted demand there was very little increase in, say, domestic US production to compensate for these disturbances.

8.3 Price Side Effects

This situation created (global) price pressures that were apparent already by end-2020 (and even earlier in some Emerging markets), and that will rage unabated until the fall of 2022 (Fig. 8.3).

The relation of those price pressures with the supply chain disruptions can be inferred from Fig. 8.4: it shows that they *precede* other price increases, including the energy-related ones (which started climbing already **a whole year before the Russian invasion of Ukraine in February 2022**).

More formally, attempts to quantify the different contributions of these components to the inflationary spike typically find a somewhat larger share for the fiscal impulse than the supply disruptions. For example, de Soyres et al. (2022) find that fiscal stimulus is responsible for 2.5 percentage points of the excess inflation in the US,[3] 1.8 in the euro area, 1.6 in the

---

[3] de Soyres, F., Santacreu, A. and Young, H. (2022), "Fiscal Policy and Excess Inflation During Covid-19: a Cross-country View", FEDS Notes, Federal Reserve Board.

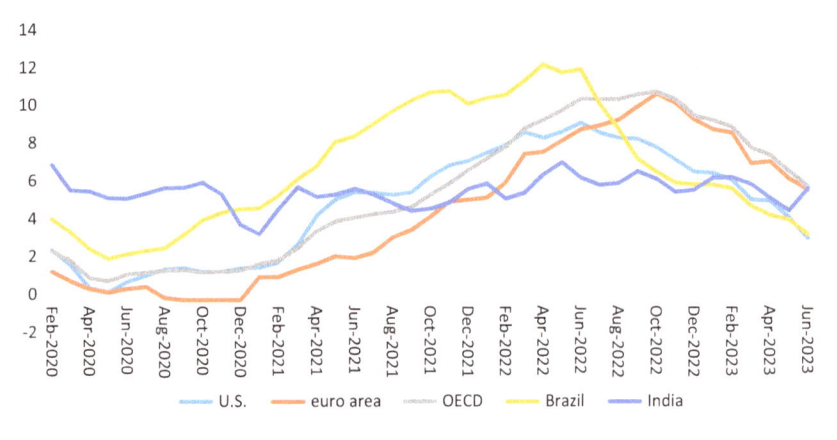

Fig. 8.3 Monthly CPI series. (Source: OECD)

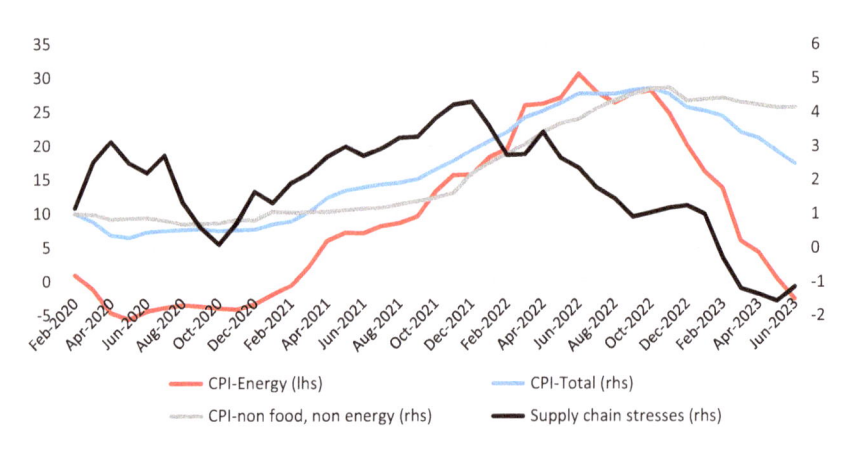

Fig. 8.4 Individual CPI items, whole OECD. (Source: OECD)

Table 8.1 Estimating the price effects of fiscal support[a]

Country/Region	Exposure type	Inflation contribution
US	Domestic Effect	2.5
US	Foreign Exposure	0.5
UK	Domestic Effect	1.6
UK	Foreign Exposure	2.3
Euro area	Domestic Effect	1.8
Euro area	Foreign Exposure	0.8
Emerging markets	Domestic Effect	1.3
Emerging markets	Foreign Exposure	0.3

Source: de Soyres et al. (2022)

[a]Aggregates are constructed using real GDP weights. The Euro area comprise of France, Germany, Italy and Spain. Emerging markets comprise 32 countries using Federal Reserve Board country classifications

UK and 1.3 in Emerging markets (Table 8.1).[4] They also estimate the indirect external effects of those domestic fiscal support packages on the trading partners of the countries that implemented then, and these can be quite significant for regions that are very open and that trade significantly with those partners (for instance, for the euro area, this is worth 0.8 percentage points of excess inflation, 0.35 of which comes from the US domestic fiscal support). As for the specific effects of supply chain stresses, Santacreu and LaBelle (2022) estimate, using a counterfactual model, that those could have added up to 20 percentage points to US PPI inflation.[5]

8.4 The (Initial) Monetary Policy (Non) Reaction

As indicated in the earlier sections, the mechanisms of the inflationary spike are fundamentally rather traditional. A more puzzling aspect of this episode, however, is why monetary authorities *in Developed countries* did

---

[4]di Giovanni et al. (2023) find comparable results for the importance of the fiscal support in the U.S. "excess inflation" during this period, and they also find that, *depending on the model used*, supply chains disruption can be even more important than the fiscal support as sources of excess inflation: see di Giovanni, J., Kalemli-Özcan, S., Silva, A. and Yildirim, M. (2023), "Quantifying the Inflationary Impact of Fiscal Stimulus Under Supply Constraints", NBER Working Paper 30892. Comin et al. (2023) also attribute roughly half of the US "excess inflation" to supply constraints (see Comin, D., Johnson, R. and Jones, C. (2023), "Supply Chain Constraints and Inflation", NBER Working Paper 31179).

[5]Santacreu, A. and LaBelle, J. (2022), "Global Supply Chain Disruptions and Inflation During the COVID-19 Pandemic", Federal Reserve Bank of St. Louis Review.

not act earlier, and why they did not foresee the effects of those measures in the financial sector when they finally did act.

For instance, only belatedly, in March 2022—over a year after the beginning of the inflation spike, during which US CPI had gone from below 2% to almost 9%—did the Fed started a tightening cycle, then proceeding to raise its policy rate **11 times within a 16-month period**. Similarly, the ECB waited until mid-2022 for inflation to breach the 9% barrier, and only then started a cycle of **ten successive interest rate hikes** within a similar time span (the UK's BoE started with a series of quarter point moves in December 2021, which became larger only after August 2022, totaling 14 successive ones by the time of writing). For the Fed, Orphanides (2023) makes the case that this "policy mistake" (yes, another one) can be traced **to decisions regarding forward guidance on policy rates:** he is quite precise as to when this happened at the Fed, pinpointing the introduction of *outcome-based forward guidance* in the FOMC statements of **September 16, 2020**, which led to a shift toward a myopic approach to policy-making (he extends the same reasoning to the ECB).[6]

Unusually, Emerging markets, and notably central banks in Latin America, showed themselves to be more willing to start a tightening cycle (Fig. 8.5): for example, in a notable demonstration of how far it had gone since its hyperinflationary days, the CBB started raising rates as soon as inflationary signs appeared in the spring of 2021 (Fig. 8.6), persisting in an aggressive trajectory that ultimately led to a *real policy rate of 10%* even in face of significant political pressures from a newly elected left-of-the-center government. In the end, the CBB was rewarded with a turning of the price cycle faster than central banks in Developed economies, and

---

[6] Orphanides, A. (2023), "The Forward Guidance Trap", Discussion Paper Series 2023-E-6, Institute for Monetary and Economic Studies, Bank of Japan, Tokyo. The corresponding section of the FOMC statement states the following: "The Committee expects to maintain this target range until it is confident that the economy has weathered recent events and *is on track to achieve* its maximum employment and price stability goals" (emphasis added).

8 SHADOWS FROM THE PAST: INFLATION AND WAR   149

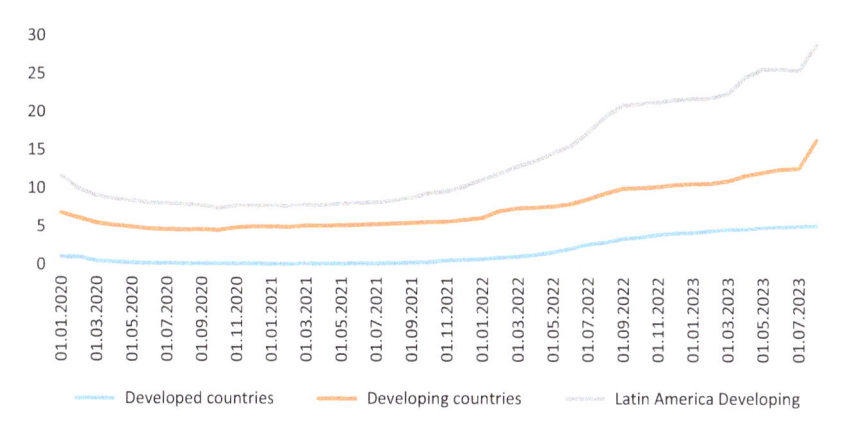

Fig. 8.5 Average policy rates, selected developed and developing countries
Developed countries: Australia, Canada, Czechia, Denmark, Euro area, Hong Kong SAR, Hungary, Israel, Iceland, Japan, Korea, New Zealand, Norway, Poland, Romania, Sweden, Switzerland, UK, US. Developing countries: Argentina, Brazil, Chile, China, Colombia, Indonesia, India, Morocco, Mexico, Malaysia, Peru, Philippines, Russia, Saudi Arabia, Serbia South Africa, Thailand, Türkiye. (Source: BIS)

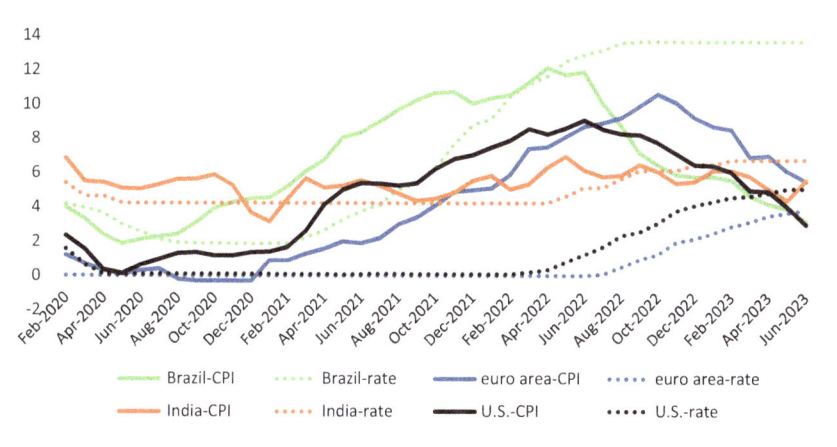

Fig. 8.6 CPI inflation and policy rates, selected countries. (Sources: OECD, FRED, CBB, RBI)

without experiencing external sustainability or banking stress episodes.[7] Showing their greater institutional maturity, Developing countries may even have been (partially) forgiven from their "original sin", successfully issuing domestic currency-denominated debt in the middle of a crisis.[8]

The fact that the combined effects of those hikes in Developed and Developing economies seem to have led to a containment of prices pressures worldwide by the summer of 2023[9] does not preclude an examination of how policy makers found themselves in this predicament, and of what are the lessons these back-to-back crises since 2007 have for monetary policy going forward. This book will attempt some concluding thoughts on this in the next, and final, chapter.

---

[7] The resolution of three US banks, First Republic in May 2023 and Signature and Silicon Valley Bank in March 2023, which went under due to exposures that were described previously in Annex 5.B, led to another proposed revision of the US banking supervisory framework, see Federal Reserve (2023), "Review of the Federal Reserve's Supervision and Regulation of Silicon Valley Bank". However, other Fed statements suggest that a consensus strategy towards that aim was still in progress at the time of this writing (see Bowman, M., (2023), "Responsive and Responsible Bank Regulation and Supervision", Federal Reserve Board, Washington). In one of the many ironies of history, former US Congressman Barney Frank, one of the authors of the 2010 Dodd-Frank Act, was actually a member of the Board of Directors of Signature Bank.

[8] Mimir, Y. and Sunel, E. (2023), "Fear (no more) of Floating: How emerging market central banks avoided a currency meltdown during the pandemic despite purchasing local-currency assets", SUERF Policy Brief, n. 684.

[9] Cavallino, P., Cornelli, G. Hördahl, P. and Zakrajšek, E. (2022), "'Front-loading' Monetary Tightening: Pros and Cons", BIS Bulletin n. 63. By the fall of 2022, more than 95% of central banks in the sample in this paper had started to increase their policy rates.

CHAPTER 9

Looking Back, Looking Forward: Monetary, Fiscal and Structural Policies for an Older, Indebted and More Fragmented World

With interest rates in Developed economies *plateauing* in the late fall of 2023 (Emerging markets like Brazil had their first rate *cuts* already in the summer of 2023), and as we seem to be approaching a so-called soft landing from the most serious inflationary episode the world has experienced since the "Great Inflation", this is more of a moment of a sigh of relief than a victory lap for central bankers (or at least for those in Developed economies).[1] There are still vast accumulated liabilities and large uncertainty about the future, with the ultimate consequences of the many ongoing shocks still unclear. Reflecting long-term underlying trends, the global economy seems to be (re)fragmenting, becoming more digital and facing long-term "transitions", while governments around the world assume a more central role in economic life, with all those elements potentially affecting again the behavior of economic agents. Are the monetary tool kits and frameworks still "fit for purpose" in this era? What needs to be

[1] One should also note that Ari et al. 2023, find that, when looking at 100 inflation episodes since the 1970s, only in 60% of the episodes was inflation sustainably brought back down within 5 years (and after an on average three-year-long tightening cycle), with most of the other episodes involving a "mission accomplished" dynamics, where inflation declined initially, leading to a premature policy easing, only to plateau at an elevated level—as is the case with the US inflation at the time of writing in the Spring of 2024—or reaccelerate later (the resolution of these relapses implied higher GDP and employment costs). See Ari, A., Mulas-Granados, C., Mylonas, V., Ratnovski, L. and Zhao, W. (2023), "One Hundred Inflation Shocks: Seven Stylized Facts", IMF Working Paper WP/23/190.

© The Author(s), under exclusive license to Springer Nature
Switzerland AG 2024
L. Vinhas de Souza, *A Century of Global Economic Crises*,
https://doi.org/10.1007/978-3-031-53460-7_9

revised and what not, and where do we need to go from here? These are questions that should be answered with both honesty and humility, while recognising the realities and constraints of policy making.

9.1 So, What Worked (and Must be Preserved)?

The history told in this book can be understood as describing the by now over a century-long effort to look for an effective anchor for monetary policy, from the "lost paradise" of the gold standard to the intermediate gold-pegged period of the Bretton Woods system, culminating in the current age of multiple floating *fiat* currencies. This process was supported by the progressive development of analytical and policy frameworks (admittedly with a few accidents along the way) that underpinned these evolving policy *choices*, leading to the current suite of micro-founded intertemporal models that incorporate expectations and different type of frictions and imperfections, and by institutional developments that progressively granted legal and functional independence to monetary authorities, while making sure that the actions and tools of those authorities are well understood by economic agents.

The global usage of frameworks like inflation forecast targeting (effectively the application of transparent types of monetary reaction functions with Taylor-like rules—even if those are underpinned by more complex, even opaque models—to "anchor" the current *fiat* floating system) by independent central banks described in this book *is a remarkable success and should be recognized as such*. These elements, therefore, should be preserved and reinforced, notably in the case of the independence (*de jure* and *de facto*) of monetary authorities.

This is specially the case when one recognizes again that the anchor in the *fiat* system is an exogenous one, and that it only guarantees a stable equilibrium under particular conditions (all underpinned by the independence of the monetary authority), while, as shown in Annex 2.A, that anchor under the classic "Gold Standard" is endogenous, unique and stable[2]: this non-automaticity, at national and system levels, implies a related need for a heavy governance framework (both in sheer numbers of

---

[2] Another dear Harvard colleague, (Sir) Paul Tucker (former Deputy Governor of the Bank of England), pointed out in an informal conversation that in the *fiat* system, ultimately, "they are the anchor" (by which he meant the heads of the monetary authorities).

staff[3] and in terms of the multiplicity of institutions—both domestic and international—related to monetary and financial policies).

9.2 What Did Not Work?

From a *policy* point of view, two key matters arise from the past crises that are arguably in need of recalibration. One is the continued importance of properly understanding the evolving links between monetary policy and the financial sector, and the implications of monetary policy actions for financial institutions. While bearing in mind the primacy of the price stability mandate, a string of episodes, from the Great Depression bank runs to the S&L crisis in the US, to the real estate bubbles and the multiple bailouts of financial institutions preceding and throughout the GFC around the world, to the resolution of banks in the US during the first half on 2023, all indicate that a forward-looking understanding of the transmission of monetary policy decisions to the banking sector still needs to be improved, but without falling in the trap of "financial dominance" (e.g., having monetary policy hampered by financial sector vulnerabilities). The other is an old danger, namely, the increased intertwining of the balance sheets of central banks and their fiscal principals, national governments, so "fiscal dominance". In the end, both of those policy vulnerabilities (themselves, if not partially created, at least enhanced by *past* central bank actions) may constrain *future* monetary policy actions.

From an *analytical* point of view, looking at the extended lags in the policy response during the last crisis and the misdiagnosis of the shock as a temporary one by monetary authorities, wedded to a data-driven (and therefore necessarily backward-looking) fear of deflation, points out to the need of some refining or recalibration in the tools described in this book. One of those recalibrations relates to the proper estimation of (forward-looking) expectations and their adequate incorporation in monetary policy frameworks (expectations were indeed a recurring theme in this book). How can this be done?

---

[3] As an example of this, when the Bank of England was founded in 1694 it had a staff of 17 (plus two gatekeepers): in 1900, the heyday of the "Classic Gold Standard" and when the UK was the center of the global monetary and financial system, the figure was 1560, while in 2020 it was 4395. See Anson, M., and Capie, F. (2022), "The Bank of England's Profits across 300 Years: Wars, Financial Crises and Distribution", *Financial History Review*, 29(1): 98–119.

The Fisher equation allows us to see the real interest rate relation to the Taylor rule, using $r_t = i_t - \pi_t$, where $i_t$the is the main monetary policy instrument (and exogenous anchor) of the framework, the short-term interest rate. As indicated in Annex 7.A, the π_t that is targeted by the monetary authority is actually a *forecast* of inflation, which is formed by economic agents based on different expectation mechanisms. As shown in Annex 4.A, these can be biased, noisy or staggered (and possibly all the three), and if an improper measure of inflation expectations is used in monetary policy reaction functions, this will lead to incorrect policies. Notably, already during early 2021, after the real demand shocks described in Chap. 8 increased contemporaneously observed inflation rates, measures of inflation expectations, while still seemingly "well-anchored", had started to shift, first via the skewness of those measures—as subgroups of agents had started changing their expectations about the future, albeit in a staggered fashion, then their standard deviation shifted, and finally the median itself moved, but this last one only by mid-2022.[4]

Another mismeasurement in the policy functions was on r_t^*, or the equilibrium real rate of interest (r-star, the one that equal savings and investments with output at potential). Having a $r_t^* < r_t$, with r_t given by the Fischer equation above implies a non-accommodative policy by the monetary authority, which is the normative stabilizing implication of a Taylor rule. A misreading of the level and/or trajectory of r_t^* could equally imply incorrect policy actions. As it turns out, different measures of r_t^* can show *both,* different levels and trends (Fig. 9.1).[5] Finally, international spillovers are inadequately represented in current central bank models, which still largely operate as closed economy ones, and when present tend to concentrate on links with legacy Developed countries.

---

[4] The same had happened during the "Great Inflation", argues Reis, R. (2021), "Losing the Inflation Anchor", Brookings Papers on Economic Activity, Fall, 307–361 (this author also points that expectations by households were more accurate in forecasting these structural breaks than the estimates by professional forecasters).

[5] Baker, K., Casey, L., Del Negro, M., Gleich, A. and Nallamotu, R. (2023) "The Post-Pandemic r*" Federal Reserve Bank of New York *Liberty Street Economics*.

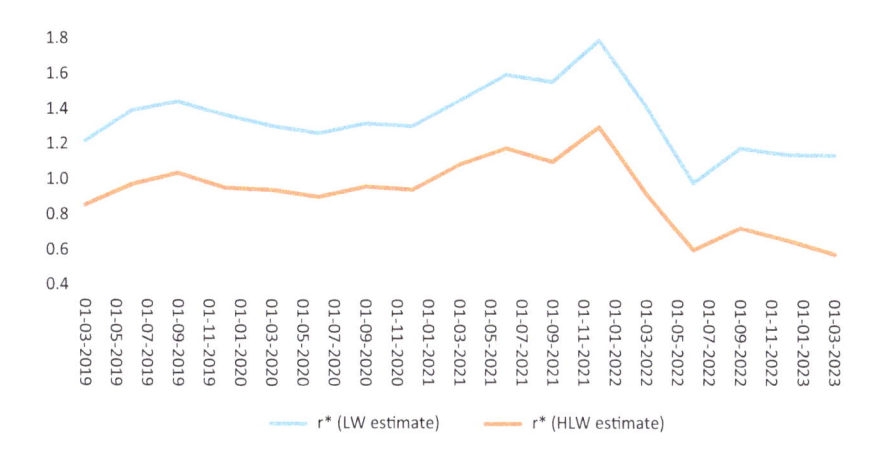

Fig. 9.1 Different estimates of r_t^*. (Source: New York Fed)

9.3 What Can (Credibly) Change?

From the points raised in Sect. 9.2, technical changes and adjustments to analytical policy tools are feasible and are already happening (as shown by Baker et al. 2023 and by Aidala et al. 2023[6], and are to be part of the upcoming formal Fed and ECB policy strategy reviews): this is the natural process of the continuous refinement of the monetary authority toolbox (which unfortunately, as the historical experience shown here demonstrated, is largely crisis-driven). Much more complex to address are the *policy (and political) constraints*, some of which are long-standing (as indicated above, "fiscal dominance" is a perennial one), but also because those are linked to ongoing, fundamental changes in the way the global economy operates: monetary policy has also to be thought of within this wider context.

9.3.1 An Older, More Indebted, More Fragmented, Slower Growing and More Digital Economy

The main theme of the global economic dynamics since the 1970s is the **smaller economic relevance of the traditional (or legacy) set of Developed nations**—still the main players in the odyssey told in this

---

[6] Aidala, F., Armantier, O., Boumahdi, F. Kosar, G. Lall, D., Somerville, J., Topa, G. and van der Klaauw, W. (2023) "Consumers' Perspectives on the Recent Movements in Inflation", Federal Reserve Bank of New York Liberty Street Economics.

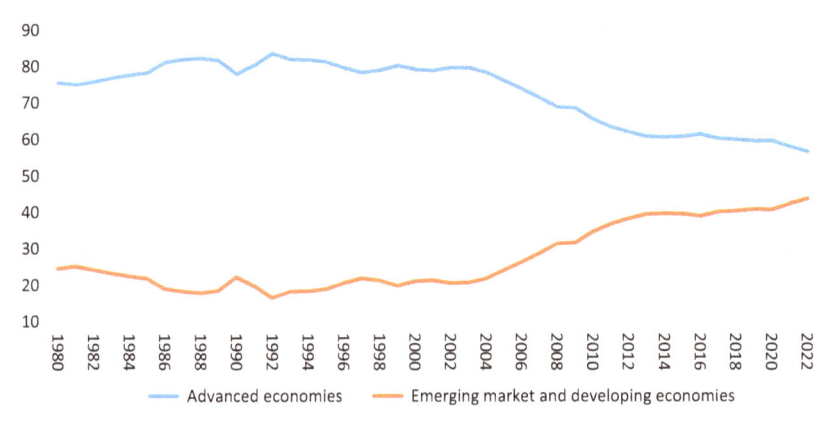

Fig. 9.2 Global GDP shares, developed & developing countries (current $). (Source: IMF)

book, parallel to the increasing importance of Developing (or "Emerging", if you will), nations (Fig. 9.2). At around the early 2000s—coinciding with the entry of China into the World Trade Organization at end-2001—Developing nations became *the* major driving force of the global economy, a process that is still ongoing.[7]

Population Dynamics Reinforces This Shift
Traditional Developed nations' share of the global population has fallen by a third since 1980 and is now less than 16% (Fig. 9.3). Not only this will continue, but among developing regions Africa—the poorest among those—is to become responsible for almost 60% of the global population growth. The earlier "demographic dividend" and the associated global price benefits from the integration of large, previously nonmarket economies with very particular features into the global supply chains—notably China, helped drive output up (mostly in the Developing economies) and push inflation down (mostly in Developed ones, at least initially).

---

[7] In purchasing power parity (PPP), Developing countries overtook Developed economies *already in 2007*. This said, a large part of the relative fall in GDP share of "legacy" Developed economies is concentrated in Europe and in north Asia (Japan), while the US has showed greater resilience.

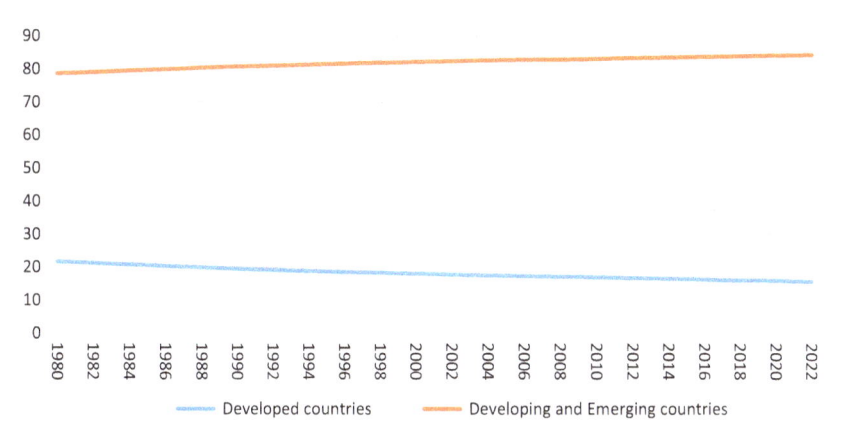

Fig. 9.3 Global population shares, developed and developing and emerging countries. (Source: World Bank)

Globalization Has Stalled

If measured by the share of global trade to world GDP, globalization (the interconnectedness of economies around the world) increased from 25% in 1970 to a high of 61% in 2008 and has since fluctuated within a 60%–50% range (Fig. 9.4). Not only global integration may have plateaued, but some signs of *economic fragmentation* are also appearing: when one looks at the status of Global Value Chains (GVCs), the intersectorial built between countries—and notably those between the US and China—are fraying, being replaced by policy-driven movements toward "friend-shoring" (e.g., Vietnam) and "near-shoring" (e.g., Mexico): similar policy moves (or at least policy *statements*) are being developed in the EU.[8] This process (which was actually started by Xi Jinping, the president of the People's Republic of China in his 2015 "Made in China 2025" strategy) implies a reverse of the earlier "globalization" positive price (and GDP) shock that has potentially huge GDP costs,[9] and may also affect the sensitivity of agents to price changes, increasing instability in pricing

[8] European Commission and High Representative of the EU for Foreign Affairs and Security Policy (2023), "Joint Communication on a European Economic Security Strategy", Brussels (this author was involved in the production of this Joint Communication).

[9] Different studies estimate that, depending on the extent of fragmentation, costs can be anywhere between **1% and 12% of global GDP**: Aiyar, S., Chen, J., Ebeke, C., Garcia-Saltos, R., Gudmundsson, T., Ilyina, A., Kangur, A., Kunaratskul, T., Rodriguez, S., Ruta, M., Schulze, T., Soderberg, G., and Trevino, J. (2023), "Geoeconomic Fragmentation and the Future of Multilateralism", IMF Staff Discussion Notes, SDN/2023/001.

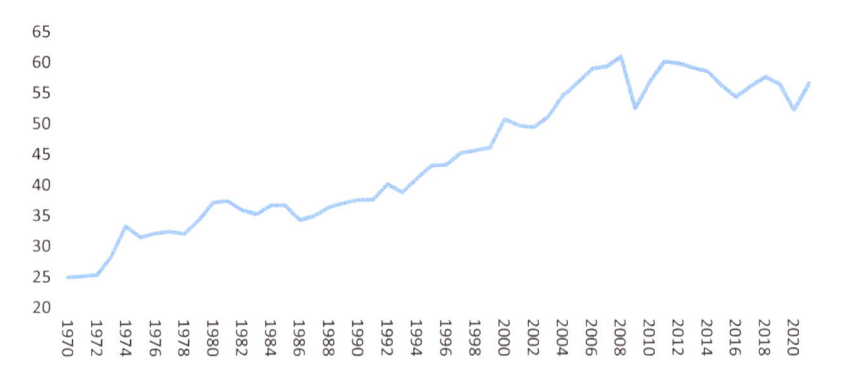

Fig. 9.4 Trade as a share of global GDP (%). (Source: World Bank)

patterns and potentially affecting again the transmission mechanism of monetary policy, like happened at the demise of the "Gold Standard".[10]

Beyond this, the economic and financial "global commons" represented by institutions like the IMF and the World Bank are facing regional alternatives (or challengers, depending on your point of view) like the New Development Bank (or NDB, the BRICS bank) and the Asian Infrastructure Investment Bank, or AIIB, both of which recently expanded their memberships, while global payment networks like SWIFT—part of the plumbing of global finance—face potential regional alternatives like China's Cross-Border Interbank Payment System (CIPS) and the dominance of the US dollar as *the* global reference currency slowly erodes (as an example of that, its' share of hard currency reserves in central banks fell from 71% to 59% in the last quarter of a century, due to the increase of a basket of other currencies).[11]

---

[10] Alfaro, L. and Chor, D. (2023), "Global Supply Chains: The Looming "Great Reallocation", Federal Reserve Jackson Hole Symposium. This paper also warns that "friend-shoring" and "near-shoring" does not necessarily reduces linkages with China, but may just add an intermediate link to those.

[11] This said, recent analyses show either no or rather limited *current* moves toward global financial fragmentation: see Weiss, C. (2023), "Financial Flows to the United States in 2022: Was There Fragmentation?", FEDS Notes, Federal Reserve Board and Bertaut, C., von Beschwitz, B., and Curcuru, S. (2023), "The International Role of the U.S. Dollar" Post-COVID Edition", FEDS Notes, Federal Reserve Board. In any case, a potential future loss of the US dollar role as the main global currency will likely be a reflection of much more serious underlying problems with the US economy (thanks to another Harvard colleague, Larry Summers, for this point).

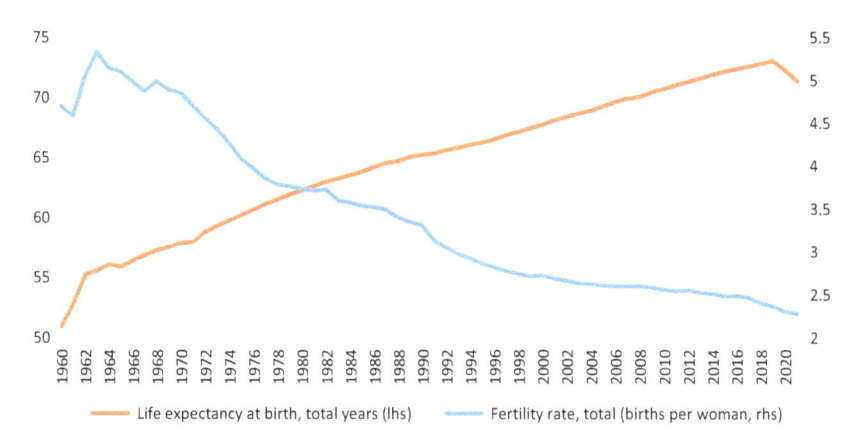

Fig. 9.5 Less (eventually) and older: life expectancy and fertility. (Source: World Bank)

A further point is what the projected slowing down of China's economy[12] may mean going forward: if that country's weight in the global economy does not increase substantially further, this will affect its role as an engine of global growth and the very dynamics of globalization itself. This slowdown is related to another feature of the long-term global trends, **aging** (which, together with the fall of natality, will eventually lead to a sustained reversal of the global population growth within the lifetime of some of the readers of this book, and which is already happening in several countries in Europe and North Asia: Fig. 9.5).[13]

Living longer and healthier lives is a blessing, in personal and societal terms, and a hallmark of the progress of human civilization. **However, there are downsides to aging**. In addition to reducing labor supply (with

---

[12] This slowdown is not a given, as structural reforms may increase China's medium-term growth rate, albeit not to its earlier 10% *pa,* and as Annex 7.B points out, China punches seriously below its weight in terms of global financial integration, so further integration may have growth effects: see World Bank, Washington, D.C., and Development Research Center of the State Council, People's Republic of China, Beijing (2013), "China 2030: Building a Modern, Harmonious, and Creative High-Income Society" (this author wrote the financial integration chapter in this work).

[13] Population shrinking in China has also already started, namely, in 2022, and the fall of China's active population may lead to a reduced demand for import goods from its trading partners, and therefore for global growth.

the associated potential of permanently tighter labor markets), population aging reduces the savings rate: the mechanism for that is described by the so-called life-cycle model, where individuals' smooth consumption over their lifetimes, while income, on the other hand, follows a hump-shaped pattern. Typically, as a population ages, youth dependency decreases and old age dependency increases (a decrease in the youth dependency ratio raises the savings rate, as the young move into the working-age category, while a declining savings rate is associated with a larger old age dependency ratio). Eventually, the benefits of a declining youth dependency ratio are outweighed by the increased retired population, permanently bringing down the savings rate and thereby growth.[14]

Conditional on what might happen in India (which overtook China as the most populous country in the world in 2023, and has shown higher GDP growth than China since 2021) and down the road with Africa, and disregarding potential increases in productivity related to technological development, these demographic trends may eventually lead to overall growth reduction and price pressures—due to higher production and labor costs and lower savings, feeding into higher nominal interest rates and tighter fiscal constraints, as age-related expenditures increase.

Still on the growth point, it is important to stress the historical uniqueness of the experience the global economy has had since the beginning of the industrial revolution in the early nineteenth century. Maddison (2001) estimates that during the millennium between the birth of Christ and the year 1000, while the world population grew by around 17%, **per capita income grew by 0%** (and actually fell during prolonged periods of time). From the year 1000 to 1820, per capita income increased by about 50%—or a somewhat underwhelming compounded rate of 0.0005% *pa*, and population by 400%.[15] **However, from 1820 to 2018, per capita income rose more than 1300%, and population more than seven times.**

A by now centuries-old question has been if this impressive record can be maintained, as this growth performance is perceived by several authors as inherently temporary, usually due to demography-related concerns (in the earlier versions of this "growth pessimistic" literature, from Malthus in

---

[14] Mc Morrow, K., and Roeger, W. (2004), "The Economic and Financial Market Consequences of Global Ageing", Springer Verlag.

[15] Maddison, A. (2001), "The World Economy: A Millennial Perspective", OECD.

1798[16] to the "Club of Rome" in 1972,[17] the culprit would be *continued population growth*). Modern growth theory concentrates on the non-explained part of growth accounting exercises (e.g., once the contributions of labor and capital are taken into account), the so-called Solow Residual,[18] also known as total factor productivity (TFP), and more specifically on innovation, or "ideas" (Romer 1990)[19]: the accumulation of physical and human capital is seen as having upper bounds, having recently demonstrated a downward trend partially linked to the fall in population growth (e.g., the opposite of previous concerns), while ideas, although "non-rival" goods, are also affected by a presumed observation that they "are getting harder to find" (Jones 2023,[20] uses as an illustration of this the anecdote that to uphold "Moore's Law"—an assertion that the number of transistors in each CPU, the core of a computer, would double every two years, the IT industry needed in the 2010s 18 times more researchers than in the 1970s). On the other hand, the increased role of populous countries like China and India in the production of innovation is one of the factors that could counteract (even if temporarily) this possible fall in the production of "good ideas" (Jones 2023, ibid.).

This older (and possibly smaller) population will also have to shoulder **a large and increasing debt load,** which, from 1974 to 2021 is estimated to have more than doubled, from 150% of GDP to over 350% (Fig. 9.6: the 2021 figure equals around *$81 trillion*) with a shrinking savings pool and lower aggregate growth (as global GDP growth and global per capita GDP growth both more than halved between the 1960s and the 2010s: the integration of countries like China into the global economy from the 1990s onward halted the fall, more than reversed it). As was highlighted in Annex 5.B, primary surpluses (supported by faster growth, but with an important fiscal adjustment component) were the main element for debt reduction among Developed economies post-World War II, and other

---

[16] Malthus, T. (1798), "An Essay on the Principle of Population", J. Johnson, St. Paul's Church-Yard, London.

[17] Meadows, D., Meadows D., Randers, J. and Behrens III, W. (1972), "Limits to Growth", Potomac Associates.

[18] Solow, R. (1957), "Technical Change and the Aggregate Production Function", Review of Economics and Statistics, 39(3):312–320.

[19] Romer, P. (1990), "Endogenous Technological Change", Journal of Political Economy, 98(5):S71–S102.

[20] Jones, C. (2023), "The Outlook for Long-Term Economic Growth", Federal Reserve Jackson Hole Symposium.

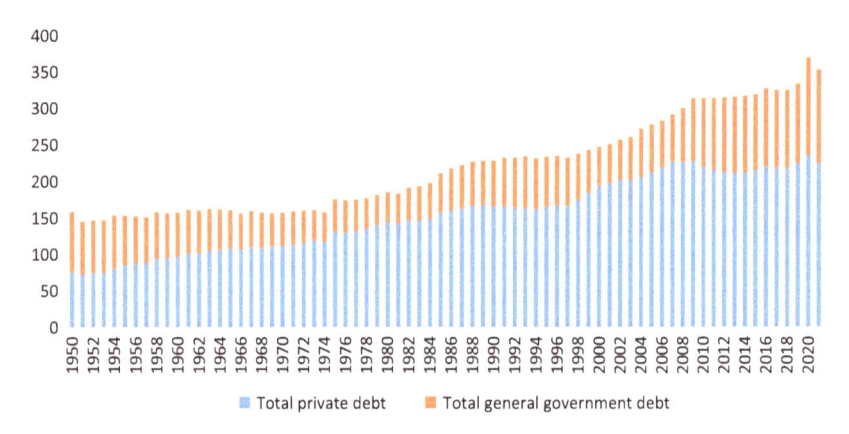

Fig. 9.6 Percentage of public and private debt in global GDP. (Source: IMF, "Global Debt Database")

avenues (from financial repression to inflation and debt restructuring) do not seem neither feasible nor, given the negative side effects, desirable (e.g., only inflation surprises can affect the stock of debt, and these inflation surprises would have to be of *a very high magnitude* to meaningfully reduce the current stocks of debt, and the large systemically destabilization effects of, say, a restructuring of the US or Italian government debts are hopefully self-evident: see Arslanalp and Eichengreen 2023, ibid.).

As the current political and economic equilibrium seems to constrain the necessary level of prolonged primary surpluses[21] to reduce debt, the corollary of the above would seem to be that the global economy will have to live with very high stocks of debt for the foreseeable future, only slowly bringing them down.

Technology Shocks
The growing digitalization of the global monetary and financial system is another uncertainty and fragmentation factor—this one driven by

---

[21] As examples, to reduce the accumulate stocks of public debt from the Napoleonic Wars, the United Kingdom run primary surpluses for **over nine decades**, from 1820 to the eve of World War I. The US, to reduce the debt from the Civil War, ran budget surpluses from 1867 all the way to 1913. Both episodes happened during periods of high growth but with even higher interest rates (therefore, **r-g was actually a drag for debt reduction**: see Arslanalp and Eichengreen 2023, ibid.).

technology, given the proliferation of private digital currencies (Bitcoin, etc.) and the potential development of central bank digital currencies (CBDCs: 130 countries, representing 98% of global GDP, are "exploring" a CBDC) as an institutional response.[22] While technologies that expanded "work from home" possibilities have increased the available workforce (and thereby limiting wage pressures), a more digitalized financial system has clearly resulted in gains for consumers and economies—including in Developing economies, and notably those in Africa, who "leapfrogged" Developed economies in this area (using the lack of physical bank infrastructure as a leverage for innovation),[23] and additional innovations from block chain to Artificial Intelligence (AI) have a potential for further efficiency and costs gains,[24] the balance of costs and benefits from potential future developments in this area and their monetary policy implications are still uncertain, while the possibility of financial stability concerns is clearer.[25]

A subset of technological shocks is the ongoing **change in the global energy matrix**, which has two components of main relevance for a monetary authority, namely, the change in relative prices from this

---

[22] Sometimes seen as a defensive move to preserve the monopoly position of the central bank as concerning monetary creation, CBDCs could, for instance, potentially facilitate transfers in times of shocks (such as, say, a pandemic) and increase resilience (this said, financial systems proved largely resilient during the Pandemic shock, while monetary authorities fulfilled their mandates, both without the need of CBDCs). Their proper design is still a work in process, but some attempts have been made for common guidelines: as an example, see BIS, (2020), "Central Bank Digital Currencies: Foundational Principles and Core Features", Basel.

[23] Ndemo, B., Mkalama, B. (2023), "Digitalisation and Financial Data Governance in Africa: Challenges and Opportunities", pp. 131–153, in Ndemo, B., Ndung'u, N., Odhiambo, S., Shimeles, A. (eds), *Data Governance and Policy in Africa. Information Technology and Global Governance*, Palgrave Macmillan.

[24] See OECD (2020), "The Tokenisation of Assets and Potential Implications for Financial Markets", OECD Blockchain Policy Series, and OECD, (2021), "Artificial Intelligence, Machine Learning and Big Data in Finance: Opportunities, Challenges and Implications for Policy Makers", Paris.

[25] For instance, in May 2022, there was a run on Terra, an algorithmic "stablecoin" (digital assets whose value is pegged to that of fiat currencies) that eventually spilled over to the entire stablecoin sector: see Anadu, K., Azar, P., Cipriani, M., Eisenbach, T., Huang, C., Landoni, M., La Spada, G., Macchiavelli, M., Malfroy-Camine, A. and Wang, C. (2023), "Runs on Stablecoins", Federal Reserve Bank of New York, Liberty Street Economics.

presumably permanent supply shock[26] and the associated investment needs in relation to savings. As indicated earlier, the baseline monetary policy response to a (in this case, global) supply shock (whatever its origin) that changes relative prices is to "look through" them (albeit our old friend, the three-handed economist, recognizes the complexities of real-world policy making),[27] but the very significant investment needs (estimated at € 620 billion per year between 2023 and 2030 just for the EU and only in the energy sector,[28] not to mention additional sums for digital technology and defense) in a world of lower growth and less investable savings may imply r_t^* drifting further up.

So, the overall long-term context is a world that is older and more indebted, possibly more fragmented, growing less and eventually with less people, while still facing significant additional investment needs (but also with uncertain productivity gains from, say, digital innovations). In short, monetary authorities will therefore possibly be facing *mostly negative* supply and demand shocks, as opposed to the, on balance, largely positive ones that they had to deal with in the previous decades: all this will affect price dynamics (in different and complex ways) and hence monetary policy going forward.[29] But what can monetary policy and monetary authorities do, or at least how can it adjust to this while still delivering on their mandates?

9.4 Conclusion: Frugal Suggestions for a Possible Path Forward

It was stressed at the very beginning of this chapter that the main challenges faced by monetary authorities in our brave post-Gold Standard new world of floating fiat currencies are *political and structural*, rather them technical or analytical (as a matter of fact, developments in those later

---

[26] Del Negro, M., di Giovanni, J. and Dogra, K. (2023), "Is the Green Transition Inflationary?", Federal Reserve Bank of New York, Staff Report, n. 1053.

[27] For an example of those, see Bandera, N., Barnes, L., Chavaz, M., Tenreyro, S. and von dem Berge, L. (2023), "Monetary Policy in the Face of Supply Shocks: the Role of Inflation Expectations", ECB Forum on Central Banking, Sintra.

[28] European Commission (2023), "Strategic Foresight Report", Brussels (this author was also involved in production of this report).

[29] For more on the demographic nature of future price pressures, see Goodhart, C. and Pradhan, M. (2020), "The Great Demographic Reversal: Ageing Societies, Waning Inequality, and an Inflation Revival", SUERF Policy Note, Issue n. 197.

areas are usually a reaction to the former, as was demonstrated throughout this book).

On the structural side, the level and trend of global integration is determined by exogenous factors like technology, monetary policy also cannot affect demographic trends, and as money is neutral in the long run, it also cannot affect long-term growth, which depends on the stock of productive factors and on the "Solow residual" mentioned earlier. **Monetary authorities' core functions and capabilities are limited and specifically related to monetary and financial stability: central banks should not allow a perception that they can—or should—act beyond those to take hold.** While there are certainly many other matters deemed societally and economically relevant, they are in all likelihood better addressed by other bodies and frameworks, and not by central banks.[30] The survival of the (implicit) social contract that enables monetary authorities to operate as they do needs this clarity of mission, and its transparent conveying to their principals and to the public at large.

From an analytical point of view, a possible evolution could be toward monetary authorities using more flexible and more robust "menus" of analytical frameworks,[31] combining workhorse data-driven, backward-looking tools with more nimble forward-looking models (with properly incorporated and estimated expectations), while explicitly recognizing uncertainty, via the usage of scenarios and an honest *ex post* explaining of forecast errors.[32] Stressing what was said in the previous paragraph, is of fundamental importance that these analytical developments are done in such a way that preserves the clear and understandable communication of the aims (and limits) of the monetary authority to all economic agents.

On the policy side (or, perhaps more accurately, on the political economy side), there are some possible levers that the monetary authority could use. On the monetary and financial nexus, monetary and financial stability requires adjustments to current policy frameworks toward addressing financial imbalances *in a symmetrical fashion during the cycle*: central banks actions being seen as unidirectional bets lead to wrong incentives and "financial dominance". To avoid that, monetary authorities

---

[30] Cullen, J. (2023) "Central Banks and Climate Change: Mission Impossible?", Journal of Financial Regulation, 1–36.
[31] Lagarde, C. (2023), "Policymaking in an Age of Shifts and Breaks", Federal Reserve Jackson Hole Symposium.
[32] Lenza, M., Moutachaker, I. and Paredes, J. (2023), "Density Forecasts of Inflation: a Quantile Regression Forest Approach", Working Paper Series, n. 2830, ECB, Frankfurt.

should be supported by macro-prudential frameworks that, while not *necessarily* housed in central banks, should benefit from the same level of operational independence that traditional monetary policy bodies now benefit from.[33]

On the "fiscal dominance",[34] and bearing in mind the long-term pressures described earlier, an extension of the above should be pursued: governments should not be allowed to perceive (again) central banks as their fiscal agents,[35] and a reinforcement of operational (*de facto* and *de jure*) independence would be necessary, while fiscal authorities engage in the hard, long slog of debt reduction (with the possible help of empowered independent fiscal bodies).

Finally, frameworks for international policy cooperation, which proved of fundamental importance throughout the episodes described in this book, may also come under pressure in a fragmenting global economy, with likely different tools and diagnosis of shocks in different countries and regions complicating further this process. The solution here could be putting a premium in enhanced "minilateral" cooperative arrangements, always keeping as much as possible Developing countries as part and parcel of those arrangements, as they will inevitably be an increasingly important part of the global economy. Reflecting that, throughout this book, I tried to support this notion by **making Developing countries actors and agents of the history I have told**.

The above is neither a revolutionary agenda nor a magic solution, rather a deliberately modest but hopefully achievable set of limited suggestions, which recognizes both the high levels of uncertainty we all face and the inherent limits of monetary policy. The frugal nature of those suggestions would also in principle allow it to be implemented by Developed and Developed countries alike, large and small, open or closed.[36]

---

[33] Borio, C. (2014), "Central Banking Post-Crisis: What Compass for Uncharted Waters?" (pp. 191–216, in *Central Banking at a Crossroads: Europe and Beyond*, Goodhart, C., Gabor, D., Vestergaard, J. and Ertürk, I. (eds.), Anthem Press.

[34] Borio, C. and Disyatat, P. (2021), "Monetary and Fiscal Policy: Privileged powers, entwined responsibilities", SUERF Policy Note, Issue No 238, 2021.

[35] Cochrane, J. (2022), "Fiscal Histories", *Journal of Economic Perspectives*, 36(4):125–146.

[36] Of course, bearing in mind differences (structural or policy-driven) like shallow financial markets that constrain the transmission mechanism of monetary policy (India), lack of physical infrastructure (sub-Saharan Africa), large dependency on single-commodity exports that imply the need of sterilizing quasi-fiscal mechanisms (Chile) or not fully liberalized current and capital accounts (China), etc.

As someone that has been on both sides of the table as it comes to (public) policy makers and (private) policy takers, one thing this author has learned in his career is that taking decisions (making policy is taking decisions, after all), is, "always and everywhere" an imperfect, complex and iterative process. When you are taking decisions under significant uncertainty and likely time (and other types of) pressure, that implies that errors will be committed, that there are things *ex post* (and sometimes even *ex ante*) that you wish you would/could have done better, or just differently: that is an inescapable part of human existence. Understanding and accepting that in a transparent manner also implies seeing those moments as learning opportunities, which they are.

In the meantime, and concluding by returning to the figure of speech I used in the very first chapter of this book, let's keep that baby firmly in the bathtub.

References

Aidala, F., O. Armantier, F. Boumahdi, G. Kosar, D. Lall, J. Somerville, G. Topa, and W. van der Klaauw. 2023. *Consumers' Perspectives on the Recent Movements in Inflation*. Federal Reserve Bank of New York Liberty Street Economics.

Aiyar, S., J. Chen, C. Ebeke, R. Garcia-Saltos, T. Gudmundsson, A. Ilyina, A. Kangur, T. Kunaratskul, S. Rodriguez, M. Ruta, T. Schulze, G. Soderberg, and J. Trevino. 2023. *Geoeconomic Fragmentation and the Future of Multilateralism*. IMF Staff Discussion Notes. SDN/2023/001.

Alfaro, L., and D. Chor. 2023. *Global Supply Chains: The Looming 'Great Reallocation'*. Federal Reserve Jackson Hole Symposium.

Anadu, K., P. Azar, M. Cipriani, T. Eisenbach, C. Huang, M. Landoni, G. La Spada, M. Macchiavelli, A. Malfroy-Camine, and C. Wang. 2023. *Runs on Stablecoins*. Federal Reserve Bank of New York, Liberty Street Economics.

Anson, M., and F. Capie. 2022. The Bank of England's Profits across 300 Years: Wars, Financial Crises and Distribution. *Financial History Review* 29 (1): 98–119.

Ari, A., C. Mulas-Granados, V. Mylonas, L. Ratnovski, and W. Zhao. 2023. *One Hundred Inflation Shocks: Seven Stylized Facts*. IMF Working Paper WP/23/190.

Arslanalp, S., and B. Eichengreen. 2023. *Living with High Public Debt*. Federal Reserve Jackson Hole Symposium.

Ashcraft, A., and T. Schuerman. 2008. *Understanding the Securitization of Subrpime Mortgage Credit*. Staff Report n. 318, Federal Reserve Bank of New York.

Avery, R., and K. Brevoort. 2015. The Subprime Crisis: Is Government Housing Policy to Blame? *The Review of Economics and Statistics* 97 (2): 352–363.

Ayres, J., M. Garcia, D. Guillén, and P. Kehoe. 2019. *The Monetary and Fiscal History of Brazil, 1960–2016*. NBER Working Paper 25421.

Bacha, E. 2003. Brazil's Plano Real: A View from the Inside. In *Development Economics and Structuralist Macroeconomics: Essays in Honor of Lance Taylor*. UK: Edward Elgar.

Baily, M., R. Litan, and M. Johnson. 2008. *The Origins of the Financial Crisis*. Brookings Institution.

Baker, K., L. Casey, M. Del Negro, A. Gleich, and R. Nallamotu. 2023. *The Post-Pandemic r**. Federal Reserve Bank of New York Liberty Street Economics.

Bandera, N., L. Barnes, M. Chavaz, S. Tenreyro, and L. von dem Berge. 2023. *Monetary Policy in the Face of Supply Shocks: The Role of Inflation Expectations*. ECB Forum on Central Banking.

Bank of Japan. 2010. *The Bank of Japan's Policy Measures during the Financial Crisis*. Tokyo.

Barcelona, W., D. Cascaldi-Garcia, J. Hoek, and E. Van Leemput. 2022. *What Happens in China Does Not Stay in China*. International Finance Discussion Papers 1360, Board of Governors of the Federal Reserve System, Washington, DC.

Barlevy, G. 2007. Economic Theory and Asset Bubbles. *Economic Perspectives* 31 (3): 44–59.

Barro, R. 1979. Money and the Price Level under the Classical Gold Standard. *Economic Journal* 89: 13–33.

Barsky, R., and L. Kilian. 2004. Oil and the Macroeconomy Since the 1970s. *Journal of Economic Perspectives* 18 (4): 115–134.

Bastian, E. 2013. O PAEG e o Plano Trienal: Uma Análise Comparativa de suas Políticas de Estabilização de Curto Prazo. *Estudos Econômicos* 43 (1): 139–166.

Belhocine, N., A. Bhatia, and J.M. Frie. 2023. *Raising Rates with a Large Balance Sheet: The Eurosystem's Net Income and Its Fiscal Implications*. IMF Working Paper WP/23/145.

Bernanke, B., and F. Mishkin. 1997. *Inflation Targeting: A New Framework for Monetary Policy?* National Bureau of Economic Research Working Paper n. 5893.

Bernanke, B., T. Laubach, F. Mishkin, and A. Posen. 1999. *Inflation Targeting*. Princeton University Press.

Bertaut, C., B. von Beschwitz, and S. Curcuru. 2023. 'The International Role of the U.S. Dollar' Post-COVID Edition. FEDS Notes, Federal Reserve Board.

Beyer, A., V. Gaspar, C. Gerberding, and O. Issing. 2009. *Opting Out of the Great Inflation: German Monetary Policy after the Breakdown of Bretton Woods*. Discussion Paper Series 1: Economic Studies Deutsche Bundesbank.

BIS. 2020. *Central Bank Digital Currencies: Foundational Principles and Core Features*. Basel.

Bloomfield, A. 1959. *Monetary Policy under the Gold Standard, 1880 to 1914.* Federal Reserve Bank of New York.

Bordo, M. 1981. The Classical Gold Standard—Some Lessons for Today. *Federal Reserve Bank of St. Louis Review* 5: 2–17.

Bordo, M., and B. Eichengreen. 2008. *Bretton Woods and the Great Inflation.* NBER Working Paper Series n. 14532.

Borio, C. 2014. Central Banking Post-Crisis: What Compass for Uncharted Waters? In *Central Banking at a Crossroads: Europe and Beyond*, ed. C. Goodhart, D. Gabor, J. Vestergaard, and I. Ertürk, 191–216. Anthem Press.

Borio, C., and P. Disyatat. 2009. *Unconventional Monetary Policies: An Appraisal.* BIS Working Papers n. 292.

———. 2021. *Monetary and Fiscal Policy: Privileged Powers, Entwined Responsibilities.* SUERF Policy Note, n. 238.

Bowman, M. 2023. *Responsive and Responsible Bank Regulation and Supervision.* Washington: Federal Reserve Board.

Bruner, R., and S. Carr. 2009. *The Panic of 1907.* Darden Case No. UVA-G-0619, U of Virginia—Darden School of Business.

Burns, A. 1970. *The Basis for Lasting Prosperity.* Address at Pepperdine College.

———. 1979. The Anguish of Central Banking. *Per Jacobsson Lecture, Reprinted at Federal Reserve Bulletin*, September 1987, 73(9): 689–698.

Burns, A., and W. Mitchell. 1946. *Measuring Business Cycles.* National Bureau of Economic Research.

Buti, M., S. Deroose, V. Gaspar, and J. Nogueira Martins, eds. 2010. *The Euro: The First Decade.* Cambridge University Press.

Calvo, G. 1983. Staggered Prices in a Utility-Maximizing Framework. *Journal of Monetary Economics* 12 (3): 383–398.

———. 1988. Servicing the Public Debt: The Role of Expectations. *American Economic Review* 78 (4): 647–661.

Calvo, G., and C. Reinhart. 2000. *Fear of Floating.* NBER Working Paper 7993.

Caputo, R., and D. Saravia. 2018. *The Monetary and Fiscal History of Chile: 1960–2016.* University of Chicago, Becker Friedman Institute for Economics Working Paper No. 2018-62.

Cardoso, E. 1989. Hyperinflation in Latin America. *Challenge* 32 (1): 11–19.

Cardoso, J. 2010. Novos Elementos para a História do Banco do Brasil (1808–1829): Crónica de um Fracasso Anunciado. *Revista Brasileira de História* 30 (59): 167–192.

Carvajal, M., M. Tudela, and L. Vinhas de Souza. 2012. *Counter-cyclical Central Banking Policies and their Longer-Term Implications.* Moody's.

Cavallino, P., G. Cornelli, P. Hördahl, and E. Zakrajšek. 2022. *'Front-loading' Monetary Tightening: Pros and Cons.* BIS.

Chakraborty, L., and S. Harikrishnan. 2022. *COVID-19 and Fiscal-Monetary Policy Coordination: Empirical Evidence from India*. Levy Economics Institute, Working Papers Series 1002.

Chappell, D., and K. Dowd. 1997. A Simple Model of the Gold Standard. *Journal of Money, Credit and Banking* 29 (1): 94–105.

Chen, Q., M. Lombardi, A. Ross, and F. Zhu. 2017. *Global Impact of US and Euro Area Unconventional Monetary Policies: A Comparison*. BIS Working Paper No. 610.

Claessens, S., G. Dell'Ariccia, I. Deniz, and L. Laeven. 2010. *Lessons and Policy Implications from the Global Financial Crisis*. IMF Working Papers 10/44.

Claeys, G., and T. Linta. 2019. *The Evolution of the ECB Governing Council's Decision-Making*. Bruegel.

Clarida, R., J. Galí, and M. Gertler. 1997. *Monetary Policy Rules in Practice: Some International Evidence*. National Bureau of Economic Research Working Paper n. 6254.

Clarida, R., J. Gali, and M. Gertler. 2000. Monetary Policy Rules and Macroeconomic Stability: Evidence and Some Theory. *Quarterly Journal of Economics* 115 (1): 147–180.

Clarida, R., B. Duygan-Bump, and C. Scotti. 2021. *The COVID-19 Crisis and the Federal Reserve's Policy Response*. Finance and Economics Discussion Series 20221-035, Federal Reserve Board.

Cochrane, J. 2022. Fiscal Histories. *Journal of Economic Perspectives* 36 (4): 125–146.

Cole, H., and L. Ohanian. 2007. A Second Look at the U.S. Great Depression from a Neoclassical Perspective. In *Great Depressions of the Twentieth Century*, ed. T. Kehoe and E. Prescott, 21–57. Federal Reserve Bank of Minneapolis.

Comin, D., R. Johnson, and C. Jones. 2023. *Supply Chain Constraints and Inflation*. NBER Working Paper 31179.

Comisión Económica para América Latina y el Caribe. 2021. *Preliminary Overview of the Economies of Latin America and the Caribbean 2020*. Economic Commission for Latin America and the Caribbean.

Commission of the European Communities. 1977. *Report of the Study Group on the Role of Public Finance in European Integration*. Brussels: Commission of the European Communities.

Congressional Research Services. 2008. *Cost Estimate—Economic Stimulus Act of 2008*. Congressional Research Services.

———. 2014. *Estimated Impact of the American Recovery and Reinvestment Act on Employment and Economic Output in 2014*. Congressional Research Services.

———. 2020. *Who Regulates Whom? An Overview of the U.S. Financial Regulatory Framework*.

Consolvo, V., O. Humpage, and S. Mukherjee. 2020. *Even Keel and the Great Inflation*. Federal Reserve Bank of Cleveland, Working Paper No. 20-33.

Cullen, J. 2023. Central Banks and Climate Change: Mission Impossible? *Journal of Financial Regulation*: 1–36. https://doi.org/10.1093/jfr/fjad003.

Curry, T., and L. Shibut. 2000. The Cost of the Savings and Loan Crisis: Truth and Consequences. *FDIC Banking Review* 13 (2): 26–35.

Davis, S., and J. Kahn. 2008. Interpreting the Great Moderation: Changes in the Volatility of Economic Activity at the Macro and Micro Levels. *Journal of Economic Perspectives* 22 (4): 155–180.

De Grauwe, P. 2009. *Economics of the Monetary Union*. UK: Oxford University Press.

De Grauwe, P., and Y. Ji. 2013. Self-fulfilling Crises in the Eurozone: An Empirical Test. *Journal of International Money and Finance* 34: 15–36.

de Soyres, F., A. Santacreu, and H. Young. 2022. *Fiscal Policy and Excess Inflation During Covid-19: A Cross-country View*. FEDS Notes, Federal Reserve Board.

Decressin, J., R. Espinoza, I. Halikias, D. Leigh, P. Loungani, P. Medas, S. Mursula, M. Schindler, A. Spilimbergo, and T. Xu. 2015. *Wage Moderation in Crises: Policy Considerations and Applications to the Euro Area*. IMF Staff Discussion Note.

Del Negro, M., J. di Giovanni, and K. Dogra. 2023. *Is the Green Transition Inflationary?* Federal Reserve bank of New York, Staff Report, n. 1053.

Dellas, H., and G. Tavlas. 2013. The Gold Standard, the Euro, and the Origins of the Greek Sovereign Debt Crisis. *Cato Journal* 33 (3): 491–520.

Demetriades, P. 2017. *A Diary of the Euro Crisis in Cyprus: Lessons for Bank Recovery and Resolution*. UK: Palgrave Macmillan.

di Giovanni, J., S. Kalemli-Özcan, A. Silva, and M. Yildirim. 2023. *Quantifying the Inflationary Impact of Fiscal Stimulus Under Supply Constraints*. NBER Working Paper 30892.

Dippelsman, R., G. Semeraro, J. Cadete de Matos, J. Catz, G. Quirós, and F. Lima. 2017. Deficit and Debt of General Government and Public Sector. In *Understanding Financial Accounts*, ed. P. van de Ven and D. Fano. OECD.

Duarte, A., and J. Andrade. 2012. How the Gold Standard Functioned in Portugal: An Analysis of Some Macroeconomic Aspects. *Applied Economics* 44 (5): 617–629.

Dutton, J. 1984. The Bank of England and the Rules of the Game under the International Gold Standard: New Evidence. In *A Retrospective on the Classical Gold Standard*, ed. M. Bordo and A. Schwartz. NBER.

EBA. 2020. *On the Future Changes to the EU-wide Stress Test*. Discussion Paper EBA/DP/2020/01, Paris.

EBRD. 2008. *Transition Report*. London: EBRD.

———. 2009. *Transition Report*. London: EBRD.

Eichengreen, B., and R. Hausmann. 1999. *Exchange Rates and Financial Fragility*. National Bureau of Economic Research Working Papers n. 7418.

Eichengreen, B., A. El-Ganainy, R. Esteves, and K. Mitchener. 2021. *In Defense of Public Debt*. Oxford University Press.

ESM. 2019. *Safeguarding the Euro in Times of Crisis: The Inside Story of the ESM*. Luxembourg: ESM.

European Central Bank. 2012. Speech by Mario Draghi, President of the European Central Bank at the Global Investment Conference in London, 26 July 2012.

———. 2023. *ECB accepts Scope Ratings within Eurosystem Credit Assessment Framework*. Frankfurt am Main: European Central Bank.

European Commission. 1989. *Delors Report*. Brussels: European Commission.

———. 2012. *Four Presidents Report: Towards a Genuine Economic and Monetary Union*. Brussels: European Commission.

———. 2015. *The Five Presidents' Report: Completing Europe's Economic and Monetary Union*. Brussels: European Commission.

———. 2023. *Strategic Foresight Report*. Brussels: European Commission.

European Commission and High Representative of the EU for Foreign Affairs and Security Policy. 2023. *Joint Communication on a European Economic Security Strategy*. Brussels: European Commission and High Representative of the EU for Foreign Affairs and Security Policy.

Federal Reserve. 2023. *Review of the Federal Reserve's Supervision and Regulation of Silicon Valley Bank*. Washington: Federal Reserve.

Fernández-Villaverde, J., and D. Sanches. 2022. *A Model of the Gold Standard*. WP 22–33, Federal Reserve Bank of Philadelphia.

Fleming, M., and N. Klagge. 2010. The Federal Reserve's Foreign Exchange Swap Lines. *Current Issues in Economics and Finance, Federal Reserve Bank of New York* 16 (4): 1–7.

Franco, G. 2017. *A Moeda e a Lei: Uma História Monetária Brasileira, 1933–2013*, 414. Brazil: Editora Zahar.

Friedman, M. 1968. The Role of Monetary Policy. *American Economic Review* 58 (1): 1–17.

Friedman, M., and A. Schwartz. 1963. *A Monetary History of the United States, 1867–1960*. Princeton University Press.

Fritsch, W., and G. Franco. 1992. *Aspects of the Brazilian Experience with the Gold Standard*. PUC Rio de Janeiro. Mimeo.

Garber, P. 1991. The Collapse of the Bretton Woods Fixed Exchange Rate System. In *A Retrospective on the Bretton Woods System: Lessons for International Monetary Reform*, ed. M. Bordo and B. Eichengreen, 461–494. Press: University of Chicago.

Garcia Munhoz, D. 1997. *Inflação Brasileira: Os Ensinamentos desde a Crise dos Anos 30*. Revista de Economia Contemporânea, 1(1), UFRJ, Brazil.

Gaspar, V., and M. Buti. 2021. *Maastricht Values*. CEPR.

Ghosh, S., N. Sugawara, and J. Zalduendo. 2011. *Bank Flows and Basel III—Determinants and Regional Differences in Emerging Markets*. Economic Premise, n.56, World Bank.

Giavazzi, F., and R. Baldwin, eds. 2016. *The Eurozone crisis: A Consensus View of the Causes and a Few Possible Solutions.* CEPR.

Gill, I., and L. Vinhas de Souza. 2013. *The Flight of the European Bumblebee.* Project Syndicate and Politico.

Goodhart, C. 2017. *A Central Bank's Optimal Balance Sheet Size?* CEPR Discussion Paper n. 12272.

Goodhart, C., and M. Pradhan. 2020. *The Great Demographic Reversal: Ageing Societies, Waning Inequality, and an Inflation Revival.* SUERF Policy Note, n. 197.

Gordon, R. 1975. Alternative Responses of Policy to External Supply Shocks. *Brookings Papers on Economic Activity* 1: 183–204.

Gorton, G., and A. Metrick. 2012. Securitized Banking and The Run on Repo. *Journal of Financial Economics* 104 (3): 425–451.

Graetz, M., and O. Briffault. 2016. *A 'Barbarous Relic': The French, Gold, and the Demise of Bretton Woods.* Columbia University Law School.

Green, R., and S. Wachter. 2007. *The Housing Finance Revolution.* Paper presented at the Federal Reserve Bank of Kansas City Symposium.

Greenlaw, D., J. Hatzius, A. Kashyap, and H. Shin. 2008. *Leveraged Losses: Lessons from the Mortgage Market Meltdown.* Paper prepared for the U.S. Monetary Policy Forum, University of Chicago and the Rosenberg Institute for Global Finance at Brandeis University.

Hakkio, C. 2013. *The Great Moderation.* Federal Reserve Bank of Kansas City.

Hartmann, P., and F. Smets. 2018. *The first Twenty Years of the European Central Bank: Monetary Policy.* Working Paper Series 2219, European Central Bank.

Hattori, M., and Y. Suda. 2007. *Developments in a Cross-Border Bank Exposure Network.* Bank of Japan Working Paper no. 07-E-21.

Herby, J., L. Jonung, and S. Hanke. 2022a. A Literature Review and Meta-Analysis of the Effects of Lockdowns on Covid-19 Mortality. *Studies in Applied Economics*, SAE (200):62.

———. 2022b. A Literature Review and Meta-Analysis of the Effects of Lockdowns on Covid-19 Mortality—II. *Studies in Applied Economics, Studies in Applied Economics*, SAE (210):115

Higgins, M., and T. Klitgaard. 2011. Saving Imbalances and the Euro Area Sovereign Debt Crisis. In *Current Issues in Economics and Finance*, 17(5), Federal Reserve Bank of New York.

Holinski, N., C. Kool, and J. Muysken. 2012. Persistent Macroeconomic Imbalances in the Euro Area: Causes and Consequences. *Federal Reserve Bank of St. Louis Review* 94 (1): 1–20.

Hukkinen, J., and M. Viren. 2023. *The Stability and Growth Pact Three Decades Later.* SUERF Policy Brief n. 564.

IMF. n.d. *Policy Responses to COVID-19.* Washington, DC.

Ishi, K., M. Stone, and E. Yehoue. 2009. *Unconventional Central Bank Measures for Emerging Economies*. IMF Working Paper WP/09/226.

Ito, T. 2013. Great Inflation and Central Bank Independence in Japan. In *The Great Inflation: The Rebirth of Modern Central Banking*, ed. M. Bordo and A. Orphanides, 357–387. University of Chicago Press.

Johnston, L., and S. Williamson. 2023. *What Was the U.S. GDP Then?* MeasuringWorth.

Jones, C. 2023. *The Outlook for Long-Term Economic Growth*. Federal Reserve Jackson Hole Symposium.

Kehoe, T., and J. Nicolini, eds. 2021. *A Monetary and Fiscal History of Latin America, 1960–2017*. University of Minnesota Press.

Keynes, J. 1923. *A Tract on Monetary Reform*. UK: Macmillan and Co.

———. 1936. *The General Theory of Employment, Interest, and Money*. UK: First Harvest Hacourt Brace.

Kohn, D. 2010. *The Federal Reserve's Policy Actions during the Financial Crisis and Lessons for the Future*. Ottawa, Canada: Remarks at Carleton University.

Kok, C., F. Mongelli, and K. Hobelsberger. 2022. *A Tale of Three Crises: Synergies between ECB Tasks*. ECB Occasional Paper No. 2022/305.

Kose, A., and F. Ohnsorge, eds. 2020. *A Decade after the Global Recession: Lessons and Challenges for Emerging and Developing Economies*. World Bank.

Labonte, M. 2021. *The Federal Reserve's Response to COVID-19: Policy Issues*. Congressional Research Service, R46411.

Laeven, L., and F. Valencia. 2018. *Systemic Banking Crises Revisited*. IMF Working Paper No. 18/206.

Lagarde, C. 2023. *Policymaking in an Age of Shifts and Breaks*. Federal Reserve Jackson Hole Symposium.

Lane, P. 2013. *Capital Flows in the Euro Area*. European Commission, DG ECFIN, Economic Papers 497.

Langhammer, R., and L. Vinhas Souza, eds. 2005. *Monetary Policy and Macroeconomic Stabilization in Latin America*. Springer.

Larch, M., J. Malzubris, and S. Santacroce. 2023. Numerical Compliance with EU Fiscal Rules: Facts and Figures from a New Database. *Intereconomics: Review of European Economic Policy* 58 (1): 32–42.

Lehment, H. 1982. Economic policy response to the oil price shocks of 1974 and 1979: The German Experience. *European Economic Review* 18 (2): 235–242.

Leiderman, L., and L. Svensson, eds. 1995. *Inflation Targets*. Centre for Economic Policy Research.

Leitão, M. 2011. *Saga Brasileira: A Longa Luta de um Povo por Sua Moeda*. Brazil: Editora Record.

Lenza, M., I. Moutachaker, and J. Paredes. 2023. *Density Forecasts of Inflation: A Quantile Regression Forest Approach*. Working Paper Series, no 2830, ECB, Frankfurt.

Lucas, R. 1977. Understanding Business Cycles. *Carnegie-Rochester Conference Series on Public Policy* 5 (1): 7–29.
Maddison, A. 2001. *The World Economy: A Millennial Perspective.* OECD.
Malthus, T. 1798. *An Essay on the Principle of Population.* London: J. Johnson, St. Paul's Church-Yard.
Mariscal, R., A. Powell, and P. Tavella. 2014. *On the Credibility of Inflation Targeting Regimes in Latin America.* IDB Working Paper Series, n. IDB-WP-504, Washington.
Mathieu, E., H. Ritchie, L. Rodés-Guirao, C. Appel, C. Giattino, J. Hasell, B. Macdonald, S. Dattani, D. Beltekian, E. Ortiz-Ospina, and M. Roser. 2020. *Coronavirus Pandemic (COVID-19).* Published Online at OurWorldInData.org.
Mc Morrow, K., and W. Roeger. 2004. *The Economic and Financial Market Consequences of Global Ageing.* Springer Verlag.
McCandless, G. 2005. Argentina: Monetary Policy by Default. In *Monetary Policy and Macroeconomic Stabilization in Latin America*, ed. R. Langhammer and L. Vinhas Souza, 87–112. Springer.
McCarthy, J., and R. Peach. 2004. Are Home Prices the Next Bubble? *Federal Reserve Bank of New York, Economic Policy Review* 10 (3): 1–17.
Meadows, D., D. Meadows, J. Randers, and W. Behrens III. 1972. *Limits to Growth.* Potomac Associates.
Medina, J., E. Toni, and R. Valdes. 2023. *The Art and Science of Monetary and Fiscal Policies in Chile.* Germany: MPRA Paper 117198, University Library of Munich.
Meltzer, A. 2002. Origins of the Great Inflation. *Federal Reserve Bank of St. Louis Review* 87 (2): 145–175.
———. 2010. *A History of the Federal Reserve. Volume 2, Book 2, 1970–1986.* University of Chicago Press.
Metzler, M. 2006. Japan and the British Gold Standard, ca. 1715–1885. In *Lever of Empire*, 14–28. University of California Press.
Mimir, Y., and E. Sunel. 2023. *Fear (No More) of Floating: How Emerging Market Central Banks Avoided a Currency Meltdown during the Pandemic Despite Purchasing Local-Currency Assets.* SUERF Policy Brief, n. 684.
Minoiu, C., and J. Reyes. 2011. A Networks Analysis of Global Banking: 1978–2009. *IMF Working Paper* 74: 11–41.
Minsky, H. 1992. *The Financial Instability Hypothesis.* The Jerome Levy Economic Institute of Bard College, Working Paper n. 74.
Miranda-Agrippino, S., and H. Rey. 2021. *The Global Financial Cycle.* NBER Working Paper Series n. 29327, Boston.
Mody, A. 2014. *The Ghost of Deauville.* CEPR.
Mohan, R. 2021. *The Response of the Reserve Bank of India to Covid-19: Do whatever it Takes.* Centre for Social and Economic Progress, Working Paper 8, New Delhi.

Moody, J. 1900. *Manual of Industrial and Miscellaneous Securities.* New York: O.C. Lewis Co.

Moody's. 2022. *Rating Methodology Sovereigns.* New York: Moody's.

Moody's Analytics. 2011. *Basel III New Capital and Liquidity Standards—FAQs.* New York: Moody's Analytics.

Morceiro, P., M. Tessarin, and H. Pereira. 2022. Políticas Macroeconômicas Adotadas no Brasil em Resposta à Pandemia de COVID-19 em 2020. *Textos de Economia, Florianópolis* 25(1): 1–23, Universidade Federal de Santa Catarina.

Morozumi, A., M. Bleaney, and Z. Mumuni. 2020. *Inflation Targeting in Low-Income Countries: Does IT Work?* Review of Development Economics.

Mundell, R. 1961. A Theory of Optimum Currency Areas. *American Economic Review* 53: 657–665.

———. 2000. A Reconsideration of the Twentieth Century. *American Economic Review* 90 (3): 327–340.

Ndemo, B., and B. Mkalama. 2023. Digitalisation and Financial Data Governance in Africa: Challenges and Opportunities. In *Data Governance and Policy in Africa: Information Technology and Global Governance*, ed. B. Ndemo, N. Ndung'u, S. Odhiambo, and A. Shimeles, 131–153. Palgrave Macmillan.

Nechio, F., and B. Fernandes. 2022. Brazil: Covid-19 and the Road to Recovery. *BIS Papers* 122: 39–55.

OECD. 2020. *The Tokenisation of Assets and Potential Implications for Financial Markets.* Paris: OECD Blockchain Policy Series, OECD.

———. 2021. *Artificial Intelligence, Machine Learning and Big Data in Finance: Opportunities, Challenges and Implications for Policy Makers.* Paris: OECD.

———. n.d. *Tracking GDP Growth in Real Time.* Paris: OECD.

Orphanides, A. 2018. Independent Central Banks and the Interplay between Monetary and Fiscal Policy. *International Journal of Central Banking* 14 (3): 447–470.

———. 2023. *The Forward Guidance Trap.* Discussion Paper Series 2023-E-6, Institute for Monetary and Economic Studies, Bank of Japan, Tokyo.

Perez-Saiz, H., and L. Zhang. 2023. *Renminbi Usage in Cross-Border Payments: Regional Patterns and the Role of Swaps Lines and Offshore Clearing Banks.* IMF Working Papers Series WP/23/77.

Pesce, M., and G. Feldman. 2023. Monetary Policy Challenges over Two Decades: A View from Argentina. In *Central Banking in the Americas: Lessons from Two Decades*, 21–39. Basel: BIS.

Phelps, E. 1967. Phillips Curves, Expectations of Inflation and Optimal Unemployment Over Time. *Economica* 34 (135): 254–281.

———. 1978. Commodity-Supply Shock and Full-Employment Monetary Policy. *Journal of Money, Credit and Banking* 10: 206–221.

Phillips, A. 1958. The Relationship between Unemployment and the Rate of Change of Money Wages in the United Kingdom 1861–1957. *Economica* 25 (100): 283–299.

Pisani-Ferry, J., E. Vihriala, and G. Wolff. 2013. *Options for Euro-Area Fiscal Capacity*. Bruegel.

Portugal, M. 2017. Política Fiscal na Primeira Fase do Plano Real, 1993–1997. In *A Crise Fiscal e Monetária Brasileira*, ed. E. Bacha. Rio de Janeiro: Civilizacão Brasileira, Brazil.

Powell, J. 2020. *Current Economic Issues*. Speech at the Peterson Institute for International Economics.

———. 2023. *Central Bank Independence and The Mandate—Evolving Views*. Stockholm: Sveriges Riksbank.

Reinbold, B., and Y. Wen. 2019. *Historical U.S. Trade Deficits*. Federal Reserve.

Reinhart, C., and K. Rogoff. 2009. *This Time Is Different: Eight Centuries of Financial Folly*. Princeton University Press.

Reinhart, C., and M. Sbrancia. 2011. *The Liquidation of Government Debt*. NBER Working Paper 16893.

Reis, R. 2021. *Losing the Inflation Anchor*. Brookings Papers on Economic Activity, Fall, 307–361.

Reserve Bank of India. n.d. Monetary and Fiscal Policy Interactions in the Wake of the Pandemic. *BIS Papers* 122: 149–157.

Rieder, K. 2022. Monetary Policy Decision-Making by Committee: Why, When and How It Can Work. *European Journal of Political Economy* 72: 1–30.

Romer, P. 1990. Endogenous Technological Change. *Journal of Political Economy* 98 (5): S71–S102.

Romer, C., and D. Romer. 2002. *The Evolution of Economic Understanding and Postwar Stabilization Policy*. NBER Working Paper 9274.

Rueff, J. 1972. *The Monetary Sin of the West*. New York: Macmillan.

Rueff, J., and F. Hirsh. 1965. The Role and the Rule of Gold: An Argument. *Princeton Essays on International Finances* 47: 2–3.

Rule, G. 2015. Understanding the Central Bank Balance Sheet. *Bank of England Handbook* n. 32.

Santacreu, A., and J. LaBelle. 2022. *Global Supply Chain Disruptions and Inflation During the COVID-19 Pandemic*. Federal Reserve Bank of St. Louis Review.

Sargent, T., and N. Wallace. 1981. Some Unpleasant Monetarist Arithmetic. *Federal Reserve Bank of Minneapolis Quarterly Review* 5: 1–17.

Schulz, J. 2017. Around the British Gold Standard: Portugal and Brazil. Two Satellites?H istória e Economia, Vol. 19: 15-54.

Scope Ratings. 2023. *Scope Upgrades Greece's Long-Term Credit Ratings to BBB— And Changes the Outlook to Stable*. Berlin: Scope Ratings.

Secretaria do Tesouro Nacional, Brazil. 2009. Dívida Pública: A Experiência Brasileira.

Sims, C., and T. Zha. 2006. Were There Regime Switches in U.S. Monetary Policy? *American Economic Review* 96 (1): 54–81.

Solimano, A., and D. Calderón Guajardo. 2017. *The Copper Sector, Fiscal Rules, and Stabilization Funds in Chile: Scope and Limits*. WIDER Working Paper 2017/5.

Solow, R. 1957. Technical Change and the Aggregate Production Function. *Review of Economics and Statistics* 39 (3): 312–320.

Steil, B. 2013. *The Battle of Bretton Woods: John Maynard Keynes, Harry Dexter White, and the Making of a New World Order*. Princeton University Press.

Stock, J., and M. Watson. 2003. *Has the Business Cycle Changed? Evidence and Explanations*. Federal Reserve Bank of Kansas City.

Summers, P. 2005. *What Caused the Great Moderation? Some Cross-Country Evidence*. Federal Reserve Bank of Kansas City, Economic Review.

Svensson, L. 1996. *Inflation Forecast Targeting: Implementing and Monitoring Inflation Targets*. National Bureau of Economic Research Working Paper n. 5797.

Sylla, R. 2002. An Historical Primer on the Business of Credit Rating. In *Ratings, Rating Agencies and the Global Financial System*, ed. R. Levich, G. Majnoni, and C. Reinhart. Boston: Kluwer Academic Publishers.

Tarullo, D. 2019. Financial Regulation: Still Unsettled a Decade after the Crisis. *Journal of Economic Perspectives* 33 (1): 61–80.

Taylor, J. 1993. Discretion versus Policy Rules in Practice. *Carnegie Rochester Conference Series on Public Policy* 39: 195–214.

Tobin, J. 1972. *New Economics One Decade Older*. Princeton University Press.

Truman, E. 2021. The Road to the 1980s Write-Downs of Sovereign Debt. *Financial History Review, Cambridge University Press* 28 (3): 281–299.

Turner, D., and P. Ollivaud. 2018. *The Output Cost of the Global Financial Crisis*. OECD Economics Department.

Valia, B. 2018. *The Single Rulebook and the European Banking Authority*. University of Cambridge Faculty of Law Research Paper No. 45/2018.

Vinhas de Souza, L. 2002. *Integrated Monetary and Exchange Rate Frameworks: Are There Empirical Differences?* Working Paper Series, n° 2/2002, Bank of Estonia.

———. 2012. *CEE and CIS Countries Could be affected by Possible Euro Area Economic Shocks, Albeit to Varying Degrees*. Moody's.

———. 2013. *Limited GDP Benefits of Basel III Expected for Developing Economies*. Moody's.

———. 2014a. *QE Tapering: Impact Differs Amongst Emerging Markets*. Moody's.

———. 2014b. *Japan's Abenomics: Answers to Frequently Asked Questions about Progress 1.5 Years On*. Moody's.

Vinhas de Souza, L., and J.M. Frie. 2015a. *Regaining Citizens' Trust, Safeguarding Banks' Stability: Towards a European Deposit Insurance Scheme*. Brussels: European Commission.

———. 2015b. *Strengthening the EU's Financial System: Bridge Financing Options for the Single Resolution Fund*. Brussels: European Commission.

———. 2015c. *Severing the 'Doom Loop': Further Risk Reduction in the Banking Union*. EPSC, European Commission.

Vinhas de Souza, L., and M. Tudela. 2012. *Euro Area Periphery: Structural Reforms Have Significantly Improved External Imbalances, but Full Resolution May Still Take Years*. Moody's.

———. 2014. Voltar a Empezar: Crisis and the Renationalization of the Iberian Financial Systems. *Comparative Economic Studies* 56 (3): 337–350.

Vinhas de Souza, L., and B. van Aarle, eds. 2004. *The Euroarea and the New EU Member States*. UK: Palgrave Macmillan.

Wallison, P. 2011. *Dissent from the Majority Report of the Financial Crisis Inquiry Commission*. American Enterprise Institute.

Warin, T. 2008. Stability and Growth Pact. In *The New Palgrave Dictionary of Economics*. London: Palgrave Macmillan.

Weiss, C. 2023. *Financial Flows to the United States in 2022: Was There Fragmentation?* FEDS Notes, Federal Reserve Board.

World Bank, Washington, D.C., and Development Research Center of the State Council, People's Republic of China, Beijing. 2013. *China 2030: Building a Modern, Harmonious, and Creative High-Income Society*. The World Bank.

Zhang, L. 2023. *Capital Account Liberalization and China's Financial Integration*. Harvard Kennedy School, Working Paper Series n. 196, Cambridge.

INDEX[1]

A
Abenomics, 82
Accommodative policies, 12, 37, 46
Advanced economies, 87, 93, 122, 123, 125, 127
Aging, 159, 160
Alvorada, Palace, 59n26
American International Group (AIG), 72n8
American Recovery and Reinvestment Act (ARRA), 126
Anchor, 8, 15, 24, 28, 47, 50, 135, 136, 152, 152n2, 154
Arrow, first, 82
Arrow, second, 82
Arrow, third, 82
Articles of Agreement, IMF, 24n26, 77n18
Artificial Intelligence (AI), 163
Asia, 14, 61, 137, 156n7
Asian financial crisis, 49, 61
Asian Infrastructure Investment Bank (AIIB), 158
Asset backed securities (ABS), 68, 69
Asset-driven, 79, 105
Asset Purchase Facility (APF), 81
Asymmetric information, 73, 114
Automatic stabilizers, 112, 128n9

B
Backward-looking, 153, 165
Bailout, 71, 72n8, 96n4, 98n8, 108, 109n29, 153
Balance sheet, 7, 71, 77–79, 79n21, 80n24, 81, 81n28, 83, 86, 91n52, 93n58, 105, 105n21, 113, 125, 130, 131, 133, 153
Balance sheet, optimal size, 83
Banco do Brasil, 54, 59

---

[1] Note: Page numbers followed by 'n' refer to notes.

© The Author(s), under exclusive license to Springer Nature Switzerland AG 2024
L. Vinhas de Souza, *A Century of Global Economic Crises*,
https://doi.org/10.1007/978-3-031-53460-7

184 INDEX

Bancor, 23, 27n34
Bank for International Settlements (BIS), 85, 104
Banking Act, 1932 and 1935, 20
Banking Act, Emergency, 1933, 20, 22n19
Banking Union, 109, 110
Bank of England (BoE), 12n3, 13n5, 78, 80n24, 81, 81n28, 90n50, 131, 148, 152n2, 153n3
Bank of England Asset Purchase Facility Fund (BOEAPFF), 81n28
Bank of Japan (BoJ), 78, 82, 131
Bank of the Central African States (BEAC), 138
Bank Recovery and Resolution Directive (BRRD), 110
Bank resolution, 110
Bank runs, 72, 75, 118, 153
Basel II, III and IV, 85, 85n42, 86, 110
Bear Stearns, 71, 72
Behavior, agents, 135
Big Three, 116n48, 117n51
Bitcoin, 163
Block chain, 163
Bounded rationality, 64
Brazil, 14, 14n8, 53–62, 88, 114n45, 122, 122n1, 131–135, 136n24, 139, 149, 151
Bretton Woods system, 23, 25–27, 26n33, 41, 95, 96, 116, 152
British pound, 14, 15, 23
Bubble, 67, 68, 71, 73n12, 75, 82, 87–90, 102, 153
Bumblebee, euro, 95–96
Bureau of Economic Analysis (BEA), 36, 49, 55, 92
Business cycle, 1, 2, 5, 6, 12, 21, 37, 63

C

Calvo, Guillermo, 62, 118
Capital controls, 27n36, 61
Capital Markets Union (CMU), 103, 110, 111, 113
Capital requirements, 70, 84n38, 85n42, 129
Cartelization, 21
Casa da Moeda do Brasil, 53
Central bank, 5, 8, 12n3, 24, 26–29, 36, 42, 47n6, 51, 53, 57, 59, 76–83, 77n19, 79n21, 80n25, 83n32, 90, 90n51, 91n52, 113, 119, 129, 132, 135, 136, 140, 140n31, 148, 150n9, 152–154, 158, 163n22, 165, 166
Central bank digital currencies (CBDCs), 163, 163n22
Central Bank of Brazil (CBB), 54, 59, 59n26, 133, 134, 148, 149
Central Bank of Chile, 61
Central Bank of the West African States (BCEAO), 138
Chile, 53, 60–62, 88, 122, 136n24, 149, 166n36
China, 6, 45–64, 74, 139–141, 144n2, 149, 156–161, 158n10, 159n12, 159n13, 166n36
Civil War, 162n21
Closed economy, 60, 154
Collateralized Debt Obligation (CDO), 69, 69n5, 76
Colonies, 13, 32, 54, 115
Commodity Futures Trading Commission (CFTC), 70n6
Common Equity Tier 1 (CET1), 86, 129
Competitiveness, 11, 99, 102
Comprehensive Capital Analysis and Review (CCAR), 81, 93n58
Congressional Research Services (CRS), 70n6

Constrained discretion, 136
Consumer Financial Protection Bureau (CFPB), 70n6
Consumer price index (CPI), 36, 42, 43, 46n4, 52, 53, 55, 81, 125, 146, 148, 149
Contagion, 67, 75, 77
Contraction, GDP, 17, 20, 77, 132
Convergence, 96–98, 139, 139n29
Core countries, 101
The Coronavirus Aid, Relief, and Economic Security Act (CARES), 126n4
Coronavirus Preparedness and Response Supplemental Appropriations Act (CPRSAA), 127
Coronavirus Response and Relief Supplemental Appropriations Act (Response and Relief, or CRRSAA), 127
Covered Bond Purchase Programs (CBPP), 105
COVID Pandemic, 126n4
Crawling band, 61
Credit default swaps (CDS), 69n5, 98n8, 99
Cross-Border Interbank Payment System (CIPS), 158
Current account balance, 100
Current account surplus, 61
Cyprus, 32, 97, 100, 108n27, 117

D
De Gaulle, Charles, 25
Deauville, Summit, 98n8
Debt, 2, 4, 7, 8, 20, 38, 38n8, 49, 57n25, 68, 70, 72, 79, 80n25, 81, 83, 83n32, 88n44, 91–93, 103, 104, 112–114, 114n45, 116, 119, 126, 150, 161, 162, 162n21, 166

Debt, restructuring, 162
De facto, 13–15, 152, 166
Default, debt, 2, 4, 97
Deflation, 20, 81, 153
De juri, 152
Delors Report, 96
Demand shock, 154, 164
Demographic dividend, 156
Demographics, 6, 8, 122n1, 160, 165
Dependency ratio, 160
Deustche Bundesbank, 91n52
Developed economies, 12–14, 24n29, 42, 52, 53, 87, 88n44, 114, 128, 129, 131, 133, 148, 151, 156n7, 161, 163
Developing countries, 5, 8, 52–53, 79, 79n21, 87, 92n55, 97n7, 123, 125, 131n12, 133, 135, 137, 149, 150, 156, 156n7, 166
Digitalization, 6, 162
Direct exposures, 75, 83, 97
Disposable income, 143, 144
Dodd-Frank Act, 70n6, 84, 150n7
Doom loop, 80, 104
Dot-com stock market bubble, 70
Draghi, Mario, 113, 119
Dual mandate, 36, 37, 40, 41, 45
Dutch disease, 60

E
Eastern Caribbean Central Bank (ECCB), 138
Economic and Social Stabilization Fund (ESSF), 61
Economic cycle, 1, 12n3
Economist, one-handed, 40
Economist, three-handed, 164
Effective lower bound (ELB), 77, 79
Emerging markets, 77, 88, 122, 123, 125, 131–133, 131n12, 136, 136n24, 137, 139, 145, 147, 148, 151

Empires, 11, 13, 14, 76
Employment Act, 36, 41
Endogenous shock, 1, 42, 124
Energy matrix, 7, 163
Energy price shock, 39, 42
Enhanced Conditions Credit Line (ECCL), 109
Enhanced Minimum Capital, 85
Euro, 16n12, 26, 79n21, 88, 95, 96, 97n6, 107, 138, 140
Euro area, 7, 74–76, 79, 82, 82n31, 83, 83n32, 91n52, 91n53, 96–105, 96n4, 97n6, 97n7, 99n10, 107–114, 108n25, 108n27, 108n28, 109n29, 110n35, 110n36, 117–119, 122n1, 127–129, 131, 138, 144, 145, 147, 149
Euro area, common fiscal capacity, 112
Euro area deposit guarantee scheme, 110
Euro area sovereign crisis, 6, 95–119, 128n9
European Banking Authority (EBA), 104, 109, 109n31
European Central Bank (ECB), 78, 79, 82–84, 90, 91n52, 96, 104–111, 108n27, 108n28, 113, 117n51, 126n6, 127–131, 133, 141, 148
European Commission (EC), 82n30, 96n3, 110n36
European Deposit Insurance Scheme (EDIS), 110, 110n36
European Economic Recovery Plan (EERP), 128n9
European Financial Stability Facility (EFSF), 97n6, 108, 108n28, 109
European Insurance and Occupational Pensions Authority (EIOPA), 110n35
European Investment Bank (EIB), 128

European Monetary Institute, 96
European Monetary System, 95
European Securities and Markets Authority (ESMA), 110n35
European Systemic Risk Board (ESRB), 109, 110
European Union (EU), 26, 49, 74, 82n31, 97, 97n6, 97n7, 98n8, 99, 99n10, 101, 103, 104, 108–112, 109n29, 110n34, 112n41, 122n1, 127, 128, 128n9, 138–140, 139n29, 157, 164
Even keel policy, 38, 38n8, 91n54
Excess inflation, 145, 147
Excessive Debt Procedure (EDP), 109
Exchange rate, 11, 12, 23, 24, 27, 57n24, 60, 61, 76, 77, 79n21, 80n25, 87, 111, 116, 119, 133, 135, 137, 138
Exchange Rate Mechanism (ERM), 49, 96, 138
Exit strategy, 7
Exogenous shock, 8
Expectations, 6, 7, 16, 29, 37, 42, 45–47, 46n4, 50, 62–64, 68, 89, 91, 97n7, 101, 108, 118–119, 135, 152–154, 154n4, 165
Expectations, self-fulfilling, 119
External sustainability, 118, 133, 135, 150

F
The Families First Coronavirus Response Act (FFCRA), 127
Fannie Mae, Federal National Mortgage Association, 69, 69n3
Farm Credit Administration (FCA), 70n6
Fear of floating, 24n29

Federal Deposit Insurance Corporation (FDIC), 17, 70n6
Federal Funds Effective Rate, 46, 46n4
Federal Housing Finance Agency (FHFA), 70n6
Federal Open Market Committee (FOMC), 41n13, 50, 50n9, 51, 91n54, 148
Federal Reserve (Fed), 15, 17–20, 26n33, 41, 45, 46, 50, 70n6, 71, 72, 78, 81, 107, 122, 126
Federal Reserve Board, 45, 147
Fiat money, 8, 14, 23, 24
Financial dominance, 153, 165
Financial innovations, 68, 70, 72n8, 115, 135
Fire asset sale, 76, 93
First Globalization, 15, 22
Fiscal adjustment, 161
Fiscal agent, 19, 90, 166
Fiscal capacity, 111–113
Fiscal dominance, 5, 6, 55, 59, 153, 155, 166
Fiscal rule, 61, 88, 112, 133
Fiscal space, 112, 128, 131
Fiscal stimulus, 82, 132, 133, 145
Fiscal support, 82, 124–129, 133, 143, 147, 147n4
Fiscal year, 131n13
Five Presidents Report, 108n26
Flexibility, 136
Flexible inflation targeter, 132
Floating exchange rate, 24, 61
Forecast, 41n13, 63, 64, 135–137, 152, 154
Forecast errors, 165
Forward guidance, 8, 51, 148
Forward-looking, 153, 165
Four Presidents Report, 108n26
Fragmentation, 107, 109, 127, 157, 157n9, 158n11, 162

Freddie Mac, Federal Home Loan Mortgage Corporation, 69, 69n3
Friedman, Milton, 16n12, 18, 19n16, 37, 38, 41, 47, 62
Friend-shoring, 157, 158n10
Fundação Getúlio Vargas (FGV), 55
Fundamentals, 25, 47n6, 88, 89, 111, 114, 119, 155, 165, 166

G
Germany, 13n4, 14, 20, 42, 100, 102, 114n45, 122, 128, 147
Glass-Steagall Act, 67
Global commons, 158
Global Financial Crisis (GFC), 6, 7, 49, 55, 67–94, 96, 97, 97n7, 99–102, 105, 108, 108n25, 111–113, 117, 123–127, 141, 153
Global Financial Cycle, 141
Globalization, 114, 157–162
Global Supply Chain Pressure Index (GSCPI), 144, 144n1, 145
Global Trade and Commodity Cycle, 141
Global Value Chains (GVCs), 157
Gold Exchange Standard, 15–22, 73n12
Gold-pegged systems, 35, 152
Gold pool, 26n33
Gold Reserve Act, 1934, 20
Gold standard, 11–32, 36, 36n2, 51, 55, 76, 114, 136, 152
Good luck, 48, 49
Google mobility data, 122
Governing Council, ECB, 83n33
Government Plan for Economic Action (PAEG), 57
Government securities, 132
Government-sponsored enterprises (GES), 69, 69n3, 70n6

Great Depression, 2, 5, 11–32, 36, 37, 45, 67, 69n3, 69n4, 70n6, 72, 72n10, 73, 83n33, 84, 97, 115, 118, 153
Great inflation, 2n1, 5, 25–27, 35–44, 46, 47, 62, 135, 151, 154n4
Great Moderation (GM), 5, 6, 8, 44–64, 67
Greece, 97, 97n6, 100–102, 117, 117n51
Guarantees, 69, 108n28, 110, 124, 128n9, 129, 132, 133, 135, 136, 152

H
Hard currency, 57, 57n24, 140n31, 158
Hemingway, Ernest, 25, 27n36
Heterodox plans, 59n26
High Representative of the EU for Foreign Affairs and Security Policy, 157n8
Households, 4, 5, 129, 133, 144, 154n4
Human capital, 161
Humphrey-Hawkins Act, 36
Hyperinflation, 53, 55, 60–62

I
Ideas, 161
Incentives, 73, 113, 165
Income transfer programs, 133
Incompleteness, EMU, 108–113
Independent and identically distributed (i.i.d.), 63, 119
Indexation, 57, 59
India, 6, 53, 122n1, 131–132, 139, 149, 160, 161, 166n36
Inertial inflation, 57

Inflation, 2, 4, 5, 7, 16, 26n33, 28, 35–37, 37n4, 42–48, 45n2, 46n4, 50–55, 50n9, 57, 61, 62, 88, 91, 100n12, 102, 104, 122n1, 132, 133, 135–138, 136n24, 143–149, 151n1, 154, 156, 162
Inflationary spiral, 37, 41, 91
Inflation forecast targeting, 135, 136, 152
Inflation targeting, 5–6, 47, 51, 88, 135–138
Information friction, 63, 64, 73
Information state, 63
Innovation, 67–70, 72n8, 115, 135, 161, 163, 164
Instituto Brasileiro de Geografia e Estatística (IBGE), 55, 59n27
Integration, debt-based, 99
Integration, equity-based, 99
Interconnectedness, 49, 71, 74–76, 157
Interest rate hikes, 148
International Monetary Fund (IMF), 23, 23n24, 24n26, 27n34, 59, 60, 77, 77n18, 97, 97n6, 111n38, 125, 128, 131n12, 132, 133, 140n31, 141, 158
International policy cooperation, 166
Investment grade, 117n51
Iran, Imperial State of, 39
Ireland, 97, 100, 102, 112, 117
Italy, 13n4, 98, 100, 102, 117, 122, 147

J
Japan, 14, 15, 39, 43, 78, 79n23, 82, 122, 148n6, 149, 156n7
Juncker, Jean-Claude, 82n30, 97n6, 108n26, 110n36
Just in time, 48, 49

K
Keynes, John Maynard, 23, 37
Keynesian policies, 37
Kuwait, 49

L
Labor mobility, 111, 111n38
Large-scale asset purchases (LSAP), 81
Latin America, 14, 20, 44, 45, 53, 55, 56, 58, 60–62, 88, 136n24, 137, 148
Latin America debt crisis, 49, 57n25
Leapfrogged, 163
Lehman Brothers, 73, 76
Lender of last resort, 19, 119
Leverage, 70, 85n42, 86, 163
Liabilities, 28, 69n5, 79, 151
Liability-driven, 79
Life-cycle model, 160
Light bulb recession, 121–124
Limited Liability Companies (LLC), 72n8, 126
Liquidity, 16, 19, 19n16, 20, 25, 76, 77, 80n25, 82, 84–86, 90n51, 104, 105, 107, 109, 118, 126, 128, 129, 132, 133
Liquidity Coverage Ratio (LCR), 84n38, 86
Lockdown, 7, 49, 121, 122n1, 123, 129, 131, 132, 143, 144, 144n2
Long-term liquidity operations (LTRO), 83, 105, 105n21, 129, 132
Lost Decade, 57
Low income Developing countries (LIDC), 125, 137

M
Maastricht Criteria, 100n12
Maastricht Treaty, 82n31, 112
MacDougall report, 112
Macroprudential framework, 80n25, 85
Maddison, Angus, 160
Maiden Lane, 72n8, 80n24, 126
Market distortions, 4
Maturity transformation, 93
Member state, EU, 97n6, 104, 109, 110, 128, 128n9
Microfoundations, 30n38
Middle East, 39, 137
Milreis, 14
Monetary authority, 5–8, 12, 15–16, 21, 24, 27n36, 29, 37, 38, 40, 42, 43, 43n17, 47, 47n6, 48, 50, 54, 57n24, 59, 77, 82, 83, 88, 90, 91, 91n52, 91n53, 101, 105n21, 118, 124, 130, 133, 135–138, 143, 147, 152–155, 152n2, 163–165, 163n22
Monetary Snake, 95
Money creation, 59
Mono-line insurance companies, 69n5
Moody, John, 114–118, 116n48, 117n52
Moody's Investor Services (MIS), 73n13
Moore's Law, 161
Moral suasion, 76, 80n25
Morgan, J.P., 36, 71
Mortgage-backed Security (MBS), 69, 70, 79, 80n24, 81
Mortgage financing, 70
Multiannual Financial Framework (MFF), 112n41
Mundell, Robert, 16n12

N
Napoleonic Wars, 13, 15, 90n50, 162n21
National Bank of Belgium (NBB), 91n53

National Credit Union Administration (NCUA), 70n6
Near-shoring, 157, 158n10
Net current transfers, 103
Net interest margin (NIM), 92
Net private savings, 101, 102
Net Stable Funding Ratio (NSFR), 86
New Development Bank (NDB), 158
New Liquidity and Leverage standards, 85
New York Federal Reserve, 19, 144
New Zealand, 13n4, 20, 137, 149
Next Generation EU (NGEU), 127, 128, 128n8
Noisy information, 63, 64
Nominal indexation, 56
Non-conforming loans, 69
Non-interest bearing checking accounts, 4
Nonlinear relationship, 119
Non-rival goods, 161
Normalization, 7, 125
North Africa, 137

O
Off-balance sheet entity, 70
Office of the Comptroller of the Currency (OCC), 70n6
Oil embargo, 39
Operational independence, 90n50, 166
Operation Twist, 81
Optimum currency area theory, 111
Organization for Economic Co-operation and Development (OECD), 42, 60, 101, 137, 146
Organization of Arab Petroleum Exporting Countries (OAPEC), 39
Original sin, 92, 92n55, 150
Orthodox plans, 59

Output gap, 136
Outright Monetary Transactions (OMT), 105, 105n22, 133

P
Pandemic Crisis Support (PCS), 128
Pandemic Emergency Longer-Term Refinancing Operations (PELTROs), 129
Pan-European Guarantee Fund (EGF), 128
The Paycheck Protection Program and Health Care Enhancement Act (PPHCEA), 127
Pension Reserve Fund (PRF), 61
Peoples' Bank of China (PBOC), 141
Per capita GDP, 139n29, 161
Perfect information, 63, 64
Perfect substitutes, 98
Periphery countries, 100, 101, 104
Phelps, Edmund, 37, 38, 47, 62
Phillips, Alban, 37n4
Phillips curve, 8, 37, 37n4, 42
Physical capital, 161
Pillar, I, II and III, 85
Plano de Ação Econômica do Governo (PAEG), 57
Plano Real, 59
Policy buffers, 88
Policy constraints, 35, 155
Political constraints, 155
Political economy, 165
Population dynamics, 156
Population growth, 156, 159, 161
Portugal, 13, 15, 53, 54, 97, 100–102, 117
Potential output, 136
Precautionary Conditions Credit Line (PCCL), 109
Price controls, 45

Primary surpluses, 92, 161, 162, 162n21
Private creditors, losses on, 98n8
Private digital currencies, 163
Public Sector Purchase Program (PSPP), 105, 107, 109
Purchasing power parity (PPP), 54, 156n7

Q
Qualitative and quantitative easing (QE2), 82
Quantitative easing (QE), 7, 77
Quotas, 23n24

R
Rating categories, 115
Rating methodology, 117n52
Rating outlook, 115
Ratings agencies, 73n13, 116n48
Rating, triple A (AAA), 69n5, 117
Rationality, 64
Real bills doctrine, 8, 20
Real estate, bubble, 68n2, 75, 82, 153
Recalibration, 153
Recession, 7, 61, 123
Reconstruction Finance Corporation Act, 20
Recovery and Resilience Facility (RRF), 127, 128
Refinancing facility, 132
Regime change, 51
Regling, Klaus, 109n29
Regulation, financial, 87
Regulatory forbearance, 132
Relief, regulatory, 93n58, 129
Relief, supervisory, 129
Renminbi, 139
Repo facility, 129

Repression, financial, 38n8, 80, 80n25, 91, 92, 162
Reserve Bank of India (RBI), 132–134
Residual term, 119
Retired population, 160
Risk mispricing, 98
Risk-sharing, 112
Risk-weighted assets (RWA), 86
Roosevelt, Franklyn Delano, 17, 20, 22n19, 24n27
R-star, 154
Rueff, Jacques, 25
Russia, 149

S
Savings, 4, 6, 99–102, 143, 144, 154, 160, 161, 164
Savings and loans crisis, 49, 69
Savings, rate, 93
Scenarios, 86, 165
Second Globalization, 144
Second-round effects, 40, 141
Securities and Exchange Commission (SEC), 70n6
Securities Market Program (SMP), 82, 105
Securitization chain, 72, 73
Seigniorage, 90, 90n51
Shadow banking, 71, 72, 84
Shocks, 1, 5, 7, 8, 11, 12, 21, 22, 39–40, 42–45, 43n17, 49, 50, 52, 54–57, 60–62, 111, 112, 122–124, 128n8, 133, 139–141, 151, 153, 154, 157, 162–164, 166
Shoe-leather costs, 4
Shortages, 76, 143, 144
Short-term repurchase agreements, 70
Sigma-convergence, 96
Signaling, 119, 133

Single Resolution Mechanism (SRM), 110, 110n34
Single rulebook, 109–110
Single Supervisory Mechanism (SSM), 110
Six-pack, 109
Slowdown, 46, 139, 159, 159n12
Smithsonian Agreement, 27n36
Smoot-Hawley Tariff Act, 16n12
Soft landing, 151
Solow residual, 161, 165
Solvency concerns, 76
Sovereign default, 115
Sovereign ratings, 114–117, 117n52
Sovereign Wealth Fund (SWF), 60, 61
Soviet Union, 6, 49, 76, 97n7, 115n47, 116
Spain, 14, 97, 100, 102, 112, 117, 122
Special Drawing Rights (SDR), 27n34, 141
Special Liquidity Scheme (SLS), 80n24
Special Purpose Vehicles (SPV), 108, 126
Speculative grade, 115, 117n50, 118
Spillovers, international, 154
Spreads, 22, 73–77, 79, 98, 98n8, 99, 119, 121, 122
Stability and Growth Pact (SGP), 99, 99n10, 100, 109, 112, 128
Stabilization plan, 57, 57n22, 58
Stablecoin, 163n25
Staggered learning, 64, 73
Standard deviation, 13, 47, 53, 98, 154
State-contingent bonds, 89
State of the world, 89
Sticky information, 63, 64
Structural reform, 82, 128, 159n12
Structured Investment Vehicles (SIVs), 70

Structure of the economy, changes to, 48
Subprime borrowers, 68
Sub-Saharan Africa, 137, 166n36
Sudden stop, 77, 87, 97n7, 105, 111, 118, 131, 133
Superintendence of Currency and Credit (SUMOC), 54
Supply chains stresses, 143
Supply shock, 40, 164
Support to Mitigate Unemployment Risks (SURE), 128
Svensson, Lars, 135
Swap lines, 81, 126, 129, 141
SWIFT, 139, 140, 140n30, 158
Swiss National Bank (SNB), 79n21, 91n53
Switzerland, 43n17, 77, 85, 149
Systemic Stress Composite Indicator (SSCI), 96
Systemic tool, 111

T
Targeted long-term refinancing operations (TLTRO), 105, 105n21
Taylor rule, 5, 50n9, 136, 137, 154
Technology shocks, 162–164
Tennessee Valley Authority, 17
Terms of trade, 61
Terra, run on, 163n25
Toolbox, 109, 155
Total factor productivity (TFP), 161
Trading partners, 147, 159n13
Tranches, 69, 69n5
Transmission mechanism, 75, 137, 158, 166n36
Transparency, 4, 85, 135, 136
Treasury-Fed Accord, 91n54
Triffin dilemma, 25

Triffin, Robert, 25
Troubled Asset Relief Program (TARP), 126
Truman, Harry, 40
Two-dip recession, 97

U
Ukraine, 7, 49, 55, 145
Uncertainty, 8, 72, 73n12, 122n1, 151, 162, 165–167
United Kingdom (UK), 13, 13n4, 15, 19, 22, 23, 23n22, 23n23, 39, 54, 75, 80n24, 90n50, 96n4, 108n27, 111, 122, 147–149, 153n3, 162n21
U.S. Congress, 22n19, 25
U.S. government, 17
U.S. Social Security System, 17

V
Vaccines, 121, 124n2
Vietnam War, 157
Volcker, Paul, 45–64, 71

W
Weekly Tracker, 123
Werner Report, 95, 95n2
Whatever it takes, 105n22, 113, 119
White, Harry Dexter, 23
White Plan, 23
Working-age, 160
World Bank, 23n24, 40, 43, 58, 97n7, 128, 157–159
World Health Organization, 121
World Trade Organization, 156
World War I, 14–16, 115, 162n21
World War II, 2, 17, 22–24, 54, 74, 116

Y
Yen, 15
Yield, 46n4, 79, 80, 84, 88, 93, 98, 98n8
Yield, search for, 93
Yom Kippur War, 39

Z
Zero COVID, 144n2

Printed in the USA
CPSIA information can be obtained
at www.ICGtesting.com
CBHW051431070724
11253CB00005B/248